KERALA
Insurgency for Politics

KERALA
Insurgency for Politics

KV THOMAS
Former Assistant Director
Intelligence Bureau, India

Manas Publications
(We Convert Fighters into Writers)
New Delhi - 110 002 (INDIA)

MANAS PUBLICATIONS
(We Convert Fighters into Writers)
(Publishers, Library Suppliers, Importers & Exporters)
4402/5-A, Ansari Road (Opp. HDFC Bank)
Darya Ganj, New Delhi - 110 002 (India)
Phones: Off.: 011-23260783, 23265523, Res.: 011-23842660
E-mail: manaspublications@gmail.com
manaspublications@yahoo.com
Website: www.manaspublications.in

ISBN 978-81-7049-547-5
₹ 795

Designed at
Manas Publications

Printed in India at
R.K. Print Services, Delhi
and published by Mrs Suman Lata for
Manas Publications, 4402/5-A,
Ansari Road (Opp HDFC Bank),
Darya Ganj, New Delhi - 110002 (INDIA)

Preface

The Maoist insurgency is the single biggest internal security challenge ever faced by the country. No less a person than India's former Prime Minister Dr Manmohan Singh made this pronouncement in April 2006, when the country was reeling under the pressure of other internal security threats such as cross-border terrorism, violence in Kashmir and ethnic conflicts and insurgency in the North-East.

As Maoist threat continues unabated with macabre killings, ambushes, encounters, sabotage and kidnapping, many crucial questions come to our mind. What prompts Maoist insurgency? Whether it is the upshot of the omissions and commissions of our democratic polity and institutions? Does it a mere law and order issue or a socio-economic problem? To what extent the Adivasis and the marginalized sections support the movement? What is the viable solution to tackle the Maoist challenge?

The existing literature on Maoist insurgency in India had attempted to find answers of such questions on conventional lines. There exist two distinct schools: one that vigorously interpret and propagate the movement as a law and order or internal security issue and the other which intertwines it with poverty, development and political disenfranchisement. There is much dichotomy in their approach in tackling it. While the law and order school prescribes a strategy of total elimination of Maoists by force even by engaging the armed forces in the worst affected States or areas, others advocate for a more holistic and humanitarian approach stressing the need for poverty reduction, land reforms, better governance and delivery.

We notice such divergence on the policies and strategies of the governments in dealing with the Maoist challenge. The government officially subscribe 'people-centric approach' which essentially is 'carrot and stick policy' of using force as well as adopting developmental strategies to win over the hearts of the people influenced by the movement. But, on the ground, the emphasis is more on military strength to fight the Maoists. The lack of perspective in properly addressing the movement especially its major stake-holders and the socio-economic and developmental issues contributing to its growth appears to be the major flaws in finding a permanent solution to the Maoist threat.

Thus, a serious attempt has been made to address such issues in this book. In Chapter 1, the theoretical framework of the problem is laid down through a comprehensive analysis of the historical evolution of the Maoist movement on pan-India level. Deviating from the conventional approach, an analysis of the demographic profile of the Maoist-affected districts in nine States shows that Tribals and Dalits continue to be their traditional source of support due to a confluence of factors. The Human Poverty Index (HPI) of these sections remains high, whereas their Human Development Index (HDI) is abysmally low clearly indicating that they are the victims of deprivation, discrimination and under-development.

The HDI/HPI or the socio-economic condition of Dalits and Tribals are closely intertwined with the land and agrarian structure. The mainstream parties, dominated by feudal landlord interests and vote bank politics, were in power for over the last six decades, virtually failed to safeguard the land rights of Tribals and Dalits, which adversely affected the process of their political mobilization and integration in national mainstream. The civil society adopts a lukewarm approach towards the 'outlier' communities of Tribals and Dalits. Thus, the alienation of these communities and their long pending issues such as restoration of alienated Tribal land and land rights have been exploited by the Maoists.

Any macro analysis of the problem, based on national or sub-national level data has the limitation to properly assess the spatial heterogeneity of Maoist movement. On the other hand, micro level study focusing specific area or target groups has the advantage to closely examine the above issues. Thus, the focused area of research was two northern districts of Kerala – socially and economically backward with sizeable Adivasi population – where the Maoist insurgency made strong ripples during its early phase.

Mapping the research field, Chapter 2 unfolds as how the 'red-terror' created strong resonance in the southern State of Kerala, which was a home to a vibrant Communist movement with an epoch-making history of agrarian and working class mobilization. The genesis of the movement was mainly due to the internal contradictions and differences in the Communist party. The cadres of Communist Party of India (Marxist) who were ideologically opposed to the party's strategy of using parliamentary forum for establishing proletarian regime sow the seeds of Maoist movement in Kerala. The feudal landlord set-up in some parts of the State coupled with the oppression and exploitation of the Adivasis and Dalits by the landed gentry, created fertile ground for Maoists.

While analysing the history of the Maoist insurgency in Kerala, we can identify four distinct phases namely:

(a) First phase of blindly following Charu Majumdar's line of annihilation of class enemies.

(b) The second phase of challenging National Emergency by attacking centres of State power.

(c) Post-Emergency phase of ideological differences and internal contradictions leading to the formation of different groups.

(d) The current phase of unity and co-ordination through the Strategic United Front etc.

Following the merger of the CPI (Maoist) and the CPI(ML) Naxalbari in May 2014, the movement has broad-based its activities by opening a new front of the people's war in the tri-junction of Kerala, Karnataka and Tamil Nadu. The Maoist strategy is now focused on the task of winning over the support of Adivasis, Dalits and other exploited or oppressed sections. Instead of perpetrating large scale violence or actions, their operational strategy is to strengthen their base in the area through non-violent mobilization.

In this backdrop, our ground level study was focused on the main themes namely the extent of support by Adivasis to Maoist insurgency, the socio-economic and developmental issues impacting the movement, the political mobilization of Adivasis and the role of indigenous outfits in countering the movement. Both quantitative and qualitative tools of research were used. Literature including authentic research works relevant to the hypotheses has been extensively reviewed. Interview with ex-Maoists, ideologues of the movement and prominent Adivasi leaders spearheading historic struggles in the State on issues like the restoration of alienated Tribal land and case study of indigenous Adivasi outfit could bring out useful inputs which were tested through an empirical survey on the basis of 5-point scale 'Likert' model questionnaire.

The Adivasi support to Maoists is discussed in detail in Chapter 4. Though Adivasis constituted less than 2% of total population in Kerala, they along with the marginalized sections were the traditional sources of support for the movement during its different phases. Neglected and betrayed by the mainstream political parties for many decades, these sections supported the Maoist insurgency without understanding the ideology or anticipating its ramifications. The lack of indoctrination coupled with lack of proper training on Maoist strategy incapacitated them to withstand the repressive measures of the State. Thus, slowly and steadily large majority of them have started dissociating with the movement. The present strategy of Maoists is to undo such trends. The scores of Adivasis, Dalits and landless poor farmers who are subjected to extreme exploitation and oppression are the main targets of the Western Ghats Special Zonal Committee (WGSZC) of Maoists operating in the tri-junction of Kerala, Tamil Nadu and Karnataka.

The co-relation between socio-economic conditions and the spread of Maoist insurgency is discussed in detail in Chapter 5. The life of Adivasis and for that matter their socio-economic conditions are inextricably intertwined with '*Jal, Jameen* and *Jungle*' (water, land and forest). Of the various socio-economic issues, the Adivasi land alienation has opened a vicious circle of maladies such as malnutrition, addiction to liquor, health hazards, and indebtedness and different forms of exploitation of Adivasis. The deprivation or deficiencies in respect of basic amenities and infrastructural facilities such as health, education, sanitation, drinking water, communication etc, in Adivasi areas are equally glaring. The Maoists try to exploit such issues attributing that such maladies as the result of neglect and indifference of the successive State Governments and the major political parties on the development agenda meant for Adivasis and other weaker sections.

The emergence of apolitical indigenous organizations strongly espousing the issues of Adivasis through a series of struggles and campaigns could considerably checkmate the Maoists. A detailed case study of Adivasi Gothra Maha Sabha (AGMS), an indigenous outfit of Adivasis in Kerala, formed in 2001 clearly revealed the above trend. But, in a political system with parties vigorously pursuing vote bank politics, the survival of apolitical outfits like AGMS was a great challenge. Such vote bank based political mobilization especially of Adivasis and Dalits without addressing their grievances and issues, but fostering an illegal nexus of political middlemen, contractors and bureaucrats creates enough space for the Maoists and other radical groups to build up their organization among these sections. Perhaps, the best example is the case of Attappadi, the first Tribal block in Kerala, where large majority of Adivasis are victims of deprivation and exploitation.

In the wake of the renewed efforts by the Maoists to woo the Adivasis and the marginalized in the northern districts of Kerala, we made a deep prognostic analysis of the major themes of the study in Chapter 8. Besides the empirical data collected by using different research tools, the views of founding leaders of Maoist movement in the State, constitutional experts, prominent Adivasi leaders and civil liberty activists etc, were also incorporated. The analysis of the data unfolded certain conclusions based on which we have come out with a number of recommendations on Maoist insurgency and Adivasi paradigm in Kerala.

Though large areas of Kerala and the major chunk of the population are 'Maoist-free', any attempt to describe the State as 'post-Naxalite' or 'post-Maoist' would be a misnomer considering the ground level realities and the incipient challenges that we face from such groups. Thus, the State and its agencies need to develop better understanding of the problem in order to formulate right strategies and policies to combat the Maoist threat. In any such strategy the focus should be more on the people-centric projects and programmes like planned development, better governance, public perception management and protection of rights and privileges of the indigenous communities than the enemy-centric measures such as reinforced police security apparatus and logistics.

That does not mean that the police and security agencies would remain as passive spectators of the violence perpetrated by the Maoists whose ultimate aim is to establish power through armed struggle. The State has every right to exercise its power and resources against the Maoists. But, that should be in accordance with the constitutional and legal provisions. The encounter or extra-judicial killings, witch-hunts of people who are Human Rights activists, intellectuals, lawyers etc, in the name of anti-Maoist operations, should be avoided. Any sort of militarization in the name of fighting Maoism is not generally endorsed by the civil society. Such measures will alienate the State and its agencies, much to the advantage of Maoists.

On the other hand, success of the people-centric strategy depends on the manner how the State machinery overcomes its weakness in the norms of administration and governance. The first and foremost task is to demolish the illegal nexus of bureaucrats, political intermediaries and the middlemen who are instrumental for siphoning off the lion's share of the funds earmarked for a variety of welfare and developmental schemes of the Adivasis, Dalits and the under-privileged. Ironically, the successive governments in the State including the present one could not do much in this direction.

In this connection, the restoration of alienated Adivasi land and proper resettlement and rehabilitation of Adivasis assume paramount importance. Keeping apart the Constitutional and legal impediments, the lack of sincerity from the part of the governments and political parties act as major stumbling block in achieving tangible results. Moreover, the mere resettlement or rehabilitation will not be of much help in resolving the vexed issues. Instead, this should be followed by effective schemes for their better education and skills development that would enable them to explore labour in secondary or tertiary sectors thereby facilitating them to come out of the vicious circle of poverty, indebtedness and social isolation.

Along with material well-being of the Adivasis and the marginalized, the State should ensure dignity and natural justice to these sections through the effective implementation of various protective legislations such as Protection of Civil Rights, Scheduled Caste and Scheduled Tribe (Prevention of Atrocities) Act, 1989, Panchayats (Extension to Scheduled Areas) Act, 1996 (PESA); Scheduled Tribes and Other Traditional Forest Dwellers (Recognition of Forest Rights) Act, 2006, The National Rehabilitation and Resettlement Policy, 2007 and so on. This will help to contain the social humiliation, indignity and injustice that the Adivasis, Dalits and the rural poor are subjected to. Very often marginalization of these communities and the resultant discontentment and distress among these sections has been exploited by Maoists and other militant groups.

Above all, the organized political violence and killings and the virtual collapse of the edifice of the law and order machinery that we have recently witnessed in many parts of the State including the State capital, create conducive climate for Maoists and other insurgents to build up their organizational network. Thus, the need of the hour is that the political executive, instead of pursuing sectarian approach should show political acumen and audacity in rallying the masses on a common platform of patriotism and nationalism in successfully combating the threat of insurgent secessionist forces like Maoists and militants.

KV Thomas

Acknowledgements

As the popular dictum goes that behind every successful man there is a woman, every popular work of literature or art is the joint effort of a set of brains. A number of respectable personalities, in one way or other, have made noteworthy contributions to bring out this work *Kerala-Insurgency for Politics*. First and foremost, I express my profound gratitude to the pioneer leaders of the Maoist movement in Kerala such as K Venu, Ms Ajitha, Gro Vasu, Civic Chandran, M Geethanandan etc, who shared their valuable experiences and insights on the Left Extremist movement. Late VR Krishna Iyer, retired Justice of the Supreme Court, despite his fragile health, had not disappointed me. I have no words to express my gratitude to this doyen of Indian judiciary, who enlightened me with his frank and candid views on the main theme of this book. There were many others like Ms CK Janu, the great symbol of indigenous movement and dozens of others from different walks of life whose contributions are gratefully acknowledged.

I acknowledge the role of The Hindu Centre for Politics and Public Policy, Chennai, for providing the initial logistics and resources for the collection of the basic data of this work. I place on record my sincere gratitude and great appreciation to

Shri VS Sambandan, Chief Administrative Officer of the Centre for his unstinted support and assistance to me.

I am very grateful to young and dynamic 'think-tanks' namely Ms Janani Krishnaswamy (International Centre for Parliamentary Studies, Kings College, London), Ms Simran Kalra (Professor, Jindal School of Government and Public Policy), Dr Nikhil Moro (University of North Texas, USA) and Mr Rajgopal Saikumar (Research Scholar, New York University), whose insights on many issues have found expression in this book.

Last but not the least, I express my gratitude to all those who helped me to bring out this book in the present format.

KV Thomas

Contents

Preface 5

Acknowledgements 15

Abbreviations 19

1. Mapping the Research Field – Historical Evolution of Maoist Movement 23

2. How the 'Red-Terror' Spread in Kerala? 77

3. Maoist Insurgency in Kerala – A Ground Level Study 103

4. Maoists and Adivasis 126

5. Socio-Economic Condition of Adivasis and Maoist Insurgency 136

6. Adivasi Organizations/NGOs versus Maoist Groups 149

7. Maoist Insurgency and Political Mobilization of Adivasis 167

8. Looking Ahead 176

9. Kerala – The Current Scenario 186

10. Conclusion 214

Annexures

1. Special Questionnaire for Survey 229
2. Personal Interview of Ex-Maoists, Civil Rights Activists and Adivasi Leaders 231

Bibliography 275

Index 283

Abbreviations

AGMS	Adivasi Gothra Maha Sabha
APRCC	Andhra Pradesh Revolutionary Communist Committee
AICCCR	All India Coordination Committee of Communist Revolutionaries
AIPRF	All India People's Resistance Forum
AHADS	Attapaddi Hill Area Development Society
ADSS	Adivasi Samyuktha Samara Samiti
BPL	Below the Poverty Line
BSP	Bahujan Samaj Party
BPR&D	Bureau of Police Research and Development
CIC	Centre of Indian Communists
COC	Central Organizing Committee
CRC	Central Reorganizing Committee
CM	Chief Minister
CPC	Communist Party of China
CPI	Communist Party of India
CPI(M)	Communist Party of India (Marxist)
CPI(ML)	Communist Party of India (Marxist-Leninist)
CUC	Communist Unity Centre
CPRs	Common Property Resources
GDP	Gross Domestic Product

GSDP	Gross State Domestic Product
HDI	Human Development Index
HPI	Human Poverty Index
IAS	Indian Administrative Service
IEDs	Improvised Explosive Devices
IPS	Indian Police Service
IPCS	Institute of Peace and Conflict Studies'
INC	Indian National Congress
IAP	Integrated Action Plan
JRS	Janadhipathya Rashtriya Sabha
JSP	Janakeeya Samskarika Vedi
KCP	Kerala Communist Party
KILA	Kerala Institute of Local Administration
KSKTU	Kerala State Karshaka Thozilali Union
LF	Left Front
LDF	Left Democratic Front
LSG	Local Self Government
LWE	Left Wing Extremism
MCP	Maharashtra Communist Party
MNREGP	Mahatma Gandhi National Rural Employment Guarantee Programme
MCC	Maoist Communist Centre
MCCI	Maoist Communist Centre of India
MUC	Maoist Unity Centre
MSP	Malabar Special Police
NDA	National Democratic Alliance
NPMO	National Platform of Mass Organizations
NGO	Non-Governmental Organizations
NTR	NT Rama Rao
OBCs	Other Backward Castes
PESA	Panchayat (Extension of Scheduled Areas) Act, 1996

PDS	Public Distribution System
PHRM	People's Human Rights Movement
PCR	Protection of Civil Rights
PRC	Peoples Republic of China
PWG	People's War Group
RMS	Rashtriya Maha Sabha
RSS	Rashtriya Swayamsevak Sangh
RCC	Revolutionary Communist Committee
RDF	Revolutionary Democratic Front
RCCI	Revolutionary Communist Centre of India
REC	Regional Engineering College
RSM	Revolutionary Students' Movement
RWM	Revolutionary Women's Movement
RWA	Revolutionary Writers Association
RIM	Revolutionary International Movement
SC	Scheduled Castes
ST	Scheduled Tribes
SRE	Security Related Expenditure
SSSC	Shreyas Social Service Centre
SEZ	Special Economic Zone
SIMI	Students Islamic Movement of India
TDP	Telugu Desam Party
UDF	United Democratic Front
UF	United Fronts
UCCR	Unity Centre of Communist Revolutionaries
UNDP	United Nations Development Programme
WGSZC	Western Ghats Special Zonal Committee
WSSS	Wayanad Social Service Society

1

Mapping the Research Field – Historical Evolution of Maoist Movement

The Left Wing Extremism (LWE) or the Maoist insurgency is the most serious challenge confronting the nation in the present millennium. The geographical expanse of Maoist influence affects around 40% of India. However, the extent or the geographical spread of Maoist threat remains to be a contentious issue. The Ministry of Home Affairs in 2010 stated that 34 districts were virtually controlled by Maoists[1] whereas 2010 Planning Commission Report on the LWE claimed that 223 districts in 28 States were reported to be struggling with the menace – 67 districts being categorized as worst affected.[2] The Institute of Conflict Management holds that the LWE groups have their presence in 194 districts in 16 States.[3] Foreign sources put the figure as high as 192 out of the total 602 districts.[4] They hold that the Maoists with around 25,000 regular cadres and over 40,000 supporters are spread across an area of 92,000 square kilometres in the Red Corridor stretching from the Nepal border to India's South West coast.

As long as the government and analysts adopt different yardsticks in identifying Maoist-affected areas, such differences do exist. Some of these assessments are based on the degree of Maoist violence; whereas the others are based on their mere presence. Many extraneous factors influence such assessments which very often fail to reflect the real ground level situation. Obviously, there is increasing demand from the States to include more and more districts as Maoist-affected in order to facilitate them to get substantial Central funds in the name of combating Maoist threat. Thus the number of districts covered under various schemes like Integrated Action Plan (IAP),[5] Security Related Expenditure (SRE)[6] and Special Infrastructure[7] etc, showed steady increase without any corresponding achievements in containing LWE violence or their presence in those States. The lack of consensus among various agencies/departments[8] on the implementation of these schemes or the improper utilization or misuse of funds had adversely affected governments' people-centric strategies to counter the threat in their citadels.

This speaks of the need of better understanding of the problem through proper conceptual and empirical analysis. Historical evolution of the Maoist movement, its social base especially the traditional supporters, socio-economic and developmental factors impacting its growth and the approach of mainstream political parties, NGOs and civil society towards the movement need closer analysis.

Broadly, three distinct phases in the evolution of the movement can be traced – the initial phase beginning in 1967 to its suppression in 1972; the period of ideological differences and physical fragmentation during 1972-1991 and the current phase of consolidation leading to the formation of CPI (Maoist) through the merger of People's War Group (PWG) and Maoist Communist Centre (MCC) in 2004.[9]

HISTORICAL EVOLUTION OF MAOIST MOVEMENT

The legacy of the Maoist insurgency and armed struggles can be traced to the Communist Party of India (CPI). Since the genesis of the party in 1925, differences existed on issues such as ideology, strategy and tactics. Inspired by the Russian and Chinese Revolutions, section of the rank and file in the party was in favour of adopting the path of violence during the freedom struggle. Such cadres played heroic role in The Meerut Conspiracy case of 1929[10] and the Chittagong Armoury raid of 1930[11] which in many respects were unique in the history of the freedom struggle. The 'Tebhaga movement',[12] Telangana uprisings[13] and 'Punnappara-Vayalar' struggles[14] were other major armed struggles of pre-Independence period in which peasants, landless tenants and share-croppers under the banner of the CPI fought against landlords and capitalists.

The theoretical foundation of the Telangana movement – the first major armed struggle inspired by the Left radicals – was based on Maoism and Mao's thesis on democracy and the application of Marxism on Chinese conditions. The Andhra thesis found that "Indian conditions are more akin to Chinese conditions because of the peasant country, agrarian country, colonial country and the semi-colonial country."[15] Initially started in 1946 as an uprising of peasants and rural poor against Nizam of Hyderabad and his army, the movement soon developed into a full-fledged insurgency as noted by Basava Punnaiah, one of its key architects:

> "When we had to fight against Nizam, his Razakars, his army, his police and all that, then we were compelled to go in for guerrilla warfare, armed warfare and with all these ideas; we had to go through Mao's theory of partisan warfare, guerrilla warfare, peasant warfare etc."[16]

The movement opened a floodgate of theoretical, strategic and actical issues which intensified the polemics in the party. Basava Punnaiah rightly observed; "We had to go into theoretical discussion – whether it is a democratic revolution or Socialist revolution or Peoples' Democratic Revolution?"[17]

Such inner party conflicts prominently figured in the Second Party Congress held in Calcutta during 1948 when BT Ranadive's thesis denouncing the strategy of co-operation with 'national bourgeoisie' in pursuance of democratic revolution found acceptance. Interpreting the victory of the working class movements in many East European countries as the 'transition phase of socialism',[18] Ranadive strongly advocated for the 'Socialist revolution' by fostering urban struggles. Such struggles by workers and toiling masses would lead to the ultimate victory of revolutionary forces; he argued. This new revolutionary line gave a fillip to the Telangana struggles which, however, failed to withstand the pressure of massive counter-extremist operations by Indian armed forces.

With divergent approach on Telangana struggles and Calcutta thesis, the party confronted serious internal conflicts mainly on the question of its tactical line. They looked towards Soviet leadership[19] to resolve such inner party conflicts; a new strategy ushering in an era of constructive alliance or co-operation with the progressive sections of national bourgeoisie was formulated. The party which was getting ready to participate in 1952 General elections called off Telangana struggle in October 1951. Thus, the Communist Party of India sowed the seeds of armed struggles in Telangana which later became the cradle of Maoist movement in the country.

The party was in the whirlpool of intense debate during the next one decade (1950-60) mainly on the question of 1951 new programme. The protractors of the new tactical line vigorously pursued the path of peaceful transition to socialism through participation in parliamentary system of government. On the other hand, the more radical cadres, inspired by the memories of Telangana struggle were drifting more and more towards the Maoist line of Marxism-Leninism. They interpreted party's strategy of establishing Communist rule through democratic conduct as betrayal of its revolutionary heritage.

The CPI's sterling performance in 1957 Kerala assembly polls and the formation of first Communist government through democratic exercise was a turning point. The dominant camp advocating the democratic path hailed it as the victory of the new tactical line; the radicals claimed that the anti-Communist liberation struggle in the State and subsequent dismissal of the government by the Centre in 1959 manifested the futility of parliamentary path in pursuing Communist agenda.

The dismissal of the Communist government in Kerala intensified the ideological differences in the party. The radicals sent a clear message to party comrades in different States that the bourgeois-landlord classes could be defeated only through protracted people's war and armed national liberation struggles[20] for which the Communists should shun the parliamentary path and switch over to armed struggle.

The developments in the International Communist movement especially the growing schism between the Soviet Union and Peoples' Republic of China on issues like peaceful transition[21] and peaceful coexistence[22] sharpened the inner party conflicts. These differences had further escalated during the Indo-China conflict in 1962 leading to the split in the party in 1964 and the formation of pro-Soviet Communist Party of India (CPI) and pro-Chinese Communist Party of India – Marxist (CPI-M).

The formation of CPI(M) and the adoption of 1964 policies and programmes upholding peoples' democratic revolution[23] gave an impetus to the Radicals who envisaged that the new leadership, influenced by Maoism and Maoist thought, would lead the party in the path of revolutionary struggles. But their expectations were short-lived. Lured by dominating parliamentary ambitions, the party was keen to work out electoral alliances/understanding with those parties and groups even ideologically opposed to the basics of Marxism-Leninism. Such United Front governments came into power in its citadels like West Bengal, Kerala and Tripura in 1960s. Political exigencies coupled with the sensitive task of cobbling together of alliance partners forced the party to make compromises. The promises made by the party to the landless poor, tenants and the marginalized in respect of land reforms, social equality and egalitarianism could not be fulfilled.

West Bengal was the crucial cubicle of CPI-M's alliance politics. The socio-economic situation in the State was highly feudalistic with rigid caste-class barriers. "In a system that had its roots in the *Zamindars* of the British colonial era, most of the smaller farmers were in fact sharecroppers, forced to give up as much as 50% of their harvest in rent to their *jotedars*, or landlords."[24] The share-croppers and landless peasants devoid of any regular source of income had been so exploited by the money lending class that their survival has become precarious. By 1967, many Bengali newspapers carried accounts of impoverished rural citizens driven to suicide by their dire economic straits.[25]

Despite the enactment of a number of progressive legislations, the Left Front (LF) government in West Bengal could not resolve many of these issues. The district level radical cadres of CPI(M) like Kanu Sanyal and Charu Majumdar who had been propagating Maoist line among share-croppers and agrarian labourers since the middle of 1960s stepped up their organized campaigns. "This brought intra-CPI(M) conflict to a head; the Central Committee claimed they were using the government as an instrument of peoples' struggle but the Maoist faction accused them of indirectly strengthening the State system."[26]

Thus, the sleepy village of Naxalbari in North Bengal witnessed the first spark of the Maoist insurgency in March 1967. The Radical cadres inspired by the teachings of Sanyal and Majumdar forcibly occupied lands; harvested the crops; destroyed land records and debt agreements; executed oppressive landlords and claimed the control of over 300 square miles of territory. But with the intensive police operations, the insurgency was quickly defeated. However, Majumdar emerged as a revolutionary leader and his ideology attracted more and more sections especially the poor and the marginalized.

Emboldened by the open support by the Communist Party of China (CPC), Majumdar floated All India Coordination Committee of Revolutionaries (AICCR) in 1967, which was later rechristened as All India Coordination Committee of Communist Revolutionaries (AICCCR) with a view to bringing together different shades of supporters of Maoist movement under the banner of a revolutionary party. Despite differences in the movement, Majumdar with the blessings of CPC formed CPI(ML) in April 1969 and called for Maoist-inspired violent overthrow of the Indian government by establishing liberated bases in the countryside, surrounding the cities, and eventually subsuming all of India within its people's democratic revolution.[27]

For the next couple of years, the CPML created a reign of terror in many parts of the country. Different shades of Maoist activities and violence were reported from down South to the North and East to West, when Andhra Pradesh and West Bengal accounted for the largest number of killings and violent incidents. The cadres from the States indoctrinated and inspired by Charu Majumdar's strategy of annihilation of class enemies[28] resorted to reckless killing and violence. The brutal murder of *jotedars*, moneylenders, and agents of the government spread 'Red-Terror' throughout the countryside.[29]

The fire had soon spread to Srikakulam district of Andhra Pradesh which witnessed the CPI(M)-led Tribal struggles against the economic exploitation by the landlords as early as in 1961. Inspired by the Naxalbari uprisings and the strategy of the annihilation of class enemies, they resorted to Naxalbari model movement in 1969; killed landlords and moneylenders and captured the control of around 500 square miles. But the movement fizzled out in 1970 due to the coordinated action by security forces, leading to the arrest/killing of senior leaders.

The Revolutionary Communist Committee (RCC) disaffiliated from AICCCR in 1969 was instrumental for another uprising in the hilly forest region bordering Telangana during 1969-70. Though the group with the support of poor Girijans and agrarian workers could liberate an area of 7,000-8,000 square miles, the movement withered away when their leaders were arrested and exiled from the area. Despite such set back, the different shades of Maoist insurgency had taken deep roots in Srikakulam and other parts of Northern Telangana.

The movement had escalated to more and more areas: Midnapore and Birbhum in West Bengal; Muzaffarpur in Bihar; Palia in Uttar Pradesh; Dharmapuri in Tamil Nadu and Thalassery in Kerala where party cadres blindly pursued annihilation strategy and let lose large scale violence. In West Bengal, students and intellectuals from many urban based alma centres joined the movement and gave it an intellectual halo and idealism. New second line leaders like Ashit Chatterjee and Santhosh Rana[30] emerged in Bengal.

In view of the serious setback faced by the movement in their rural/agrarian campaigns, the party adopted strategic reverses such as Cultural Revolution in urban centres like

Calcutta in the form of the destruction of all symbols of bourgeoisie culture. Their targets included the statues of iconic figures and freedom fighters, traditional theatre and cinema, renowned universities and educational institutions etc.

In the wake of large scale violent activities in Calcutta during 1970, the police and the Central forces stepped up their operations that had virtually decimated the movement when the ideologically committed cadres and intellectuals supporting it were put behind the bars or eliminated in fake encounters. The entry of a large number of anti-social elements, criminals and goons into the movement masquerading as revolutionaries and their nefarious activities such as kidnapping of businessmen for ransom, extortion and cold-blooded killing of innocent persons branding them as class enemies or police informers further alienated the movement from the masses. Thus, with the arrest and subsequent death of Charu Majumdar in Calcutta during 1972, the fire lit by the CPML had been temporarily doused.

Ironically, CPML from the very beginning was in a whirlpool of ideological differences. Charu Majumdar's strategy for Indian revolution was the main target of criticism. His blind conviction on annihilation theory; total negation of urban proletariat in struggles and last but not the least the rejection of all mass organizations in building up struggles were challenged by leaders from time to time leading to the emergence of splinter groups.

The first shot was fired in 1969 by T Nagi Reddy of Andhra Pradesh who disagreed with Charu Majumdar on such issues and formed Andhra Pradesh Revolutionary Communist Committee (APRCC). It had broken into other splinter groups such as Unity Centre of Communist Revolutionaries (UCCR) controlled by Reddy himself and Chandra Pulla Reddy's Revolutionary Communist Centre (RCC) – both having their main bases in Andhra Pradesh. Just like Nagi Reddy, Amulya Sen and Kanhai Chatterjee of West Bengal disagreeing with Majumdar on the issue of mass organizations formed Dakshin Desh which was rechristened as Maoist Communist Centre (MCC) in 1975 while shifting its operational bases from West Bengal to Bihar.

With Majumdar's death, the Maoist movement in the country was clearly polarized into two major camps – those who supported the strategy/tactics of Majumdar and those who ideologically opposed him. But the fall of Lin Biao,[31] the designated successor of Mao during the Cultural Revolution from the grace of the Chinese Communist Party, had its ripples in the pro-Majumdar camp. Claiming the legacy of Majumdar, Mahadev Mukherjee of West Bengal became the strong protagonist of pro-Lin Biao faction. He kept alive the revolutionary line of Majumdar in West Bengal with occasional attack on Police Stations and the looting of firearms, till his arrest in 1974.

The anti-Lin Biao camp dominated the scene when the CPML (Liberation) and the Central Organizing Committee (COC), CPML established their strong presence in Bihar and Andhra Pradesh respectively. The COC/CPML that split in 1977 had subsequently emerged as People's War Group (PWG) led by Kondapalli Seetharamaiah. Satyanarayan Singh, Bihar State Committee Secretary of CPML who had been at logger heads with Majumdar since 1971 over the latter's strategy, emerged as the most potential leader in the anti-Majumdar camp. His group became the most mass-based Maoist outfit in Bihar during 1970s. Their main opponent in the State was CPML (Unity Committee) which in 1982 merged with the Bihar State unit of COI/ML leading to the formation of CPML (Party Unity) with Naveen Prasad as its leader.

Various other splinter groups such as Central Reorganizing Committee (CRC) CPML, Centre of Indian Communists (CIC), Communist Unity Centre (CUC), Maoist Unity Centre (MUC), CPML, Red Flag etc were formed in Southern States, Madhya Pradesh, Maharashtra, and Bihar and so on, by interpreting Maoism and Marxism-Leninism, in bits and pieces. The ideological differences, internecine conflicts and disillusionment of cadres virtually emasculated the movement. Added to this were the stepped up operations by police and security forces during National Emergency (1975-77), which decimated the movement in many States except in Andhra Pradesh and Bihar.

In Andhra Pradesh, Kondapalli Seetharamaiah, who formed People's War Group (PWG) in 1980, steadily built up the movement by adopting a two pronged strategy. Though a supporter of Majumdar's annihilation theory, he discarded Majumdar's strategy and concentrated on the organizational consolidation by building up revolutionary mass bodies of the Adivasis, rural peasants and the under-privileged. Operating from the dense forests of the Telangana region conducive for guerrilla warfare, he built up the movement, which maintained its violent profile "with attacks on *jotedars*, police, and police informants."[32] Simultaneously, by rallying the support of radical intellectuals, writers and civil liberty activists, he could effectively pursue social reformist role opposing social evils like prostitution, gender violence, illicit brewing, and atrocities against Adivasis and Dalits etc. With the ground level solidarity and support of those sections, PWG could successfully withstand the police operations for more than one decade.

But, the State of Bihar witnessed an entirely different scenario during 1980s and 1990s, when Maoist Communist Centre (MCC), CPML (Party Unity) and CPML (Liberation) established their bases as a counter-movement against the

'Caste Senas' (private armies) floated by the Upper castes and the landed backward communities targeting Dalits and Adivasis. The Liberation which slowly switched over to a line of normalization, embraced electoral politics in early 1990s, by floating the over ground outfit, the Indian People's Front (IPF). On the other hand, the MCC and the Party Unity, exclusively committed to armed struggles continued their killings of upper caste landlords and their families. Rather than class ideology on Marxist-Leninist lines, they were guided by caste compulsions and exigencies that helped them to broaden their support base among Dalits and rural poor who were the victims of oppression and exploitation by upper caste for centuries.

With their main citadels in Andhra Pradesh and Bihar, the above three groups accounted for 80-90% of Naxalite violence in the country during 1990s.[33] Confronted with ideological differences, they remained antagonistic with each other in their areas of influence and failed to create any major impact at national level. The change of guard in PWG leadership during 1992 gave an impetus for the unity moves. The elevation of Muppalla Lakshmana Rao alias Ganapathy to the leadership, replacing the legendary leader Seetharamaiah accelerated the entire process. Ganapathy, aware of the ground level realities of the Indian polity was fully convinced that "unification (of groups) is the only way to advance the cause of the revolution."[34]

Thus, in 1993, all the three groups were brought together on a common platform under the banner of All India People's Resistance Forum (AIPRF) in order to coordinate their activities in their main areas of operation. However, the AIPRF failed to take off any serious unity moves, except organizing joint rally/campaigns against the neo-colonial and anti-people policies and programmes of ruling class surrendering the interests of the country to the imperialists and multinationals. When the controversies centring around Economic Reforms and liberalization slowly subsided in 1996, the Forum lost its teeth and the groups dissociated themselves from the body and pursued their independent strategy/tactics.

Meanwhile, Ganapathy undeterred by his unity moves could work out the merger between PWG and Party Unity (PU) leading to the emergence of CPML (People's War) in 1998. Similarly, MCC joined hands with a small group, Revolutionary Communist Centre of India (RCCI) and formed Maoist Communist Centre of India (MCCI). After many rounds of negotiations between the PW and the MCCI during 2002-2004, both the groups merged in September 2004 and formed CPI (Maoist) which dominated the Maoist movement in the country during the last one decade.

In the backdrop of the historical transition of Maoist movement with three distinct phases, it is relevant to examine their traditional sources of support; the socio-economic factors impacting its growth; the approach of mainstream political parties towards the movement and the role of civil society and NGOs in countering them.

DALITS AND ADIVASIS: TRADITIONAL SOURCES OF SUPPORT OF MAOIST MOVEMENT

The spread of Maoist movement in India reveals that it draws its main strength from Adivasis, Dalits and the marginalized especially of the backward and under-developed areas of the country. The report of Government of India underlined that "the main support of the Naxalite movement comes from Dalits (Scheduled Castes) and Adivasis."[35] Despite ideological differences within the movement or its geographical shift, this trend was obvious during the different phases of the movement.

For example, more than 65% of the population in Naxalbari village[36] of Siliguri sub-division in Darjeeling district, West Bengal where the first spark of the movement was triggered in 1967 belonged to Adivasis/Dalits, traditionally the 'baghchashis' or share-croppers exploited by big jotedars for centuries. The immediate reason for the uprising was the attack on a Tribal youth who went to plough his land on the strength of a judicial order. The Tribal peasants retaliated forcibly capturing the land and foodgrain stocks of the landlords that led to the death of around one dozen Tribals in the subsequent clashes.

A similar situation developed in Srikakulam, the hilly forested Tribal belt in the North East of Andhra Pradesh, described by the Maoists as the Yunnan of India. The Girijans/Tribals constituted more than 70%[37] of the population in the area. The Girijan Sangham organized at the instance of Vempatapu Satyanarayana and Adibhatla Kailasam became the main source of inspiration for the Tribals to demand their genuine land and other rights that sparked the controversy. Just as in the case of Naxalbari, the killing of two Tribals at Levidi village by local landlords during October 1967 ignited the fire which rapidly spread to more villages at the instance of the newly formed All India Coordination Committee of Communist Revolutionaries (AICCCR). Over the next couple of years Srikakulam had turned into a battle ground of Maoist insurgency and counter-Maoist operations by security forces in which hundreds of Tribals and peasants perished and over 120 police personnel killed.

Situation was not different in other major areas of Maoist conflict during this phase. The Santhals, Oraons, Lodhas and other Tribals were the backbone of Maoist uprisings in Birbhum, Murshidabad, Midnapore and Santhal Parganas (West Bengal) during 1969-70. The Dalits and Tribals were in the forefront of 'Mushahari conflict' in Muzaffarpur, Bihar during 1968; whereas the Dalits and other backward sections played the pivotal role in Lakhimpur Kheri (Terai region/Uttar Pradesh) struggles in 1968 and last but not the least the Adivasis of the Northern Kerala were one of the major sources of support for the early phase of Naxalite movement (1967-70) in Kerala.

The Adivasi Dalit belt in Andhra Pradesh, Bihar and West Bengal was the main pockets of influence of Maoist groups during the second phase of the movement infested by internal contradictions, ideological differences and fragmentation. Since 1980, People's War Group (PWG) dominated the scene in Andhra and their cadres operated in the forested border regions of Telangana where they had strong support base among the Adivasis. By availing Adivasi support and using local terrain conducive for 'guerrilla warfare', they slowly spread their wings to Bastar area of the present Chhattisgarh. Similarly, the rugged terrain coupled with the support of Adivasis helped the Maoist Communist Centre (MCC) to establish strong foothold on the Bengal-Bihar border and subsequently in the plain areas where they enjoyed the support of low caste agricultural workers in struggle with the upper caste land owners.

During the third phase of the Maoist movement commencing from early 1990s, they expanded their base from Andhra Pradesh and Bihar to contiguous areas of the Central Tribal belt in Madhya Pradesh, Maharashtra, Odisha, and what became Chhattisgarh and Jharkhand in 2001.[38] A study of the Ministry of Tribal Affairs revealed that these areas are notable for their rugged terrain and high proportion of Adivasis.[39] West Bengal has figured in the insurgency map, when the Adivasi dominated forest areas bordering Odisha and Jharkhand witnessed their organized campaigns and activities opposing the acquisition of agrarian land for establishing Multinational ventures.

As per 2011 Census, the Scheduled Castes (SC) constitutes 16.9% of total population in India. In fact, Bihar, Odisha, MP, Chhattisgarh, West Bengal and UP accounted for 58% of the Dalit population. Similarly, of the total Scheduled Tribe (ST) population (8.6%) in the country, 68% are in 7 States namely Madhya Pradesh (14.5%); Maharashtra (10.2%); Odisha (9.7%); Gujarat (8.9%); Rajasthan (8.4%); Jharkhand (8.4%) and Chhattisgarh (7.8%).[40]

An analysis of the demographic pattern of 83 Maoist affected districts covered under Security Related Expenditure (SRE) scheme of Government of India[41] revealed that Adivasis (Tribals) and Dalits (SCs) constituted the major chunk of population in these districts. 35 of these districts in 9 States, (Andhra Pradesh – 1; Bihar – 6; Chhattisgarh – 7; Jharkhand – 11; Madhya Pradesh – 1; Maharashtra – 2; Odisha – 5; Uttar Pradesh – 1 and West Bengal – 1) have high intensity of Maoist activities/violence. Notably, majority of these districts have high percentage of ST and SC population as delineated below (Table 1.1):

TABLE 1: ST/SC Population (in percentage) in 35 focused/SRE Districts

State	District	ST (%)	SC (%)	Total (%)
Andhra Pradesh	Khammam	27.37	16.54	43.91
Bihar	Arwal	0.08	20.16	20.24
	Aurangabad	0.04	26.57	26.61
	Gaya	0.07	30.38	30.45
	Jamui	4.48	17.24	21.72
	Jehanabad	0.10	19.81	19.91
	Rohtas	1.07	18.56	19.63

(Contd.)

State	District	ST (%)	SC (%)	Total (%)
Chhattisgarh	Bastar	65.93	2.68	68.61
	Bijapur	80	3.96	83.96
	Dantewada	76.88	2.42	79.30
	Khanker	55.38	4.21	59.59
	Narayanpur	77.36	3.56	80.92
	Rajnandgaon	26.36	10.18	36.54
	Sarguja	55.11	4.90	60.01
Jharkhand	Bokaro	12.40	14.50	26.90
	Chabra	4.37	32.65	37.02
	E/Singhbhum	28.51	4.85	33.36
Jharkhand	Garhwa	15.56	24.18	39.74
	Gumla	68.94	3.16	72.10
	Hazaribagh	7.02	17.5	24.52
	Latehar	45.54	21.3	66.84
	Lohardagga	56.89	3.13	60.20
	Palamu	9.34	27.65	36.99
	Ramgarh	21.19	11.2	32.39
	W/Singhbhum	67.31	3.79	71.01
Madhya Pradesh	Balaghat	22.51	7.37	29.88
Maharashtra	Gadchiroli	38.71	11.25	49.96
	Gondia	16.2	13.2	29.40
Odisha	Gajapati	54.29	6.77	61.06
	Malkangiri	57.83	22.55	60. 38
	Rayagada	66.01	16.99	83.00
	Sambalpur	34.12	18.42	52.54
	Debagarh	35.32	16.67	51.99
Uttar Pradesh	Sonbhadra	20.67	22.63	43.30
West Bengal	Midnapore	14.88	19.07	33.95

(Based on State Primary Abstract – Census 2011.)

The SC/ST population in these districts ranged from 20-84%. 3 districts (Bijapur, Narayanpur and Bastar) of Chhattisgarh; 3 districts (Gumla, West Singhbhum and

Latehar) of Jharkhand and one district (Rayagada) of Odisha, noted for high intensity of Maoist activities and violence, have the highest concentration of these sections.

Demographically, all these districts from Chhattisgarh, Jharkhand, Odisha, Maharashtra, Madhya Pradesh and Andhra Pradesh have high concentration of Adivasi/Tribal population, whereas Maoist infested districts in Bihar showed high percentage of Dalit (SC) population. The Tribal-Dalit population is almost fifty-fifty in Maoist affected districts from Uttar Pradesh and West Bengal.

Thus, a different pattern emerges in respect of the support base of Maoist groups in their main citadels. From the very beginning, the Tribals were the mainstay of various Maoist groups in the whole of Central India except Bihar where the conflicts between lower castes (mainly Dalits) and upper castes contributed to the genesis, growth and consolidation of the movement. For example, the creation of Caste Senas by upper caste landlords and their atrocities against Dalits helped the CPML (Liberation) and the CPML (Party Unity) to build up their strong bases in Central Bihar and the Maoist Communist Centre (MCC) in South Bihar.

The Adivasi support to Maoist insurgency is inextricably interwoven with geography, history, sub nationalist trends, governance, development and socio-economic political factors. An analysis of Forest Survey of India Report[42] revealed that around 160 districts fall under the Red corridor, stretching from upper Gangetic plain bordering Nepal straddling through the plains of Bihar and the forested hills that parallel the East coast of India down as far as the northern Tamil Nadu.[43] Adivasis, Dalits and other backward groups constitute the major chunk of the population in this corridor covering almost 1/5 of the total forest area in the country. Such inaccessible dense forest belt is conducive for guerrilla warfare (Fearon and Laitin[44]).

Obviously, the CPI (Maoist), while formulating their strategy and tactics identified "these hilly regions with dense forest cover; with sufficient economic resources, a vast population and a vast forest area spreading over thousands of square kilometres"[45] as their strategic areas for building up the underground guerrilla apparatus.

By virtue of their traditional habitat, the Tribals adopt an indigenous way of life in which land and forests are their main sources of livelihood. With the advent of the concept of modern State – initially as colonial and later as national – steady deprivation of their traditional resources started and virtually made their survival difficult. Their indigenous identity was in crisis. The exodus of immigrant population to Tribal heart land, extensive alienation of Tribal land, introduction of commercial crops, depletion of forest and water resources, large scale displacement in the name of developmental projects, attack against their customs and culture and extensive exploitation and oppression posed the greatest challenge to their very existence. This led to the emergence of 'sub-nationalist trends' and conflicts between the Tribal community and the State apparatus.

Thus Arundhati Roy[46] has commented that the Tribal people of Central India have a big history of resistance that predates Mao Zedong by centuries. The present citadels of Maoists in Chhattisgarh witnessed series of such movements like Halba rebellion (1774-79), Bhopalpatnam Struggle (1795) Paralkot rebellion (1825); Maria revolt (1842-63); Koi revolt (1859); Muria rebellion (1876); Tarapur rebellion (1848-54), Rani rebellion (1878-82) and Bhumkal revolt (1910).[47] Augul rebellion (1846-47), Kalahandi rebellion (1855) and Sabara rebellion (1856-56) were the major Tribal struggles in the interior areas of Odisha now infested by Maoists.[48] The Maoist affected areas of Jharkhand witnessed such movements like the Kol uprising (1831-1832) and Santhal insurrection (1855)[49] etc.

> "All these rebellions were focused and asserted the traditionally inalienable right of the Tribals on the local resources, land and forests. Often the mobilization was around the issues of tradition, culture and the Tribal way of life. These rebellions were also in protest against an alien system of governance and an alien political, economic and social order that had been forced upon them by the British."[50]

Despite constitutional safeguards and a plethora of legislations, many of these issues such as Tribal land alienation, depletion of forests, displacement and dislocation of Tribals in the name of development and their social and cultural exploitation continued in independent India. Thus, the contradiction between the Tribal community and the State led to frequent conflicts especially in the North East and in the Tribal belt in various States such as Andhra Pradesh, Madhya Pradesh, Chhattisgarh, Odisha and Jharkhand. Ironically, the governments instead of resolving their genuine issues, tried to suppress such movements treating their struggles as basic law and order problem or a threat to internal security. Portraying such movements as national liberation struggles, the Maoists capitalized them to build up their support base among those sections.

Just as in the case of Tribals, the Maoist could successfully exploit the Dalit issues especially their confrontation with landowning upper caste forces in many States where feudal landlords dominated the socio-economic and political spectrum. Around 70% Dalits in India are poor. On a comparative scale, over 10% of Dalits are totally landless and another 77% nearly landless. The high incidence of landlessness coupled with the lack of other productive assets plunged them into extreme poverty, deprivation and exploitation as a result of which large majority of them are engaged in traditional or low status occupation such as sweepers, scavengers, cobblers, washermen etc. More healthy among them were enslaved as farm workers or tillers by landlords for decades; a small section was engaged as tenants or share-croppers under extreme exploitative conditions.

Placed at the lowest level of the social ladder, Dalits are subjected to various discriminatory and exclusionary practices in all walks of life. While untouchability practices continue unabated in many rural and urban areas, there is no let-up in the incidence of atrocities against Dalits. According to Anand,[51] two Dalits are assaulted every hour; three Dalit women are raped and two Dalits are murdered and two Dalit houses are burnt every day. The enforcement of the Protection of Civil Rights (PCR) Act, 1955 and the Atrocities Act is far from satisfactory as manifest by the conviction and acquittal rate of cases registered under these Acts. In the case of the PCR, the conviction rate is merely 2.72% while the acquittal rate is 23.24% with nearly 75% cases pending for trial.[52] Similarly the conviction rate in the cases under the Atrocities Act is 11.04% while the acquittal rate is 88.96%.[53]

The non-registration of cases, apathetic attitude of police personnel towards Dalit victims, political interference and intimidation of the victims to compromise with the perpetrators of violence, indifferent and haphazardous investigation of cases, registration of false counter cases against the victims and the poor quality of prosecution and even prejudiced trial and judgment so on are some of the common issues that go against the interests of Dalits. More intense is the social and economic exploitation. Thus, Professor Sukhadeo Thorat who conducted extensive empirical studies on Dalit paradigm in India had identified a concept of caste and untouchability based on economic discrimination through market and non-market exchange leading to unequal opportunity and poverty among Dalits. Such discrimination in almost every field has virtually stunted the upward mobility of Dalits for centuries.

In fact, the plight of the Dalits is compounded due to the lack of sincerity from the side of political leadership on many vexed Dalit issues coupled with the collusion of the State super structures with the landlords and more powerful and privileged sections. Such trends were more pronounced in States where feudal and semi-feudal forces had dominating influence over the centres of power and State institutions. There the Dalits were evicted from disputed lands; their hutments were set on fire and made them shelter less or were hunted and butchered by the 'Armed Senas' of the upper castes; their women flock were molested or raped and their children were engaged as bonded or child labour and were socially boycotted and ostracized on flimsy grounds. The irony is that such crimes and injustices are not punished. Ms Mary Tyler, the British lady who was arrested along with a group of extremists in Chotanagpur during 1970 unfurled such poignant images:

> "The Naxalite crime was the crime of all those who cannot remain unmoved on an India where a child crawls in the dust with a begging bowl; where a poor girl can be sold as a rich man's plaything; where an old woman should half-starved in order to buy social acceptance; where countless people die of sheer neglect...; where justice is the exception and injustice the rule."[54]

Over the last four decades, the overall plight of Dalits or Adivasis has not changed much. The greatest challenge is the justice administration system which has virtually crumbled and collapsed especially in protecting the legal and constitutional safeguards of these sections. There are bitter stories from

Maoist infested areas of Andhra, Chhattisgarh, Jharkhand and Odisha about Dalits and Adivasis who joined the rank of Maoists when confronted with gross injustices like dispossession from their traditional land, constant harassment by forest officials, rape of their womenfolk, incarceration in false cases or cold-blooded killings of their kith and kin in fake encounters with no action against the perpetrators either by the law enforcement agencies or by the institutions of justice administration.

In many remote areas, there is growing feeling among these sections that the criminal justice system is not meant for them, but for the rich, influential and the powerful. Naturally they look for alternative channels of justice system and see a light at the end of the tunnel in the Maoist's strategy of dispensation of instant justice through 'Peoples Court' and 'Public trial'. Thus, the "fight against the social oppression that the Dalits (lower castes) and the lower among Other Backward Castes (OBCs) have been regularly subjected to is perhaps the most significant among the issues used by the Naxalite movement."[55]

SOCIO-ECONOMIC ISSUES INFLUENCING THE GROWTH OF MAOIST MOVEMENT

The Maoist movement or any other social or political movement does not arise in vacuum. "They are rooted in the objective conditions of life and respond to the deep seated frustrations of the people with the existing social, economic and political order, its institutions and practices and the notion of development, participation and governance which they challenge and seek to change."[56] It will be pertinent to examine as how the various socio-economic and developmental issues contribute to the growth of Maoist movement in India.

Since the genesis of the movement in 1967, a number of government committees, academic scholars and civil society groups studied the issue in detail and found that the Maoist movement has been greatly influenced by various socio-economic developmental issues especially of the Tribals/Dalits and the under-privileged sections. The Expert Panel of the Planning Commission observed:

> "Lack of development coincides with the rise of Maoist movement and the Maoists gain support primarily from impoverished rural population that suffer from under-development, social injustice and discrimination. Maoists exploit the wide gap between the socio-economic and developmental promises made by the government to the poorest and the actual ground level implementation."[57]

Academics like Ramachandra Guha[58] felt that the exclusion of Tribals and the under-privileged from the growth history of India during the last 60 years sparked conflicts such as Naxalite uprisings. The words of former Prime Minister Manmohan Singh echoed such views as:

> "We recognize that Naxalism is not merely a law and order issue. In many areas, the phenomenon of Naxalism is directly related to underdevelopment. It is not a coincidence that it is the Tribal areas that are the main battle grounds of Left Wing Extremism (LWE) today. Large numbers of Tribal areas have become the hunting grounds of Left Wing extremists. Exploitation, artificially depressed wages, iniquitous socio-political circumstances, inadequate employment opportunities, lack of access to resources, under-developed agriculture, geographic isolation, lack of land reforms, all contribute significantly to the growth of Naxalite movement."[59]

The co-relation between socio-economic backwardness and the growth of Maoist movement is evident from ground level data from the affected States. According to Oxford University Multidimensional Poverty Index (2010), a staggering 55% of the Indian population live Below the Poverty Line (BPL) of US dollar 1.25. Those sections numbering around 400 million are mainly concentrated in eight States – Chhattisgarh, Jharkhand, Bihar, Odisha, MP, UP, West Bengal and Rajasthan.[60] Except Rajasthan, the other seven States affected by Maoist insurgency are economically backward with the largest number of Below Poverty Line (BPL) category, as manifest from the following figures (Table 1.2):

TABLE 1.2: Poverty Index and BPL category

State	Monthly per capita		No of BPL people (in lakhs)	% of BPL people
	Rural	Urban		
AP	**860**	**1,009**	78.78	9.20
Bihar	**778**	923	358.15	33.74
Chhattisgarh	**738**	**849**	104.11	39.93
Jharkhand	748	974	124.38	36.96
MP	771	897	234.66	31.65
Maharashtra	967	1,126	197.92	17.35
Odisha	695	861	138.53	32.59
Rajasthan	905	1,002	102.92	14.71
UP	768	941	598.19	29.45
West Bengal	783	981	184.98	19.98
ALL India	**816**	**1,000**	**2,697.83**	**21.92**

(State specific poverty lines for 2011-12, Planning Commission.)

The poverty index and percentage of people living below the poverty line in Maoist infested States like Chhattisgarh, Jharkhand, Odisha, Bihar and MP are higher than that of all India figures. Another notable feature is that the bulk of such poor belonged to Tribals and Dalits. The Human Poverty Index

(HPI), the yardstick to assess the level of deprivation among a given social group remains high among these sections. The all India HPI for Scheduled Castes (SCs) and Scheduled Tribes (STs) was estimated to be 41.47% and 47.79% respectively, as against 31.34% for other categories. The HPI for SCs and STs in respect of Maoist affected States is as follows (Table 1.3):

TABLE 1.3: HPI for SCs/STs

State	HPI for SCs %	HPI for STs %
Andhra Pradesh	36.54	46.61
MP (including Chhattisgarh)	43.68	55.08
West Bengal	37.72	47.72
Odisha	47.66	60.69
Bihar (including Jharkhand)	59.36	60.47
Maharashtra	31.48	43.88
UP	50.03	55.45
All India	41.47	47.79

(Human Poverty Index for SC/ST – Regional variation 2000.)

The comparatively high HPI of SCs and STs speaks of the lack of basic amenities or facilities to these sections as manifest from the following Table 1.4:

TABLE 1.4: Parameters that determine HPI (SCs, STs and General)

Parameters	Dalits	Tribals	Others
Landlessness	10%	12%	4.8%
No of Households with consumption up to ₹ 340	40%	50%	17%
Literacy	67% (M)	59% (M)	79 (M)
	42% (F)	35% (F)	58% (F)
Attendance in schools (5-14 years)	68%	61%	81%
Infant Mortality Rate (per 1,000 lives)	83	84	61

(*Contd.*)

Parameters	Dalits	Tribals	Others
Antenatal care	42%	18%	64%
Mortality of children (up to 5 years) per 1,000	119	127	83
% of Children with anaemia	78%	79%	40%
Availability of drinking water	27%	15.2%	45.2%
Availability of Tap water	32%	20%	40.1%
Having Latrine facilities	23.7%	17%	42.2%
Connect with waste water outlay	42.9%	21.8%	50.6%
Pacca houses	42.8%	24.4%	57.7%
Access to Electricity	44.3%	36.5%	61.4%

Source: Based on the reports of Planning Commission, GOI, 2008 and Ministry of Tribal Affairs, 2005.

These figures are more precarious in respect of Maoist affected States like Chhattisgarh, Odisha etc. Chhattisgarh is a typical example: The State is having the highest overall poverty ratio of any major Indian State with around 40% of people live below poverty line; 10 out of 16 districts do not have a district hospital; one health care centre services 40,000 people; infant mortality rate is the highest (68%); 90% of the population work in the rural farm sector; 68% of households do not have electricity; 49% of households have no access to water; only 19% of agriculture land is irrigated; hardly 1% of the population has a telephone; 40% of rural villages are not serviced by roads; 53% of children do not attend primary schools and 64% school dropout rate among STs.[61] No doubt, during the last decade there is marginal improvement in overall situation. But the State is lagging behind in infrastructural development particularly in Maoist affected areas despite the best efforts of the present government to launch a number of developmental projects.

Such indicators strongly reflect on the Human Development Index (HDI). According to the UNDP India Report (2011)[62] on Human Poverty and Socially Disadvantaged Groups in India, the HDI at all India level for SCs is estimated to be 0.303, which is lower than the HDI for non-SC/ST at 0.393 for the period 1980-2000. The "STs along with other marginalized groups especially in States affected by extremist violence (like Andhra Pradesh, Bihar, Chhattisgarh, Jharkhand, Madhya Pradesh, Maharashtra, Odisha and West Bengal) are not only worse than other groups in their respective States, but also their counterparts in other parts of the country."[63]

The wide variation in the HDI of individual districts of the same State explains as how Maoists have established their pockets in certain areas of a developed State. A unique example is Maharashtra. Mumbai city is assessed to have the highest HDI (1.0). Considering this as absolute, Thane district with HDI, 0.82 is rated as second highest in the State. Gadchiroli district which is considered to be the citadel of Maoists, has the lowest HDI (0.210). Similar pattern of Maoist presence and activities can be found in West Bengal, Odisha and Andhra Pradesh indicating that "Maoist conflicts are often localized and depended on unequal spatial distribution of resources within the country."[64] Thus, in the present citadels of Maoists, there exists an "established link between underdevelopment, regional imbalances, economic disparity and gun culture."[65]

The HDI or the socio-economic conditions of Dalits and Tribals are closely intertwined with the agrarian structure. As per Planning Commission data, 45.6% of Dalits and 38.13% of Tribals are agricultural workers. More than 70% of Tribals depend upon agriculture. The percentage of Dalits and Tribals in non-agrarian occupations or activities continues to remain nominal. Thus their main source of income and livelihood depends on the pattern of land holding and the availability of land for cultivation and other productive assets. In the absence of viable employment opportunities, they are forced to depend upon the landowning class for their livelihood. Many of them work as tenants or share-croppers of landlords who exploit them through long hours of work with low wages, debt bondage and denial of due share of produce to them. In the caste based social structure with upper caste landed gentry enjoying all pervasive powers, Dalits are always subjected to humiliating treatment and physical punishment with social immunity.

The case of Tribals is not much different. They have been deprived of their traditional rights over the Forest and other natural resources. This is mainly through the extensive alienation of Tribal land by force, fraud or manipulation and their displacement from the traditional land or habitat through government acquisition. Over the years after independence, the Tribal land has substantially dwindled in almost all States. The more challenging phenomenon is their steady displacement due to government's compulsory acquisition. More than 40% of the approximately 60 million displaced persons between 1947 and 2,000 are Tribals.[66]

It is significant that Maoists could establish their strong bases precisely in those States like Andhra Pradesh, Chhattisgarh or Odisha where there has been large scale displacement of Tribals. Despite such challenges and a mosaic of resistance movements and mass struggles, the acquisition of such land rich in minerals and natural resources constitutes one of the major agenda of the government's crony capitalism. Organized efforts are made to circumvent constitutional and legal impediments that have come up while pursuing such a policy. A typical example is the landmark judgment in Samatha case[67] which categorically stated:

> "The object of the Fifth and Sixth Schedule is not only to prevent acquisition, but also to ensure that Tribals remain

> in possession and enjoyment of lands in Scheduled Areas for their economic empowerment, social status and dignity of their person: The Constitution intends that land always should remain with the Tribals. Even the government land should increasingly get allotted to them individually and collectively."

The governments greatly influenced by the compulsions of globalization and liberalization adopted a negative approach on this judgment. Initially, on the lines of a secret Note (No 16/48/97-M-VI) dated July 10, 2000, by the Ministry of Mines, the government moved the Apex Court for an amendment in Article 244, Clause 5(2) for removing the prohibitions and restrictions on the transfer of land by Adivasis to non-Adivasis for undertaking any operations including prospecting and mining. Later, the government strategy was to get reversed the judgment in respect of similar other cases like, POSCO, BALCO and Vedanta in Chhattisgarh and Odisha. Thus a civil rights activist Late Balagopal has rightly commented: "the State Governments circumvented the judgment through the subterfuge of creating a legal fiction of State enterprise as the agency to which the land could be transferred which in turn leased it out to Corporates."[68]

Influenced by neo-capitalist and corporate policies of the liberalization era, the governments showed a lukewarm approach in safeguarding the genuine interests of Tribals. A study by the Ministry of Rural Development (2004) revealed that out of 3.75 lakh cases of alienated Tribal land measuring 8.5 lakh acres registered for restoration, only 1.62 lakhs covering an area of 4.41 lakh acres were decided in favour of Tribals. 1.55 lakh cases with an area of 3.62 lakh acres were rejected.

In many States, the politically backed non-Tribals' lobby who occupied bulk of the Tribal land by force or fraud virtually defeated restoration orders by filing appeals etc. Thus, the Expert Group on Prevention of Alienation of Tribal Land and its Restoration[69] has identified major anomalies in the disposal of such cases especially corruption and malpractices at the instance of non-Tribal lobby, long pendency, dismissal of cases of Tribals on flimsy grounds and major difficulties in getting possessions delivered.

Similar procedural flaws had virtually defeated the effective implementation of other legislations such as The Scheduled Tribes and Other Traditional Forest Dwellers (Recognition of Forest Rights) Act, 2006 (Forest Rights Act), the Panchayats (Extension to the Scheduled Areas) Act, 1996 (PESA) and the Land Acquisition, Rehabilitation and Resettlement Act, 2011, which are aimed at dousing the flames of unrest among Tribals by ensuring their rights over forest/natural resources and the effective decentralization of governance with their participation.

The alienated Tribals and those displaced by the compulsory government acquisitions were allotted alternate land which in many respects was not conducive for the traditional cultivation or crops. In fact, lion's share of Tribal land – whether traditional or restored – are less cultivable or fertile due to lack of irrigation facilities, fluctuating climatic conditions and environmental hazards. For example, only 26% Tribal land has irrigation facilities as compared to 53% in respect of other Communities.[70] The naked corruption and other malpractices coupled with political intervention and nepotism virtually defeated governments' rehabilitation and resettlement programmes leading the Tribals and other displaced sections to utter frustration and despair, which to a great extent, could be exploited by the Maoists in building up their pockets among the affected groups.

LAND RIGHTS OF DALITS AND TRIBALS – FERTILE GROUND FOR MAOIST EXPLOITATION

Beginning from the Telangana uprisings of late 1940s, the land and land related issues constituted an integral part of the revolutionary struggles by the Communist parties. They identified the landless peasants and small scale agrarian workers as the frontline soldiers of proletarian struggles on Marxist-Leninist lines. These sections actively participated in a number of major armed struggles of pre-Independence period such as 'Tebhaga movement', Telangana and Srikakulam uprisings and 'Punnappara-Vayalar' struggles under the command of the undivided Communist party. Thus, the Communists coined catchy slogans like "Land to the landless; land to the tillers" and included such themes in their policies and programmes. For example, the Communist Party of India (Marxist) ever since their formation in 1964 stood for abolishing landlordism by implementing radical land reforms and giving land free of cost to agricultural labourers and poor peasants.[71]

No doubt, the CPM-led governments in Kerala and West Bengal introduced radical land reforms and made serious efforts for the distribution of surplus land to landless poor. But, on many instances, compelled by parliamentary ambitions, they made compromises on the implementation of these reforms. On the other hand, Congress after its historical split in 1969 by wearing a facade of progressive ideas went ahead with half-baked land reforms in other States especially in the light of the growing unrest and struggles by Tribals, Dalits and landless for land rights. Influenced by electoral politics and compulsions, almost all the mainstream parties failed to implement the land reforms in their true letter and spirit protecting the inalienable rights of Tribals, Dalits and other marginalized sections.

The Maoists could effectively exploit the deviations of mainstream parties in respect of the implementation of land reforms. A close look at on such issues is imperative for better appreciation of land reforms vis-a-vis Maoist strategy. In the Zamindari system of British colonial period, majority of the landless peasants were tenants or share-croppers who were forced to shelve more than 50% of their harvest to landlords or jotedars. In the highly caste-oriented society with upper caste hegemony in all walks of life, the Dalits, Tribals and other lower castes were the most exploited lot who were treated like slaves for many decades. The dawn of independence had brought a ray of hope to these sections; but with landlordism and feudalism having decisive sway over the socio-political and economic set up in the country, their fate had not changed much. Exploitation and oppression of downtrodden sections continued in one form or other as a result of which the land reforms and land redistribution efforts have virtually bypassed majority of Dalits, Tribals and the landless peasants.

The reforms had abolished Zamindari and tenancy systems. But the large majority of illiterate Dalits and Tribals who functioned as tenants of big landlords failed to get the ownership or possession of land as they lacked any records or documents to establish their long years of cultivating status. Similarly, after the implementation of tenancy reforms, the landlords/absentee landlords resorted to large scale informal tenancy through oral orders to defeat the land reforms. Majority of such tenants especially Dalits and Tribals bereft of any records to prove their tenancy failed to get the protection of laws. A corrupt revenue bureaucracy with pro-landlord proclivities very often played in the hands of landowning class detrimental to the interests of tenants.

Similarly, the Dalits, Tribals and the landless poor were not much benefited out of the redistribution of land acquired through ceiling, Bhoodan movement or from the general pool of governmental land. Hardly 2% of land could be acquired through such schemes. In many States, the land so acquired and located in far flung areas without any infrastructure or basic amenities were virtually barren and uncultivable. Despite the proclaimed government policy of preference to Dalits and Tribals in allotment of land, the upper crust of the peasantry from other lower castes managed to get sizeable chunk of such land. Moreover, in view of a series of litigations on the acquisition of surplus land and its ownership, even those who got allotment were subsequently evicted from their dwellings.

Many States launched the ambitious programme of land to shelter less, in order to better the housing facilities of the landless poor. What mattered more in such schemes was political exigencies and populism, which ultimately led to the emergence of a number of sprawling slums and housing colonies of the under-privileged without any infrastructure or basic amenities such as electricity or drinking water. Such colonies with majority of residents devoid of any sustainable source of income had soon transformed into typical 'ghettos', prone to criminal and extremist activities.

One major fall out of the land reforms was the social tension and intensification of class/caste conflicts. This was more acute in States like Bihar, Madhya Pradesh, Uttar Pradesh, Odisha, Maharashtra and Andhra Pradesh where upper caste oriented feudal landlordism backed by mainstream parties was not prepared to reconcile with the land reforms or interrelated measures. Not only that tenancy rights were denied to tenants belonging to lower castes, but even the land allotted to them under government schemes were also encroached upon by the landlords or their private armies.

Discrimination and deprivation increased on the use of Common facilities by the under-privileged. The Upper and middle castes denied access to Common Property Resources (CPRs) such as grazing field, drinking water ponds, irrigation facilities, Fish ponds, play grounds, Community Halls, Burial grounds etc to the Dalits, Tribals and the poor so that these sections found their survival in the newly allotted land or colonies difficult. Any resistance by Dalits or Tribals was suppressed by the Upper caste lobby with the patronage of political parties or law enforcement officials. The long saga of caste conflicts in many of those States arose out of land related issues or the urge of the Dalits and the landless poor to uphold their identity and to ensure livelihood.

The plight of Tribals was more arduous. On one hand, the steady alienation of Tribal land by the powerful non-Tribal lobby has uprooted them from their traditional habitat. The promise of restoration of alienated Tribal land and its redistribution remained as mirage because of the diabolical designs and vote bank politics by mainstream parties. The amendment in Indian Forest Act coupled with the enactment of new forest laws such as The Forest Conservation Act, 1980, The Wildlife Protection Act 1972 and a plethora of legislations on Environment and Ecology have curtailed or denied access of Tribals to various Forest resources. Other policy decisions such as allocation of forest land for private industry, establishment of Wildlife sanctuaries or National Parks displacing Tribals from their traditional land, plantation policy favouring commercial crops/cultivation in the place of natural vegetation etc added the dilemma of Tribals. The forest officials harassed and haunted the Tribals in the name of implementing these policies. Millions of Adivasis and Dalits were displaced or evicted from their traditional habitat without proper rehabilitation or resettlement package.

In such a socio-economic milieu when Dalits, Tribals and the landed poor were fighting for land rights, the Maoists seriously took up the issue with their popular slogan *"Khet par adhikar ke liye lado, desh men janwad ke liye bado"* (fight for land rights, march towards democracy in the country).[72]

Regardless of ideological contradictions or differences in strategy, land related issues especially its redistribution among the Dalits, Tribals and the landless poor remained one of the major tasks of Maoist movement in the country. For example, despite strong reservations among a section of comrades, Charu Majumdar, father of the Maoist movement in the country, was deeply committed to the ideological line that feudal landlordism which is the principal contradiction in the Indian context should be fought with and eradicated through the annihilation of landlords.

For more than three decades since the Naxalbari uprisings in 1967, the CPML vigorously pursued this strategy which boomeranged against the movement in some States where it was at incipient stage. The other CPML groups like the Maoist Communist Centre (MCC), Liberation, CPML (Party Unity) etc, though having different tactical approach, built up their bases by actively involving in various struggles on land related issues. Fundamentally, some of these groups which followed the phase-wise theory of revolution identified the first stage as the struggle to ensure the right to land; the second phase being the resistance struggle to protect their economic interests and the third stage of political struggles leading to the armed revolution for overthrowing the government in power. For example, MCC and Liberation, focusing on the inequality in land distribution and constant conflicts between landlords and landless peasants were successful in strengthening their movements in States like Bihar, whereas the other Maoist groups like People's War Group (PWG) built up their strong bases in Andhra Pradesh, Chhattisgarh, Odisha etc, by taking up the issues of Tribals like land alienation, denial of minimum wages and harassment by forest and revenue officials.

The protection of land rights and redistribution of land to the landless especially the Dalits and Tribals continue to be the main focus area of Maoists. For example, the People's War Group (PWG) of Andhra Pradesh during 1980-1990 distributed around 400 acres of land (forcibly captured from landlords) to the landless in Karimnagar and Nizamabad districts, besides protecting the interests of Tribals in over 18000 acres of forest land in Telangana region. Similarly, the MCC and CPML (Party Unity) built up their strong bases in Bihar through land related struggles by the landless poor.

The CPI (Maoist) have identified that one of their main tasks is "to redistribute land among landless poor, Adivasis and agricultural workers on the basis of the slogan land to the tillers and ensure equal right of women over the ownership of land."[73] While vigorously pursuing the Maoist agenda of redistribution of land among the landless poor, they have recently opened new fronts against the move of governments to acquire large areas of land in Tribal dominated Scheduled areas for dams, mining and Multinational corporations. The Maoists could successfully exploit such movements/struggles by agrarian workers, peasants and Tribals in Nandigram, Singur and Lalgarh (West Bengal), Dhinkia, Niyamgiri and Kalinganagar (Odisha) and Baniladile and Lohandiguda (Chhattisgarh) to broaden their base in those areas. Inspired by these movements, the Maoists are engaged in building up Strategic United Fronts by actively involving in various struggles by Tribals, Dalits and other under-privileged groups. As part of this strategy, the Maoists have floated a number of Front and extension organizations such as Revolutionary Democratic Front (RDF) to broaden their mass base.

POLITICAL MOBILIZATION OF TRIBALS AND DALITS – STRATEGIES TO COUNTER MAOISM

The genesis and spread of any violent movement or struggle like Maoism is sometimes attributed to the failure of democracy, described by many as the greatest antidote to contain social unrest and turmoil through institutional mechanisms like regular elections and formation of popular governments. The political parties play a pivotal role in any democratic set up. The failure of institutional democracy and its processes are reflective of the fact that these parties cannot rise up to the expectations of all sections of the masses. Slowly and steadily, undemocratic trends and tendencies such as criminalization of politics with money and muscle power usurping democratic processes, corruption and mal-governance creep into the system.

Overdependence on caste/community based vote bank politics virtually makes them incapable of properly using democratic space to engineer social change and promote measures empowering the marginalized sections. Even the political equality of Dalits and Tribals in exercising free and fair franchise has been jeopardized. Influencing the poor and illiterate voters in the elections by distributing cash, food or alcohol; booth capturing and intimidation of voters to deny access to voting; physical assault and social boycott of voters who fail to comply the 'dictates' of dominant caste/group etc, weaken the democratic fabric of any country.

The functioning of much trumpeted Panchayati Raj Institutions falls short of the expectations of the marginalized. The mainstream parties with dominant castes at the helm of affairs stage-manage the elections to three-tier bodies filling the reserved quota of Scheduled Castes, Scheduled Tribes and women with their own puppets virtually keeping these sections away from any decision/policy making process. Moreover, many crucial provisions of Panchayat (Extension of Scheduled Areas) Act, 1996 (PESA) are either diluted or misinterpreted so that decentralization at grassroots level with the active participation of Dalits and Tribals remains a myth. A bureaucracy subservient to dominant and middle castes very often defeats such progressive legislations much to the discontent and frustration of the marginalized.

While the mainstream parties are successful in sabotaging various constitutional safeguards of the Dalits and Tribals in the arena of governance, they adopt ingenious methods to keep them away from key positions in the party organization. There is no serious effort to mobilize members of these communities and elevate them to key positions. Instead, a few upcoming leaders are accommodated in petty positions and use as pawns to pursue party's 'vote bank politics'. Similarly, by elevating a handful of Dalits or Tribals as figure heads of Constitutional or Statutory bodies, these parties effectively disseminate a message that they are the real messiahs of the poor and downtrodden! Ironically those who adore such constitutional posts are keener to obey the 'dictates' of their masters than to work for the genuine rights of their suffering brethren.

Those leaders who occupy major political space through various struggles espousing the Tribal cause very often betray the larger interest of the community. The rise and fall of leaders like Madhu Koda, Shibu Soren (Jharkhand), Mahindra Karma (Chhattisgarh) etc, speaks volume of such trends. Another set of Dalit leaders who built up mass based political parties like the Bahujan Samaj Party (BSP) riding high on the wave of sensitive Dalit issues, slowly abandon the Dalit agenda and emerge as apostles of 'Social Engineering'[74] and other political gimmicks in order to ensure their seats of power.

In nut shell, the mainstream political parties virtually failed in the major task of political mobilization of Dalits, Tribals and the under-privileged by winning over their confidence. This, to a great extent, has influenced the growth of Maoists in States like Maharashtra, Andhra Pradesh, Madhya Pradesh, Chhattisgarh, Odisha and Jharkhand. The Andhra Pradesh High Court[75] which examined the role of political parties in the context of mounting Naxalite activities in the State during 1980s rightly observed that political parties lost touch with the people at grass roots. The political vacuum so created was filled by Naxalites who through their strategy of reckless violence against the 'class enemies' created a reign of terror.

Ironically, the political parties, instead of resisting such challenges and defending the affected sections, virtually withdraw from the main citadels of Maoists and suspend their organizational activities thereby helping the consolidation of the movement. For example, in Telangana belt of Andhra Pradesh, political activities came to a standstill during late 1980s and early 1990s when 'red-terror' spread its wings. In many parts of Telangana like Karimnagar and Mehboobnagar, the political parties were forced to seek permission from the People's War Group (PWG), before conducting any programme – be it canvassing for votes or holding meeting in their strongholds. For many years, the situation was not different in Maoist strongholds in Chhattisgarh and Jharkhand where the 'dictates' of ultras went unquestioned. Even now, many parts of Chhattisgarh remain inaccessible to mainstream political parties because of the concentrated activities of Maoists.

The political exigencies very often influence the approach of parties towards Maoists. Perhaps, convinced by such ground level realities of his own State, Koratala Suryanarayana, a senior leader of the Communist Party of India (Marxist), Andhra Pradesh had succinctly put this trend as: "the political parties which have been in power in the State for the last three or four decades have been trying to utilize or use the services of these extremist groups either to come to power or to perpetuate their power."[76] The heart of the matter is that major political parties, eager to capture the seats of power through Machiavellian politics are not susceptible to adopt a united approach or strategy to face a major challenge like Maoist insurgency.

A brief case study of the political history of Andhra Pradesh, a citadel of Maoists for more than three decades, demonstrated the above trend. During 1970s when the Indian National Congress (INC) was in power both at the Centre and State, the party led government adopted a hard line to meet the initial Maoist challenge. When the political fortunes of the party had eclipsed due to the emergence of regional parties like the Telugu Desam Party (TDP), the INC was predominantly guided by political exigencies. Dominated by electoral interests, the party led by Dr Chenna Reddy recognized the 'patriotic image' of the People's War Group (PWG) and lifted the ban on the outfit in December 1989. For more than one year, the extremists had unfettered freedom.

In the wake of large scale violence, series of extortion and destruction of public and private properties, N Janardhanan Reddy, the successor of Chenna Reddy, reimposed the ban on PWG and its front organizations during May 1992. His hard-line policies including intensive anti-PWG operations led to palpable decline in extremist violence till 1994 when NT Rama Rao of TDP returned to power. YS Rajasekhara Reddy of the INC, who was elevated as CM in 2004 adopted a dual policy of dialogue cum ceasefire and systematic security operations which broke the backbone of the newly emerged CPI (Maoist). In fact, the ceasefire negotiations personally attended by senior Maoist leaders virtually exposed the clandestine network of

CPI (Maoist) that made the security operations against Maoists easier and successful. His successor Kiran Kumar Reddy, to a great extent, could checkmate the re-grouping efforts of Maoists through his two-pronged strategy of law enforcement and socio-economic development.

The case of the Telugu Desam Party (TDP) was equally inconsistent. NT Rama Rao (NTR) who successfully led the TDP to power in the State in 1982 riding high on the wave of 'Telugu pride' adopted a policy of appeasement with the PWG ostensibly to lure them for dialogue. Describing the Maoists as "true patriots who had been misunderstood by the ruling classes" he de-escalated anti-PWG operations and to a great extent won their passive electoral support. But, soon, PWG let loose a reign of terror through killing of civilians, extortion and kidnapping including a couple of senior IAS officers. Thus NTR government was forced to switch over to hard-line approach and a special task force 'Greyhounds' was constituted in 1987. Their stepped up operations helped to contain the large scale violence by ultras. NTR who was unseated in 1989 elections, on return to power in 1994, adopted a policy of appeasement and lifted the ban on PWG leading to the recurrence of violence and their steady expansion to more and more areas including the border States of Maharashtra and Odisha. Chandrababu Naidu who replaced NTR revived the ban on PWG and its front organizations and reverted to the hard line policy of confronting the extremists by force. Side by side, his government formulated a long-term policy to tackle Maoist threat through rural development schemes especially for the Tribals and rural poor.

In fact, the recent killing of Nayeemuddin alias Nayeem, the most wanted Maoist-turned-gangster in an alleged exchange of fire with police in Telangana during August 2016 and the subsequent tirade by political parties and bureaucrats throw much light as how these parties are hand in glove with Maoists and other extremists in safeguarding narrow political interest at the cost of national security and integrity of the nation. While Telangana Rashtra Samithi (TRS) blamed the TDP for nurturing Nayeem when it was in power between 1994 and 2004, the latter alleged that section of TRS leaders in the past shielded Nayeem. The Congress party has also been accused of continuing the State support for Nayeem between 2004 and 2014. Similarly, there were allegations of nexus between political leaders and renegade Maoist Kattula Sammaiah who died in mysterious circumstances during 2001 after he was injured in an aborted take off of an aircraft at Colombo airport. Sammaiah, an accused in IPS officer KL Vyas's murder, was on his way to Frankfurt for setting up a windmill project there. Ironically, such nexus or linkages are buried under the carpet enabling the sections of political parties and Maoists/insurgents to continue their symbiotic relationships.

The lack of vision or long-term strategy by mainstream parties to tackle the Maoist threat very often helps the ultras to consolidate their base by overcoming the pressure exerted by security forces during intensive 'flushing out' operations. For example, through the process of dialogue or ceasefire, they manage to get the ban lifted; secure the release of cadres in detention and succeed in the re-grouping efforts exploiting the lull in operations. On many occasions, they try to exploit such exercises for building up their public image and acceptance through open but distorted statements denigrating the State and its superstructures for failure of dialogue.

More serious is the issue of collusion between mainstream parties and Maoists. Sometimes, the political parties use extremist cadres to advance the narrow political and personal interests of the leaders. Unfortunately, such nexus existed tacitly or otherwise in almost all States like Andhra Pradesh, Bihar, Chhattisgarh, Jharkhand, Madhya Pradesh, Odisha and West Bengal and so on, worst affected by Maoist movement. Perhaps, the statement of Balswarup Yadav alias Sridharji,[77] the area Commander of the military wing of CPI (Maoist) in Jharkhand reflected this trend: "Several members of Parliament and Legislative Assembly of Jharkhand and Bihar as well as top leaders of many political parties were in regular contact with leadership and cadres of the CPI (Maoist) and sought their help." Similar sentiments were expressed by Inder Singh Namdhari, a prominent leader of Janata Dal (United) and ex-Speaker of Jharkhand as:

> "Vast majority of politicians can be broadly placed in two categories. One section of politicians who have faith and belief in the democratic political practice stay away from the Maoists, without criticizing or supporting them. Theirs is a stay aloof policy. The other section is actually hand in glove with Maoists on a day-to-day basis. They do their political activity in constant consultation with the Maoists and with their active support. This support extends from garnering votes in elections to eliminating political and personal rivals."[78]

Essentially, both these classes of politicians undermine the smooth functioning of democratic institutions and the systematic development of Maoist affected States, by succumbing to the pressure and influence of the extremists. Thus, along with a united approach by mainstream parties in seriously fighting against the threat of Maoists, these parties and their leadership should not fall prey to the lure of short-term political gains and compromise with the Maoists. But, the crucial question is how far the mainstream parties will sincerely practice such mundane democratic values in the midst of growing influence of 'vote bank politics' in Indian polity?

Maoist Insurgency and the Civil Society

In any modern welfare State, the civil society which is independent of the government has a crucial role in nation building process. As interpreted by Antonio Gramsci,[79] the Italian political thinker and philosopher, a civil society which is in the realm of struggle has the potential to sweep away every component of the old order – cultural, economic and political – in pursuance of a Socialist revolution.

Ironically, the bulk of the civil society in our country is infested by ideological or caste-community differences. Virtually they are different reflections of the same contested set of material relations. Thus, on many occasions, civil society adopts a cynical or opportunistic approach towards Maoism or the issues of the under-privileged sections especially the Tribals and Dalits.

However, the Non-Governmental Organizations (NGOs) or 'activist groups' have become an inevitable component of the civil society. As majority of the activist groups or progressive NGOs basically work among the marginalized and under-privileged sections, conflict of interest takes place between these bodies and the Maoist groups as witnessed in many States like Andhra Pradesh, Bihar, Jharkhand, Chhattisgarh, Odisha and Maharashtra.

The Maoists are ideologically opposed to conventional NGOs which according to them hamper the growth of revolutionary movements in view of their neo-colonial and imperialist nature of campaigns and activities among the rural and downtrodden sections making them loyal and subservient to the State and its agencies. Similarly, Maoists see another set of NGOs as government-sponsored bodies functioning as the appendages of various government agencies with their narrow agenda. Thus, in early 1990s a number of Telangana-based

NGOs like Samata, Chaitanya Saravanti and Laya, working among Tribals, landless poor and the marginalized were forced to shift their area of operations when the PWG was making strong waves in that region. Similar scenario prevailed in undivided Bihar and Madhya Pradesh when many NGOs and 'activist bodies' working among Tribals and unorganized workers in agrarian and industrial sectors, attracted the wrath of Maoists.

Over the last few years when the Maoists are pursuing the idea of 'United Strategic Front' to broaden their revolutionary mass base by rallying ideologically like-minded groups, there is major shift in their approach towards NGOs/activist groups. Many Maoist groups feel that the marginalized and the under-privileged sections are the best judges in determining the presence or otherwise of NGOs or any other organization in their area on the basis of their activities and commitment to the people at the grassroots. While they continue to oppose NGOs sponsored by the government or religious/pseudo-religious or caste-community organizations, they are not antagonistic towards such bodies engaged in a myriad of activities meant for the uplift of the poor and the downtrodden. For example, Samata in Andhra Pradesh, Chhattisgarh Mukti Morcha in Chhattisgarh, Ganga Mukti Andolan of Bihar, Manthan Yuva Sansthan in Jharkhand and Adhar in Odisha are a few such NGOs which have taken up sensitive issues like Tribal empowerment, gender justice, environment stabilization, natural resource management, equality and social justice. Many ex-Maoists or pro-Left intellectuals and activists are associated with these organizations.

Significantly, these activist bodies could ignite the self-pride, ethos and identity of the vulnerable and under-privileged sections leading to the formation of autonomous organizations. Such bodies of indigenous groups, Dalits, rural poor and agrarian workers, through their various campaigns and struggles could make inroads into the space hitherto occupied by Maoists and other radical groups. The mainstream political parties and the civil society dominated by vote bank politics or class hegemony and vested interests are not favourably inclined to the spread and consolidation of such autonomous bodies. Unfortunately, on their behest, attempts are made to strangulate these bodies by dubbing them as appendages of extremist outfits or those promoting militancy and secessionism. The more such efforts by the State, the greater will be chances for Maoists and other radicals to exploit them.

NOTES AND REFERENCES

1. IPCS Conference Report, March 2012, "The Naxal Problem – Understanding the Issues, Challenges and Alternative Approaches" (speech by DR Karthikeyan, IPS).
2. Government of India, Planning Commission Report on LWE, 2010.
3. IPCS Conference Report, March 2012, "The Naxal Problem – Understanding the issues, challenges and Alternative Approaches".
4. Gouverneur, "India's Undeclared War", p 14.
5. The Integrated Action Plan (IAP) envisaged by the Planning Commission in 2010 was initially targeted for 33 districts in 9 worst LWE affected States, subsequently extended to 60 districts and now in 88 districts.
   (www.thehindu.com/national/otherstates/districts-brought under-action plan for naxalhit-states/article-5012948ece, accessed on January 26, 2014)
6. A non-plan scheme implemented since September 1996 to supplement the efforts of the States to deal with the Naxal problem effectively; initially started in 76 districts by recouping 100% of the expenditure incurred for logistics, police modernization etc.
   (pib.nic.in/newsat/ereleaseespx?relid=74332 accessed on January 26, 2014.)

7. The Special Infrastructure Scheme in LWE affected States was approved in the 11th Plan with an allocation of rupees Five hundred crores to fill the critical infrastructure gaps.
(mha.nic.in/naxal/news accessed on January 26, 2014.)
8. For example, in the case of IAP, the Union Home Ministry and the Finance Ministry felt the Scheme should be implemented through the specially constituted district level Committees, the Planning Commission and the Rural Ministry were in favour of allocation of at least 50% of the funds to the local self-governing bodies which should be entrusted with its implementation.
(www.thehindu.com/national/otherstates/districts-broughtunder-action plan for naxalhit-states/article-5012948ece, accessed on January 26, 2014.)
9. PV Ramana, "The Maoist Movement in India", *Defence and Security Analysis*, 22, No 4, December 2006), pp 435-449.
10. The controversial court case in which several Left Trade unionists including PC Joshi, Muzaffar Ahmed and SA Dange (later all elevated to the leadership of CPI) and three British were arrested and tried on charges of conspiracy for national level Rail strike.
11. The Chittagong armoury raid was attempt made on April 18, 1930 to raid the armoury of police and auxiliary forces at Chittagong in Bengal Province of British India by armed revolutionaries led by Surya Sen.
12. The 'Tebhaga movement' was a militant movement started in Bengal in 1946 under the banner of Kisan Sabha (peasant body of CPI) demanding 2/3 share of crops to tenant share-croppers instead of the then practice of 50:50 share to tenant and landowner. Charu Majumdar (who was then in CPI) led the movement.
13. The Telangana armed struggles started by the peasants of the area in 1946 against Nizam and his army continued till it was completely suppressed by the Indian army in 1951. The Andhra State unit of CPI led and conducted this struggle.
14. The 'Punnappara-Vayalar' struggle started in two villages (Punnappara and Vayalar) in Alleppey district of the then Travancore Princely State (now in Kerala) during 1946 was the first major struggle by CPI against landlords and capitalists and Sir CP Ramasamy Iyer, the then Diwan of the State.

15. AG Noorani, "Of Stalin, Telangana and Indian Revolution", *Frontline*, Volume 28, Issue 26, December 17-30, 2011. (www.scribd.com.doc/89059088/communist-memories/A-G.Noorani accessed on January 31, 2014.)
16. *Ibid*, p 46.
17. AG Noorani, "Of Stalin, Telangana and Indian Revolution", *Frontline*, Volume 28, Issue 26, December 17-30, 2011. (www.scribd.com.doc/89059088/communist-memories/A-G.Noorani accessed on January 31, 2014.)
18. Ranadive was much influenced by the achievements of Yugoslavian President Marshal Tito and his Socialist government there.
19. In the wake of differences within the party on its tactical line, a four member party delegation consisting Basava Punnaiah, C Rajeswara Rao, Ajay Ghosh and SA Dange visited Soviet Union and held interaction with the leaders of Communist Party of Soviet Union (CPSU) including Stalin. Based on these discussions, the 1951 new programme was formulated in which the selective support to the policies of Nehru government was the main agenda. (www.scribd.com.doc/89059088/communist-memories/A-G.Noorani accessed on January 31, 2014.)
20. People's War also called protracted people's war, is a military-political strategy first developed by Mao Zedong (1893-1976). The basic concept behind People's War is to maintain the support of the population and draw the enemy deep into the interior where the population will bleed them dry through a mix of Mobile Warfare and Guerrilla warfare.
21. The CPSU and its allied parties advocated using democratic and peaceful means to advance the struggles of the working class and toward winning State power wherever those means were available. The CPC, on the other hand, disparaged such methods and proposed that the need for revolutionary war in order to seize power was a universal law of class struggle.
22. Deriving from its views on the dangers of nuclear war, the CPSU saw coexistence with the West as in the mutual interest of both systems. The Chinese saw this as capitulation.
23. The most important distinguishing feature of a people's democratic

revolution is the character of the State power it establishes: a revolutionary democratic dictatorship of the revolutionary classes led by the dictatorship of the proletariat.
(www.naxistom/history/international/comintern/sino-soviet/spli accessed on February 2, 2014.)

24. Edward Duyker, *Tribal Guerrillas: The Santals of West Bengal and the Naxalite Movement* (Delhi: Oxford University Press, 1987), pp 55-57.
25. Sumanta Banerjee, *India's Simmering Revolution: The Naxalite Uprising* (London: Zed Books Ltd, 1984), pp 9-12.
26. Mahanoy 1977: p 141.
27. "Programme of the Communist Party of India (Marxist-Leninist)", May 1970, reprinted, Ghosh, 199, Jawaid, p 36.
28. Charu Majumdar, "A Few Words about Guerrilla Actions," *Liberation*, February 1970, reprinted in Ghosh, pp 290-297.
29. Dasgupta, *The Naxalite Movement*, pp 45-46.
30. Santhosh Rana and Ashit Chatterjee led the Midnapore struggles (West Bengal) during 1969, in which around 100 'class enemies' were eliminated by the Maoists.
31. Lin Biao (1907-1971) strategic man of the genius of Chinese Red Army and its successor the People's Liberation Army (PLA); played a crucial role in Chinese Cultural Revolution (1966-76) and mysteriously died in plane crash in 1971, allegedly while plotting against Mao.
32. Biplab Dasgupta, "The Naxalite: An Epilogue", published by *Social Scientist*, Volume 6, No 12, July 1978, pp 3-24. (www.istor.org/stable/3516672 accessed on February 12, 2014.)
33. Government of India, Ministry of Home Affairs, Annual Report 2004-2005, p 39.
34. Ganapathy's interview by Chindu Sreedharan, "The Rediff Interview/ Ganapathy," Rediff On the NeT, October 7, 1998. (http://www.rediff.com/news/1998/oct/07gana.htm accessed on February 16, 2017.)
35. Government of India (2008) "A Report of the Expert Panel on the challenges in the Extremist areas".
36. "Naxalism – The Malady and the Remedy".

(www.Dsaert.org/October-2010/141/naxalism-the-malady-and-the-remedy-by-en-ram-mohan, accessed on February 17, 2014.)

37. *Ibid*, p 67
38. The Report of Ministry of Home Affairs, 2010.
39. From the Report of the Ministry of Tribal Affairs, 2006
40. "Human Poverty and Socially Disadvantaged Groups in India". (www.undp.org/...intent/dam/india/docs/humanpoverty accessed on February 12, 2014.)
41. *Ibid*, p 37
42. Forest survey Report, 2011, Ministry of Forests and Environment, Government of India.
43. "What is Going on India's 'Red Corridor'? – Questions about India's Maoist Insurgency". (www.business.highbeam.com/5477/article/1G1-257765121/going-idia-red-corridor-question-india-maoist-insurgency accessed on February 14, 2017.)
44. Fearon, JD and Laitin, D, "Ethnicity, Insurgency and Civil War", *American Political Science Review*, Volume 97, pp 91-101.
45. Maoist document strategy and tactics, Central Committee (P) CPI (Maoist). (www.satp.org.saportop/communist/countries/maoist/documents/papers/strategy.htm accessed on February 20, 2016.)
46. Ms Arundhati Roy, the Booker Prize winner is noted for her crusade for the protection of civil and human rights of marginalized sections.
47. PK Mohanty, *Encyclopedia of Scheduled Tribes in India* (5 volumes) Gyan Publishing House.
48. The Khanda Revolution in Kalahandi, Odisha. (www.orissa.gov.in/e-magazine/orissareview/august2007/—/page76-77/pdf accessed on February 25, 2014.)
49. www.rebelsindia.co/-/viewArticle.aspx?ai=112 accessed on February 25, 2014.
50. www.incredible.chhattisgarh.com/Tribal-revolt-and-rebellion, accessed on February 24, 2014.
51. S Anand, "Understanding the Khairlangi Verdict", *The Hindu*, October 5, 2008.

52. http://nhrc.nic.in/Documents/Publications/nhrc_journal_2009.pdf last accessed on October 20, 2016.
53. *Ibid*, Sl No 52.
54. *Social Issues of India*, Edited by Samarak Swain, New Vishal Publications, New Delhi, 2011, "The Naxalite Movement" by Arunava Narayan Mukherjee, pp 188-92.
55. Government of India (2008), "Development Challenges in Extremist Affected Areas, Report of the Expert Panel to the Planning Commission".
56. Jerkins and Klandermans, *The Politics of Social Protest: Comparative Perspective on State and Social Movement*, Minnesota Press, Minneapolis, 1985.
57. Government of India (2008), "Development Challenges in Extremist Affected Areas, Report of the Expert Panel to the Planning Commission".
58. Guha, Ramachandra, 2007.
59. Manmohan Singh, "Prime Minister's Speech to the 2nd Meeting of the Standing Committee of Chief Ministers on Naxalism", (Speech, New Delhi, India, April 13, 2006), GoI Press Information Bureau. (http://pib.nic.in/release/rel_print_page.asp?relid=17128 accessed August 10, 2016.)
60. www.unihidelberg.de/md/awe/professurun/intwin/india-pdf-2011 accessed on March 16, 2017. (Hoelscher Kristian, Jason Miklian, Krishna Chaitanya.)
61. Rajat Kumar Kujur, "Left Extremism in India: Naxal Movement in Chhattisgarh and Orissa", Institute of Peace and Conflict Studies Special Report 25, June 2006. (http://ipcs.org/pdf_file/issue/576885354IPCS-Special-Report-25.pdf accessed on March 25, 2014.)
62. www.undp.org/ntent/dam/india/docs/humanpoverty accessed on March 25, 2014. ("Human Poverty and Socially Disadvantaged Groups in India".)
63. 2011http://www.im4change.org/docs/340IHDR_Summary.pdf accessed on March 26, 2014. (India – Human Development Index, 2011.)
64. Joseph Flavian Gomes, "The Political Economy of Maoist Conflict in

India – An Empirical Analysis", Working Paper 12-18, Economic Series, June 2012, Universidad, Carlos III, Madrid, Spain.

65. *Ibid*, p 89
66. Walter Fernandez, "Internally Displaced Persons – Challenge to Human Dignity", *Vidyajothi Journal of Theological Reflection*, 71(1), January 2007. pp 43-51.
67. The Supreme Court by majority judgment dated 11/7/1997 disposed of civil appeal Nos 4601 and 4602/97 filed by Samatha, an NGO working in East Godavari district of AP, established that government land, Tribal land and forest land in scheduled areas cannot be leased out to non-Tribals or private companies for any non-agricultural or industrial operations.
68. K Balagopal, 2007.
69. MRD, 2006, Report of the Expert Group on the alienation of Tribal land and its restoration, New Delhi: Ministry of Rural Development, Government of India.
70. Ministry of Rural Development, Government of India, 2004
71. The Communist Party of India (Marxist), New Programmes, New Delhi, March 2001.
72. The policy document of Liberation, a major Naxalite group with their strong bases in Bihar etc.
73. Maoist Documents: Party Programme – South Asia Terrorism Portal. (www.satp.org/satporgtp/countries/india/maoist/documents/papers/partyprogram.htm last accessed on October 15, 2016.)
74. Ms Mayawati, the supremo of BSP tried this strategy in UP by bringing together Dalits, OBCs and Muslims on a common electoral platform, even by sidelining sections of BSP/Dalit leaders. But, the strategy failed to take off because of dominating caste/group interests among the alliance partners.
75. Justice Madav Reddy of Andhra Pradesh High Court, while delivering the judgment of 'Secunderabad conspiracy case' in 1990 elaborately discussed the role of political parties in countering the threat of Naxalites. The case related to the meeting of pro-Naxalite writers and civil liberty activists who were charged for conspiracy and other offences against the State; filed in 1969 and trial commenced in 1984 was finally disposed in 1990.

76. KV Thomas, *Left Wing Extremism and Human Rights: The Role of Civil Liberties Organizations in Andhra Pradesh*, SAGE Publications, New Delhi, 2014.
77. Balswarup Yadav, a senior leader of CPI (Maoist) from Jharkhand, involved in several cases of murder, dacoity, arson and extortion in Bihar and Jharkhand was arrested by Jharkhand police in November 2009.
78. Venkitesh Ramakrishnan, "Maoist Connection", *Frontline*, Vol 24, Issue 25, December 22, 2007–January 4, 2008.
79. The Marxist intellectual Antonio Gramsci (1891-1937) developed the theory of cultural hegemony to further the establishment of a working class worldview.

2

How the 'Red-Terror' Spread in Kerala?

Perhaps, it is an anachronism that the echoes of the spring thunder that rocked the sleepy village of Naxalbari in West Bengal created strong resonance in the southern State of Kerala, which was a home to a vibrant Communist movement with an epoch making history of agrarian and working class mobilization. The State had a unique distinction of installing a democratically elected Communist government in 1957, which introduced radical legislations meant for the uplift of the poor and the marginalized. The dismissal of the State Government by the Centre in 1959 after prolonged anti-Communist liberation struggle by the major communities in the State came as a rude shock to sections of the Communist party and shook their confidence in electoral politics. They tried to revive the party's old line of armed struggles with the propaganda that bourgeois landlord classes strongly backed by caste, communal and sectarian forces could be defeated only through protracted people's war[1] and armed national liberation struggles for which the Communists should shun the parliamentary path.

The above strategy had sharpened the polemics and internal contradictions in the Communist party that led to its split in 1964 with the formation of pro-Soviet Communist Party of India (CPI) and the pro-Chinese Communist Party of

India (Marxist). The radicals who had high expectations on the new party CPI(M) in view of their pro-Chinese gestures and their 1964 policies and programmes upholding peoples' democratic revolution were soon disillusioned when the party vigorously pursued the idea of floating United Fronts solely for electoral gains. Thus in 1967, when the party worked out such alliance in Kerala with those parties or groups which are ideologically opposed to them and came into power, the radicals in the State were keenly waiting for an opportunity to throw down the gauntlet against the leadership. They found that opportunity when Charu Majumdar unfurled the flag of revolt against the party in Bengal during May 1967, by openly leading the landless peasants and Tribals of Naxalbari on the path of armed struggle in support of their demands.

While analysing the genesis and spread of Naxalite/Maoist movement in Kerala, we can identify four distinct phases namely:

(a) Ist phase of upholding Charu Majumdar's line of annihilation of class enemies.

(b) IInd phase of challenging National Emergency by attacking centres of State power.

(c) Post-emergency phase of ideological differences and internal contradictions leading to the formation of different groups.

(d) The current phase of unity and coordination through the Strategic United Front.[2]

The State witnessed the first incident of Left Wing Extremist violence on November 21, 1968, in the form of attacking Thalassery Police Station in the northern district of Kannur by a squad led by Kunnikkal Narayanan. After a couple of days, another team led by Philip M Prasad attacked the Wireless

Station of Pulpally Police in Wayanad district killing two police personnel. The majority of frontline leaders of the movement were the ex-cadres of the CPI(M) or its Kisan, youth or student fronts. Inspired by Charu Majumdar's slogan of annihilation of class enemies, armed peasants, workers and youth targeted landlords and estate owners in the Adivasi belt of Wayanad district. Grains seized from the granaries of those landlords were distributed among the poor. Charu Majumdar complimented the Kerala comrades hailing that the "heroism and courage displayed by the impoverished masses of Kerala have raised a new wave of enthusiasm among the revolutionary people all over India."[3]

But the rhetoric was short-lived. Most of the cadres who participated in the attack such as Kunnikkal Narayanan, Anikkad Varghese, Philip M Prasad, Mandakini, Ajitha, Gro Vasu, Thettamala Krishnankutty, Vellathoovaal Stephen and Kurichiyan Kunjiraman were arrested. Kisan Thomman, the bomb-making expert was killed in a blast, while the action squad was fleeing from the police. The killing of Varghese one of the pioneer young leaders of the Maoist movement in Kerala in a police encounter during February 1970 had subsequently developed as major controversy leading to the prosecution and incarceration of one of the Police officers involved in the operation.[4]

The early Maoists could exploit certain local issues in mobilizing Adivasis and the landless peasants on the lines of Naxalbari uprisings. The first one was the organized moves by the Forest Department and Pulpally Devaswom[5] to evict over 7,000 settlers from around 20,000 acres of forest land in Wayanad district. When the CPI(M) led government was going ahead with eviction using force, the Maoists decided to resist the move by resorting to violence. The deployment of Malabar Special Police (MSP) which is known for their ruthless methods, at Pulpally for eviction duties created volatile situation in the area. Meanwhile, in the neighbouring Kannur district – the citadel of the CPI(M) – over 20,000 impoverished 'Beedi' workers became jobless following the closure of Beedi companies by the Karnataka based owners in protest against the implementation of Minimum Wages Act for Beedi workers by the CPM-led Left Democratic Front (LDF) government in Kerala.

By taking up the cause of those farmers and workers, the Maoists decided to put into practice the first lessons of Maoist armed struggles that they learnt from Charu Majumdar and Kanu Sanyal. Their targets were a couple of Police Stations and landlords known for their brutality and inhuman treatment of their tenants and daily wage earners. As these operations were the rudimentary form of guerrilla warfare, there were lapses as well. For example, out of the 1,000 Maoists and their sympathisers scheduled to take part in the Thalassery Police Station attack, only 315 turned up. A lone grenade hurled at the Police Station did not explode and as the sentry there set off the alarm, the group was forced to flee. The lack of communication between the squads created much confusion on the post-operational plans and strategy especially the escape routes and hideouts for the squad members.

More than the operational bottlenecks and police action, what weakened the movement subsequently were the sharp differences focusing on their ideology/strategy. While Majumdar insisted on the strategy of the annihilation of class enemies including the unarmed landlords and Zamindars, leaders like Kunnikkal Narayanan wanted to remain focused on attacking the Police Stations. During the next couple of years (1969-70), the State witnessed around one dozen incidents of attack on Police Stations/killing of landlords in different districts such as Kannur, Wayanad, Calicut, Palakkad,

Idukki, Kollam and Trivandrum, which virtually created a reign of terror in the State. The spike in extremist violence led the Indian National Congress (INC) led State Government to launch intensive operations that led to the arrest of several Maoist leaders. With the senior leaders in jail, the movement lost much of its steam. That marked the end of the first phase of the Maoist insurgency in Kerala.

The ideological differences that cropped up in the Communist Party of India – Marxist-Leninist (CPI-ML) led by Charu Majumdar had reflected in Kerala too. Acknowledging the legacy of All India Coordination Committee of Communist Revolutionaries (AICCCR), KPR Gopalan, the legendary Communist leader of Kerala floated the Communist Revolutionary Party which tried tc use parliamentary forum to broaden the base of the Maoists. The party which unsuccessfully contested the 1970 Kerala polls failed to make any impact. Similarly, other ex-CPM leaders like AV Aryan (Trichur), KP Kosalramadas (Trivandrum), Jos Abraham (Idukki), A Achuthan (Alapuzha) etc, floated splinter Naxalite/ Maoist groups and adopted militant line to resolve the issues of landless peasants and unorganized workers. Many of these groups perished or merged into other Maoist groups in due course.

The second phase commenced just a few months before the National Emergency when a young intellectual K Venu rallied various groups to form a Maoist party. Many students, talented youth, professionals and intellectuals opposed to the Emergency joined hands with Maoists to fight against the State's unbridled powers of curtailing the freedom of expression and personal liberty. The alma-centres like the Regional Engineering College (REC), Kozhikode, Maharajas College, Ernakulam etc, became the hot-spots of such activities. In the history of Maoist movement in the State, the REC left rich legacy as Murali Kannamballi[6] who had subsequently become one of the main pillars of Maoist movement in India and P Rajan[7] (killed in police custody) were the students of that institution.

Interpreting Police Stations as the symbols of State power, the Maoists were engaged in direct action such as attacks on Police Stations. Naturally, they became the main targets of the police. Jayaram Padikkal (IPS), who headed the Crime Branch set-up was in charge of the anti-Maoist operations. All those suspected to have any links with Maoists were taken into custody and tortured and questioned in secret interrogation camps. A few unfortunate souls like Rajan and Varkala Vijayan perished in police custody. Their mortal remains were clandestinely disposed of leaving their kith and kin in perpetual agony and despair. In the wake of such police excesses, large majority of cadres bereft of proper ideological indoctrination or guerrilla training deserted the movement.

Such a saga of excesses and brutalities against Maoists created strong ripples in Kerala polity immediately after the lifting of the emergency. The veteran Congress leader K Karunakaran, who was the then Home Minister in the State, was elevated as the Chief Minister after the 1977 Assembly polls. However, he had to resign from CM post on April 25, 1977 following adverse observations from the High Court of Kerala against him for giving false testimonies in the court as a respondent in the Rajan *habeas corpus* case. Ironically, Rajan episode haunted him all through his political career. Even after four decades, such sad story of emergency excesses continues to remain alive in Kerala society. Recently in 2016, sixteen eminent personalities, including Booker Prize winner Ms Arundhati Roy[8], have appealed to the government to initiate a fresh probe into the disappearance of Varkala

Vijayan, a Maoist activist, during the Emergency days in 1976. Unfortunately, Vijayan too had the same fate of Rajan.

Drawing lessons from the past mistakes, the Maoists worked out corrective strategies during post-Emergency phase to broaden the mass base of the party ensuring revolutionary fervour of the cadres. The systematic campaign and propaganda focused on the stories of emergency excesses particularly the Rajan episode had created pro-Maoist thinking among sections of youth, intellectuals and writers. All forms of authoritarianism and curtailment of personal freedom became an anathema to the large segments of the population. The Maoists, to a great extent, could exploit this 'mass psyche' to their advantage. They had reorganized themselves as the Central Reorganizing Committee Communist Party of India Marxist-Leninist (CRC-CPML) and resumed the publication of the party organ 'Comrade' which had been banned during the emergency.

While upholding the proletarian revolutionary line of Charu Majumdar, the CRC underlined that armed struggle is the main form of struggle and all other forms of struggle should be complimentary to it. However, the party's armed struggle and military line[9] underwent major shifts. The first one took shape during the period 1979-82, when the party came out with its line that armed struggle could be initiated only after uncovering and sharpening contradictions by intervening in ongoing mass and trade union struggles and developing them into political struggles. This was a major deviation from Charu Majumdar's well-known opposition to making economic or partial struggles a precondition for the initiation of armed struggle. The CRC highlighted Charu Majumdar's counterpoising of mass struggles and mass organisations to guerrilla struggle, ignoring the necessity of an agrarian programme and one-sided stress on secret work etc, as the major reasons for the failure of the first phase of the movement.

The second deviation was the denouncement of the Leninist stand that economic struggles cannot be developed into the political struggle for power. Despite reservation from sections of comrades; the First All India Conference of the party in 1982 approved the line. Thus, the attempt of CRC was to adopt a new style of militant mass struggle built around the slogan, "To rebel against injustice is right".

The formation of the Janakeeya Samskarika Vedi[10] (JSV/ People's Cultural Forum) in 1980 gave an impetus to the party's line of militant mass struggle and connected strategies like 'people's trial'[11]. Reiterating that revolutions should start with the attack on the moral-political order and traditional hierarchy and class status, the Vedi had identified its main task as the creation of a new democratic culture in the country by allying with all new forces of democratic revolution and struggles at various levels. While the CRC functioned as the political front representing as the vanguard for the political liberation of a people, the cultural front gave the lead for their spiritual emancipation.

One noticeable trend was the proliferation of small theatre groups and forum of progressive writers, poets and artists who through their various art forms tried to attract the masses to the Maoist movement. Serious attempts were made to incorporate indigenous customs, traditions, myths, superstition and beliefs in such literary/art forms in order to attract the Tribals and Dalits to the movement. For example, a street play 'Nadugaddika'[12] staged by the Vedi in hundreds of places in the State dramatized the oppression and exploitation that the Tribals had been subjected to for generations and their ultimate liberation from the chains of slavery at the intervention of an exorcist who was none other than Varghese, the Naxalite leader killed by the police in Wayanad during 1970.

By broadening the mass base, the Vedi and the party were engaged in serious moves in setting up parallel centres of people's political power, which according to them, can be brought into existence only by the people in each area seizing power locally to take decisions and implement them in all economic, social and political problems in their own locality. They interpreted 'people's courts' and 'people's trials' as instruments for the establishment of people's political power at the local level. The 'public trial' of corrupt doctors and bureaucrats brought unprecedented popularity for the party in Kerala. Even, the front bodies such as Democratic Youth Federation of India (DYFI/CPM), All India Youth Federation (AIYF/CPI) etc, hailed these movements interpreting as peoples' resistance against corruption and malpractices in public life. However, ideological contradictions again surfaced in the party mainly on the issue of the application of 'mass line'[13] and 'military line'.

The party leadership wary over the dilution of revolutionary fervour of the rank and file due to the preponderance of mass line activities pushed ahead the 'military line' in May 1981. The annihilation theory of class enemies was re-introduced. Madathil Mathai, a non-Tribal settler at Kenichira in Wayanad district was identified as people's enemy and was eliminated by the party's action squad. Ironically, consensus was lacking in both the CRC and the Vedi on such crucial issues including the application of mass and military lines. For example, a small section in the CRC who was opposed to the annihilation line formed dissident CRC-CPML and batted for mass-based activities for preparing the people for the protracted struggles. Similarly, within the Vedi, there was a small group who toed the official line of the party giving upper hand to the military line.

Thus, it was also a phase of 'two line struggle'[14] which in due course led to the fragmentation of the movement. However, Vedi leadership formally denounced the annihilation and dissociated itself from it holding that annihilation did not suit the civilized political sensibility of Kerala.

The 'Kenichira action' had led to severe State repression in which the party and the Vedi withered away. Their senior leaders went underground. The JSV was dissolved. Meanwhile ideological differences, once again plunged the CRC into deep crisis. This was mainly on the question of the party's approach towards the insurgent or separatist movements in Punjab, the North-East and the Gorkhaland. The party had identified some of these movements as indicators to the military potential of the nationality question. In the case of Khalistan movement, the party held that the situation had developed to the demand for national independence involving armed struggle against national oppressors.

The concept of new democratic revolution of oppressed nationalities that fractured the path of people's war into separate people's war with separate people's armies, prominently figured in the documents and deliberations of the CRC without any general consensus. These issues became the major agenda of the party during the Party Plenum held in 1985. However; the position taken by the party on the nationality question was formally incorporated in its 'strategic line' adopted in the Second All India Conference held in 1987. Accordingly, the CRC had acknowledged that in situations where nationalist forces were already engaged in armed struggles, the party could intervene only by initiating armed struggle of its own. The Conference also accepted the plan of action proposed by the leadership: initiate armed struggle in Punjab and prepare for initiation of such struggles in Kerala and Maharashtra within one year.

However, the decisions of the all India conference and the subsequent strategy – instead of restoring monolithic organizational structure – intensified the ideological differences. KN Ramachandran, one of the founder leaders of the CRC fired the first salvo opposing the strategy of armed struggle and the party's line on issues such as the nationality question. Describing many of the policies of the CRC as adventurous and helpful for the growth of secessionist and fissiparous forces, he floated the CPI-ML (Red Flag) in 1987 with the declared task of rebuilding the CPI(ML) as a true Bolshevik party based on Mao's mass line. The party which had its main bases in Kerala subsequently spread its wings to other States like Karnataka, Madhya Pradesh, Maharashtra, Chhattisgarh, West Bengal and Odisha. It adopted the new constitution and the policies and programmes in 1997 emphasising the need of building up revolutionary struggles by mobilizing masses and using parliamentary forums. Under the banner of National Platform of Mass Organizations (NPMO), the Red Flag organized campaigns and struggles focusing on issues like the globalization and imperialism, the economic reforms and liberalization adversely affecting the common people etc. Initially, the Red Flag could create some impact in Kerala by espousing the issues of the traditional fishermen and unorganized workers etc.

Differences surfaced in Red Flag too. After the All India Conference in 2000, a faction led by Rauf in Andhra Pradesh, left the party and formed CPML (Rauf). In 2003 a large section of the party in Kerala broke away from the all India set-up and formed a parallel body on the same name under the leadership of PC Unnichekkan, Kerala State Secretary. The main reason for the split was the soft line approach of the Kerala unit towards the CPI and the CPI(M), which was opposed by the Central leadership. In 2005, the Red Flag led by Ramachandran merged with Kanu Sanyal's Communist

Party of India (Marxist-Leninist) at a unity conference in January 2005. Following the merger, the party was rechristened as 'Red Star'. Both the groups (Red Star and Red Flag – Unnichekkan) have become reformist abandoning the path of revolutionary resistance and resort to open functioning including participation in the elections.

The formation of groups like CPML-RF had further weakened the CRC which went through a phase of ideological contradictions and confusion on issues such as military line, mass line, political power, nationality question etc. Thus, by the end of 1991, the CRC was liquidated. K Venu, the architect of the party, unceremoniously left the field and embraced the parliamentary institutions. He unsuccessfully contested as an INC backed candidate in the 1996 Kerala Assembly elections.

The liquidation of CRC draws some crucial lessons. The first and foremost is that whenever Marxism-Leninism-Maoism are applied in bits and pieces on strategic or tactical grounds, alien ideologies step into the party or the movement which ultimately change the character of the organization. This had happened in the case of the CRC which opened itself up to petit bourgeois and bourgeois influences in the name of resolving new questions on political power, military line or nationality issue. Once these ideologies had crept into the core element of the party, they soon spread like a virus and infested all aspects of the party such as its political line, strategies, organization and leadership virtually negating the inalienable elements of Marxism-Leninism-Maoism. Secondly, when deviations in the party are not rectified in time, they would create conditions for the growth of an alternate or wrong line that will influence the thinking of the rank and file of the organization. That is why the Communist parties attach considerable importance to the rectification campaigns, in order to rectify omissions and commissions within the party or on the code of conduct of the leaders and members. Basically, these exercises are meant to contain or eliminate bourgeois tendencies that corrupt or influence the party and its rank and file in a democratic or socialist system. But, ironically, seldom these efforts succeed to eradicate such tendencies as overwhelming parliamentary interests' corrupt Communists too.

After the dissolution of the CRC, the Maoist movement was in total disarray in Kerala. Meanwhile, modernist trends had set in the State. Globalization and liberalization had raised new challenges. This has led to the emergence of new social movements focusing on neo-colonial issues adversely affecting Adivasis, Dalits and the indigenous, women, rural poor and the environment and ecology. Those movements occupied the major space hitherto made use of by ultra Left radicals to build up their support base.

But, the splinter groups with different strategies and tactics kept alive the Maoist ideology through their sporadic actions and campaigns focusing on the issues of the marginalized and the under-privileged. The Kerala Communist Party (KCP) and the Maharashtra Communist Party (MCP) which survived the disbanding of the CRC merged to form the CPI(ML)-Maoist Unity Centre in 1997. The Maoist Unity Centre (MUC) merged with the Andhra based Rauf faction of the Red Flag and formed CPI-ML-Naxalbari in 1998.

The CPML-Naxalbari had limited pockets of influence in Kerala. Murali Kannamballi alias Ajit of Kerala, who has been active in the Maoist movement since the time of the National Emergency and had links with Revolutionary International Movement (RIM)[15], was the All India General Secretary of the party. Its front organizations like the Ayyankali Pada and Porattom kept the outfit alive through isolated operations/ violence. As an ideologue of Maoism, Murali had linkages with a number of Revolutionary Communist parties, notably the Nepalese Communist Party (Marxist-Leninist). It was at the instance of Murali that the Ayyankali Pada demonstrated its militant profile in Kerala by holding Palakkad district Collector as hostage in 1996, on the issue of restoration of alienated Tribal land. On the other hand, Porattom had targeted World Bank project offices, multi-national giants like the Coca-Cola, Citibank branches etc, in Kerala ostensibly to high light the adverse impact of globalization, liberalization and new economic reforms.

The unity among the prominent Maoist groups has given an impetus to the current phase of the Maoist movement in Kerala. Beginning with 2000, the People's War Group (PWG) had loose organizational set up in Kerala with their main bases in the Northern districts bordering Tamil Nadu and Karnataka. Following the merger of the Peoples War (PW) and the Maoist Communist Centre of India (MCCI) leading to the formation of CPI-ML (Maoists) in 2004, the inter-State tri-junction of these three States has become a focal point of their operations. Basically, the tri-junction that connects Western and Eastern Ghats with hilly terrain and dense forests is ideal for guerrilla warfare particularly for using as safe hideouts for party cadres during stepped up anti-Maoist operations by security forces in their known citadels.

Thus, more than a decade ago, the Maoists initiated their operations in the Malnad region of Karnataka in the Western Ghats. To begin with, serious attempts had been made to constitute a Special Zonal Committee with a view to organising Maoist activities in the Northern districts of Kerala; Dakshin Kannada and Coorg in Karnataka and Theni-Gudalur belt in Tamil Nadu. However, such moves could not meet with success in view of the series of setback faced by the Maoists. The party lost more than one dozen leaders and fighters including Rajamouli, Saketh Rajan (both Secretary, Karnataka), Shivlingu and Gowtham (State committee members) etc. The arrest of Malla Raji Reddy (Central Committee member from Andhra Pradesh, in underground since long) who was assigned with the task of expansion and consolidation of the movement in Kerala and Chandrasekhar Gorebal, engaged in rebuilding the party in Karnataka etc, had given severe blow to the party.

Despite these setbacks, the Maoists in this area decided to pool their capabilities in the three Southern States by forming a separate Western Ghats Special Zonal Committee (WGSZC). This committee resolved to concentrate its major force at the tri-junction of the three States in the Western Ghats, while continuing to work in Malnad. Accordingly, plans and preparations were made. The deployment from Malnad to the tri-junction which began in May 2012 was completed in May 2013. This was followed by a three months Politico-Military campaign during November 2014–January 2015 in order to mobilize the masses for the revolutionary struggles. As part of this campaign, party literature and leaflets highlighting the stand of the party on environmental issues, Endosulfan victims in Kasaragod, land-related issues of Adivasis, general plight of landless farmers and unorganized workers etc, were distributed in Adivasi hamlets and local people.

During this period the presence and movement of Maoist groups had been noticed over two dozen occasions in the districts of Malappuram, Wayanad, Palakkad and Kannur in Kerala and Mysore, Kodagu, Udupi, Chikmangalur and Shimoga in Karnataka. On a couple of occasions, the members of the groups had engaged the Thunderbolts[16], the commando wing of the Kerala police specialized in jungle warfare. However, the Thunderbolts achieved their major operational success when they gunned down Kuppu Devaraj (who was in underground since long and involved in a number of ambushes and extremist attacks in Andhra, Odisha, Chhattisgarh, Jharkhand etc) and Advocate Ajitha (woman cadre from Tamil Nadu) while imparting training to cadres in the Nilambur forests (Malappuram) during November 2016.

With the Nilambur episode, it is now established that the Maoists have been seriously trying to build up their base in the Western Ghats especially the tri-junction including the Northern districts of Kerala. According to a party document, the WGSZC have identified a number of factors conducive to organize revolutionary movement; wage armed struggle and build revolutionary army in this belt. The Sahyadri range starting from Gujarat and Maharashtra in the North and straddling through Goa, Karnataka, Tamil Nadu and ending at the Southern tip of Kerala has been the site of many a popular struggles, both armed and unarmed. The North Wayanad, one of the main areas of operation of Maoists has the proud history of fierce resistance against British colonialism in the late 18th and early 19th century in which Kurichiya Adivasis played heroic role. Moreover, Wayanad was one of the main areas of revolutionary struggles in Kerala inspired by the armed peasant uprisings in Naxalbari. The area was historically inhabited by fifty odd Adivasi tribes, who were initially exploited by the British and later by the landed gentry backed by political parties and bureaucrats. The Tribal land alienation, failure of political setup to restore the alienated land, oppression and exploitation by non-Tribal settlers, the eviction from their traditional lands in name of mega projects, National Parks and Wildlife Sanctuaries etc, have made their life miserable.

Just like the case of Adivasis, the condition of rural proletariat, landless peasants, agricultural and plantation workers living in this area are equally deplorable. The majority of the rural proletariat of the area is the migrants, who over the last many decades had transformed the hilly terrains and forest land into fertile land and are mainly engaged in agriculture for livelihood. They are the worst victims of the globalization-liberalization policies. With the entry of Multinationals and major corporate bodies into the agrarian sector, the traditional ways of cultivation and conventional crops have been replaced by mechanized means and diversified cash crops. The agrarian economy is virtually controlled by such groups detrimental to the interests of those who actually toil in the soil. Thus, majority of the poor and marginal farmers find it difficult to meet their both ends. Those who fall into debt trap cunningly operated by the 'blade mafia' or the landlords are forced to commit suicide in penury and humiliation.

In plantation and other sectors, job security has been badly affected. The true concept of collective bargaining and trade unionism has become a myth, as illegal nexus existed between the corporate management and the organized trade union leaders. Casualization – the general tendency of engaging workers on temporary or contract basis – is increasing dramatically with the ostensible aim to deny workers their genuine rights and privileges. While work load has been increased, their real wages have been reduced in many sectors. The agrarian workers mainly engaged in the small and medium holdings owned by the rich and marginal farmers remain unemployed or underemployed. Owing to the exodus of migrant workers from other States, the wage rate of agrarian workers is going down. The government's ambitious programmes such as Mahatma Gandhi National Rural Employment Guarantee Programme (MNREGP) cannot help to ameliorate the rural unemployment in the area especially in view of the large scale corruption and malpractices at their implementation. Thus, the assessment of the Maoists is that all sections of the people living in this region – Adivasis, Dalits, plantation workers, agricultural workers and peasants –

face heavy exploitation and oppression at the hands of the State machinery and various other exploiters.

Following the merger of the CPI (Maoist) and the CPI(ML) Naxalbari in May 2014, the movement has broad-based its activities, opening a new front of the people's war in Kerala. The Maoist strategy is now focused on the task of winning over the support of Adivasis, Dalits and other exploited or oppressed sections. Instead of perpetrating large scale violence or actions, their operational strategy is to strengthen their base in the area through non-violent mobilization. For that purpose, they have floated different fronts or extension organizations espousing the cause of Adivasis, Dalits, women, landless farmers, unorganized workers and the marginalized. The prominent among them include: Revolutionary Democratic Front (RDF) which was noticed opposing the neo-capitalist policies of the State. The Special Economic Zone (SEZ) and the Retail Sector are the two areas identified by them as the new realms of struggle against imperialism. Another strategy of the outfit is to actively take up local issues. Porattom, the ideological squad of CPI-ML-Naxalbari, of late, has been vigorously taking up the cause of CPI-Maoists through open and covert channels. Viplava Sthreevadi Prasthanam (Revolutionary Women's Movement), Viplava Vidyarthi Prasthanam (Revolutionary Students' Movement), Adivasi Vimochana Munnani (Adivasi Liberation Front) and Njattuvela Samskarika Samithi (Cultural Body) are at present not much active. On the other hand, the Janakeeya Manushyavakasha Samiti (People's Human Rights Movement), just like the Andhra Pradesh Civil Liberties Committee, has emerged as a strong body using legal and open channels in defending the cases/issues of Maoists in Kerala.

On many instances, the Maoists use such front or extension organizations to carry out their overt campaigns in co-operation with other outfits or groups. In the late 1970s and 1980s, such solidarity between the Maoist groups and the Students Islamic Movement of India (SIMI) was noticed in Kerala on issues such as anti-Shah movement in Iran and the Soviet occupation in Afghanistan and the installation of the puppet regime headed by Mohammed Najibullah. They had linkages with Fedayeen-e-Khalq, a Marxist-Leninist group that stood for Islamised Communism and the Iranian students in India opposed to the Pahlavi regime. There were more than 20,000 Iranians (mostly students) in India, when Iran was in the grip of an Islamic revolution. After the ban, both the SIMI and the Maoists continued their clandestine linkages for strategic purposes such as training of cadres, procurement of weapons and for safe hideouts during the operations by the security forces.

Such linkages constitute an essential component of Maoists' Strategic United Front, which according to Maoist leaders, is one of the magic weapons of the movement to achieve their ultimate goal of overthrowing the government in power. Thus, they interpret the insurgency in the Kashmir valley or in the North East as 'nationalist struggle' to uphold the identity of sub-nationalities. The main focus of the present Maoist strategy is to declare solidarity with any outfit that opposes the imperialist forces or the Indian State in particular either through peaceful means or violence. The Maoists even interpret the Islamic terrorism on such strategic lines. That is why CPI(M) General Secretary, Ganapathy, has succulently put that Islamic jihadist movements of today are a product of imperialist – particularly the US imperialist – aggression and the suppression of the oil rich Islamic and Arab countries and the persecution of the entire Muslim religious community. He further claimed that only the Maoist leadership alone can provide correct anti-imperialist orientation and achieve class unity among the Muslims as well as the people of other religious persuasions.

In the context of Kerala, the Maoists have identified certain target groups or sectors such as Adivasis/Dalits, women, youth, unorganized workers and the environment for building up their support base. During the last one decade, the Maoists along with Action Groups or Non-Governmental Organizations (NGOs) had taken up a number of issues such as illegal mining and quarrying; land acquisition for the construction of major roads; collection of tolls for roads and bridges; women empowerment and dignity against exploitation and gender-based discrimination; fascist attacks and moral policing, rehabilitation of Endosulfan victims in Kasaragod district; Adivasi-Dalit land struggles at Muthanga and Chengara and Plachimade struggles against The Coca-Cola Company and many others. Through these struggles which were launched beyond the realm of mainstream political parties or caste-communal groups, the Maoists tried to send a message across the society that people are left with no option other than mobilize themselves against the oppressor, the political establishment that includes a huge and powerful gang of industrial and business groups, leaders from various parties, corporations, dominant religious and caste groups and media.

However, the re-grouping efforts of Maoists suffered major setback due to a couple of recent developments. The first one was the arrest of Roopesh and Shyna, Kerala's most wanted Maoist couple from Tamil Nadu by Andhra Police during the first week of May 2015. The Kerala Police had over two dozen cases against the couple who were instrumental for arranging shelter to Malla Raji Reddy, the Central Committee member, arrested by Andhra Police in December 2007 from Angamali, Kerala. Since the arrest, both the leaders had gone underground and were engaged in strengthening the movement in Kerala and Tamil Nadu. Shyna, by playing the role of a woman activist was successful in floating trade union like outfits among the unorganized women workers of Cochin

Export Processing Zone, while Roopesh was successful in building up support base among Adivasis, Dalits and other marginalized sections.

Closely on the heels of their arrest, the Maoists had a severe blow with the arrest of top Maoist leader Murali Kannamballi alias Ajith, by the Maharashtra Anti-Terrorism Squad (ATS) near Pune during May 2015. In fact, after the exit of K Venu from the movement in early 1990s, Murali was the backbone of the movement in Kerala. Moreover, he maintained wide contacts with Maoists across the world and had even acted as a mediator in Nepal when Maoism was hit by dissidence. As the National Secretary of the CPI-ML (Naxalbari) and the Central Committee member of the CPI (Maoist), he has been playing a crucial role in strengthening the movement in the tri-junction of Kerala, Tamil Nadu and Karnataka. This was followed by the Thunderbolts' first major breakthrough of demolishing Maoists Training camp in Karulayi forest, near Nilambur in Malappuram district during November 2016, leading to the killing Kuppu Devaraj (who was in underground since long and involved in a number of ambushes and extremist attacks in Andhra, Odisha, Chhattisgarh, Jharkhand etc) and Advocate Ajitha (woman cadre from Tamil Nadu).

Undeterred by these setbacks, the Maoists continue their efforts to build up their support base in the tri-junction where at least three *dalams* (armed squads) namely Kabani, Nadugani and Bhavani are active; with each *dalam* comprising 10-15 members. They are equipped with sophisticated weapons such as Kalashnikovs, self-loading rifles, and shotguns. Majority of these weapons had come through the Nepal or South-East Asian routes. Meanwhile, a Special Committee of the Maoists for the Western Ghats have been constituted to recruit more youth and cadres to the movement. The members posing as the activists of Human/Civil Rights organizations or anti-fascist outfits try to attract intellectuals and youth to the fold of Maoists.

Though the Kerala Police has been quite effective against the incipient threat of a spreading Maoist presence and activities, it is useful to acknowledge enduring capacity deficits that make its task difficult. According to the latest data provided by the Bureau of Police Research and Development (BPR&D), as on January 1, 2016, the State had 53,881 policemen, as against a sanctioned 60,502 policemen, leaving 6,621 police posts vacant, a deficit of 10.94%. Further, at least 41 Indian Police Service (IPS) posts were vacant in the State, against a sanctioned strength of 163 – a deficit of a 25.15%. Also, the Police/Area Ratio (number of policemen per 100 square kilometres) is 138.64, as against the sanctioned strength of 155.68 – a deficit of 10.94%. However, the all-India ratio stands at 54.69 per 100 square kilometres, as against a sanction of 72.03. Such deficits will eventually impact adversely on the State's capacity to contain the Maoists and must be urgently addressed to.

Politics and violence bear an inextricable link in Kerala, particularly when it comes to the struggle being waged between the CPI(M) and the RSS and the BJP. As the parties come together to broker peace and make lip service to bring to an end the violence between left and right wing activists, police statistics show that political murders have held as a norm in the State, with over 170 killings in the last 17 years.

According to police records accessed by Sneha Mary Koshy of NDTV, 172 political murders have occurred since 2000. Of these, the RSS and the BJP together lost 65 party workers, while 85 of the CPI(M) workers have been killed, 11 activists each of the Congress and the IUML have also been killed in this period.

From February 2016 to July 2017, 10 RSS or BJP workers, and four CPI(M) workers have been murdered, allegedly for their political affiliations.

Though police records show that the CPI(M), DYFI, BJP and RSS cadres have been accused of most number of murders, other parties too have targeted their rivals.

For example, members of Social Democratic Party of India (SDPI) were accused of murdering Nazirudeen, an IUML man from Kuttiyadi (Calicut district) in July 2016. SDPI has the legacy of radical Muslim outfits like the National Development Front (NDF)/Popular Front of India (PFI) which since the early 1990s had made concerted efforts to augment radical and militant ideologies among Muslim youth, posing challenges to the law enforcement machinery in the State.

While political murders take place across Kerala, the northern district of Kannur remains the core arena of political violence in the State.

According to RTI information received from the police by 101reporters.com, 69 political murders were committed between 2000 and 2016. Among these, a roughly equal number of workers from the CPI(M) and the RSS-BJP were killed – 30 from the former and 31 from the latter.

The data shows that the number of killings on both sides rose higher during Left Democratic Front (LDF) regimes, and fell during UDF rule in the State. In 2000, for instance, when the LDF was in power, Kannur recorded nine deaths in a single year. In 2008, again under LDF rule, 12 persons were killed, with five workers each from the CPI(M) and the RSS-BJP being killed.

According to NCRB data, while Kannur contributed to 50% of political murders in the State during the two LDF terms between 2000 and 2016, it accounted for 20-30% of the political murders committed during the UDF regimes in this period. Overall, Kannur contributed to 36% of all political murders in Kerala between 2000 and 2015.

While the political rhetoric raised by CPI(M) and the RSS-BJP constantly seeks to pin the blame on one side over the other, the pattern of deaths is relatively equally distributed across both. While a straight comparison between only these two parties seems to suggest that more CPI(M) workers have been killed versus RSS-BJP workers, it is also important to take account of the rivalries between the CPI(M) and the Congress and IUML. The political rivalry between the major fronts – the UDF and the LDF – which had alternatively ruled the State since 1967 and the recent hectic moves of the BJP, strongly backed by the RSS to occupy a major space in the State polity have led to the trend of increased political violence in Kerala.

NOTES AND REFERENCES

1. The protracted people's war which is also called as People's War is the military-political strategy developed by the Chinese Marxist-Leninist revolutionary and political leader Mao Zedong (1893-1976). The basic concept behind the people's war is to maintain the support of the population and draw the enemy deep into the interior where the population will bleed them dry through a mix of mobile warfare and guerrilla warfare.
2. The strategic United Front is a loose association of tactical and opportunistic partnerships aimed at achieving certain intermediary objectives.
3. "Return of the Native: CPI-Maoist in Kerala", Bibhu Prasad Routray, Visiting Fellow, IPCS. (http://www.ipcs.org/article/india/return-of-the-native-cpi-maoist-in-kerala-4850.html last accessed on January 23, 2017.)
4. On the basis of the disclosures made by police personnel Ramachandran that A Varghese was killed in a fake encounter in 1970,

the CBI registered a case in 2001, against the police personnel involved in the operation. One DSP K Lakshmana who was one of the accused in the case was given life imprisonment by the Kerala High Court. However, his punishment was subsequently commuted due to old age.

5. It was a religious trust in Wayanad district which had substantial land holding during the pre-Independence period.
6. Murali Kannamballi from Kerala is considered to be one of the prominent think-tank and ideologue of the Maoist movement in India. He joined the movement in early 1970s while studying in REC Calicut; played a crucial role in drafting the various documents of the CRC-CPML; established close contacts with the Revolutionary International Movement (RIM) and worked as Editor and publisher of RIM's organ *A World to Win*. He maintained close linkages with the Nepalese Revolutionary Communist Party and was instrumental for giving clear Marxist-Leninist line for the party. Murali who played a key role in forming CPML-Naxalbari was arrested in Pune during 2014. His outfit Naxalbari formally merged into CPI-Maoists in May 2014.
7. P Rajan, a student of REC Calicut was taken into custody from college hostel in 1975 for his suspected linkages with the CPML. During interrogation/custodial torture in the infamous Kakkayum camp of the Crime Branch, he was killed. His dead body was clandestinely disposed of, but in police records he figured as missing case. Rajan's desperate father knocked at all centres of power to know the fate of his son, but none could give any convincing reply to him.
8. Arundhati Roy, the Booker Prize winner is noted for her crusade for the protection of the civil and human rights of the marginalized sections.
9. The 'military line' in Maoist parlance denotes that the armed form of struggle is the only form of struggle and armed form organization is the only form of organization and all other form of struggles and organizational activities negate the true revolutionary concept.
10. JSV was floated by Left Wing intellectuals of Kerala in late 1970s to promote Maoist ideology among masses through various cultural/literary activities.

11. The public trial is the Maoist strategy of quick dispensation of justice in the form of the open trial of those identified by the party for corrupt practices or other offences.
12. "Nadugaddika" a play staged by the JSV illustrated how the Naxalite cultural activists, unlike their predecessors, were able to use the folk traditions and myths of a people to convey, from a working class perspective, the oppression they had been going through for generations. 'Gaddika', a Tribal ritual of the Adiyars of Wayanad, was used to exorcise evil spirits.
13. The 'mass line' theory of Maoist groups advocate that the mass struggles and mass movements on revolutionary line should be organized in order to prepare the masses for 'protracted armed struggles'.
14. Mao's thesis on the two-line struggle is inextricably bound up with the whole analysis Mao made of the nature of socialist society, the class struggle under socialism, the continuing existence of the bourgeoisie and the need to carry forward the revolution even under conditions of proletarian dictatorship.
15. The Second International Conference of Marxist-Leninist Parties and Organizations officially formed the Revolutionary Internationalist Movement in March 1984, as an international association of Maoist revolutionary parties. Over the years some new member parties joined and some older ones departed. Due to growing internal problems and differences RIM ceased functioning around 2007.
16. Thunderbolts is an elite command force of the Kerala Police formed in 2012 to counter possible terror strikes and carry out counter-insurgency operations, imparted training in guerrilla and jungle warfare under NSG/SPG and other specialized forces.

3

Maoist Insurgency in Kerala – A Ground Level Study

Of all the States in India, Kerala maintains a unique status in many respects. The State occupies 1% of the total land area of India, whereas its population of 3.33 crores account for 3% of the total population of India at the 2011 census. Though its Gross Domestic Product (GDP) per capita is just over 1,000 dollars a year, the State has the highest literacy (94%) and life expectancy (72 years) in the country. Its infant mortality rate is among the lowest in the developing world. Similarly, in the field of social development, Kerala truly stands out as the Mount Everest. Thus, Nobel Laureate Dr Amartya Sen had rightly described the achievements of the State in social, economic and political fields as spectacular.[1]

The State's achievements in various fields can be largely attributed to the "constructive and combative roots of its historical background."[2] The constructive roots, no doubt, were the State's rich history and legacy and its global exposure. From time immemorial, Kerala as the land of spices attracted the Arabs and the Europeans who established cordial relations with the Princely rulers and the chieftains. The British were instrumental to the development of the infrastructure in many parts of the State to prop up their business and plantation ventures.

The combative roots can be traced to the organized struggles and campaigns by the lower and backward castes against the rigid caste system and upper caste domination. The social reformers like Sree Narayana Guru[3], Ayyankali[4], and Dr Palppu[5] and so on played a significant role in the social renaissance movement in Kerala, which had decisive impact over the social structure and class relations. Equally important was the role of Christian churches and Missionary groups whose pioneering endeavours in the educational field accelerated awareness of various sections on their rights and privileges. This had resulted in resurgence among Dalits and the low castes which had reflected in many radical social reforms such as the historic Temple Entry Proclamation in 1936 by which the low castes were allowed to enter the temples in Travancore State.

In fact, the cumulative impact of these developments had clearly reflected in the political consciousness and the social enlightenment of the large majority of the people. Thus, the seeds of the Communist ideologies which were sown in Kerala soil in early 1900s had sprouted and grown into a mammoth tree during 1950s when the Communists after decades of clandestine struggles and violent movements, were voted to power in 1957. No doubt, the first democratically elected Communist government of 1957 introduced sweeping land reforms and progressive legislations meant to improve the conditions of workers and peasants. Despite the emergence of a Communist regime upholding proletarian policies and programmes, the State witnessed the first spark of the Maoist killings and violence in 1968, just after a few months of the Naxalbari armed struggles in West Bengal that created big bangs in the Indian polity.

While studying the genesis and growth of Maoist insurgency in India, there are two distinct schools – one that interprets it as a political movement with strong base among the landless, the poor peasantry and the marginalized sections and the other which treats it as a basic law and order issue that should be dealt with an iron land by the State and its super structures. Basically, issues such as functioning of democracy, development, governance and socio-economic disparities etc, are closely intertwined with spread of Maoist insurgency. Polemics also exist on the support base of the movement. Some of them interpret the movement as "a rebellion in which people are fighting to save their land, forests, water and minerals from being grabbed and they are convinced that they have an alternative vision"[6] indicating the deep involvement of the Tribals and the indigenous sections. On the other hand, others feel that "it is not a movement of landless peasants and Tribals seeking to overthrow the State power, but a project defined by those who are neither peasants nor workers nor Tribals, but who claims to represent their rights."[7]

Against this backdrop, the theme of research assumes significance. In fact, State or area specific issues or factors considerably influence the genesis and growth of the movements. For example, the all-pervasive feudalism and landlordism that had exploited the sizeable chunk of socially and economically backward rural Tribal population for centuries virtually undermining the State and its establishments gave an impetus for its growth in Chhattisgarh, Jharkhand, Odisha and Andhra Pradesh. In Bihar, the caste conflicts coupled with the organized efforts of the landed gentry to oppress the Dalits and the under-privileged sow the seeds of the movement. The geographical proximity with the Maoist dominated areas of Chhattisgarh has considerably influenced the spread of the movement in the neighbouring States like Madhya Pradesh and Maharashtra.

Thus, instead of the conventional approach of studying the problem through macro analysis based on national or sub-national level data, a micro level study was undertaken to properly understand the spatial heterogeneity of movement and specific factors contributing to its growth.

For the micro level research, 6 Gram Panchayats[8] – three each from Wayanad and Palakkad, two socially and economically backward Northern districts of Kerala were taken. The focused area of research had some unique features relevant to the theme of study. Geographically, both the districts are situated in the tri-junction in the Western Ghats bordering Tamil Nadu and Karnataka, which in the recent past has prominently figured in the strategy of Communist Party of India (Maoists) to establish their bases. The forest cover and inaccessible terrain criss-crossed with rivers and rivulets are conducive for guerrilla operations. Around 37% of the total area in Wayanad district and 35.16% in Palakkad district are reserved forests. The Silent valley National Park, one of the last undisturbed tracts of South Western Ghats mountain rain forests and tropical moist evergreen forest in India is located in Palakkad district.

These districts which belonged to the erstwhile Madras Presidency were economically backward at the beginning of the British colonial rule, but continued to remain so even after the departure of the British in the middle of the 20th century. The economic backwardness of the districts can be mainly attributed to the British land policy which put majority of the population in utter poverty and misery. On one hand large areas of the cultivable land were accumulated by the landlords (Janmis). For example, out of 1,229,217 acres of total land in Malabar region, 6,28,921 acres (52%) were owned by 32 Janmis who belonged to upper castes such as the Namboothiris and Nairs. The landless tenants belonging to lower and backward castes were in extreme poverty. Further, under the unfavourable policies of the colonial administration, a gradual shift of the economy from primary to secondary or tertiary sector was clear. Large areas of land in these districts were converted into Coffee, tea and other plantation crops in which the Adivasis, landless peasants and migrant labourers worked like slaves. The steady exodus of the people notably from the Central Travancore to the hilly Adivasi dominated areas of these districts led to the systematic alienation of Tribal land and inter-related issues.

Another significant feature of the area is the sizeable presence of indigenous population. As per the 2011 Census, Wayanad district has the highest percentage of Adivasi population (18.5%) in Kerala, while Palakkad has around 2% of Adivasis. Atta paddy, the first Tribal Block in the State is located in Palakkad district.

The ethnic diversity of Tribal groups and their socio-economic backwardness are being exploited by the extremist and militant groups. For example, in Wayanad district, the Paniyar tribe which constitutes about 45% of the total Tribal population are the most socially and economically backward group which have been exploited for many decades. In the post-Independence period, they have become the major source of labour for the plantation groups and non-Tribal settlers with substantial land-holdings. On the other hand, the Kurichiyas (16%) are one of the most developed tribes in the district, economically and socially advanced with their own land-holdings for agriculture. With the rich legacy as the warriors of Pazhassi Raja who engaged British forces in several battles, they have traditional interest in archery and martial art. The other Tribal groups namely Kuruman (13%) Kattunayakkan (11%), Adiya (7%), Vettakuruman (4%) and Kuruman (2%) live in extreme poverty bereft of any cultivable land or employment.

In the case of Palakkad district, the plight of Tribals in Attappady area is not much different. The main tribes namely Irula (82%) Kurumba (10%) and Mudugas (7%) are economically and socially backward. Historically, the entire Atta paddy belt was under the rule of the Zamorin of Calicut, who distributed the land to the traditional upper caste families. Three landlords had absolute ownership of the land for centuries. Over the years, they converted vast areas into Tea, Coffee and Rubber plantations with the help of the British. This led to the steady influx of non-Tribal settlers for land and Adivasis for labour, to the area.

Thus, influx of non-Tribals and the inter-connected socio-economic issues such as exploitation of Tribals, land alienation and a series of land related struggles figured prominently in our area of study. The Adivasis were the victims of this influx. For example, the Adivasis who constituted more than 95% of the total population in Attapaddy Tribal belt in Palakkad district during 1951 were reduced to a minority (40.98%) in 2001. Similarly, Wayanad district witnessed a decadal growth rate of 62.5% during 1951-61, as a result of which the Adivasis became a minority. Over the years, the number of non-Tribals has further increased with the new ventures in the fields of eco-tourism, plantations and small-scale units in Adivasi belts. Inter-related with the influx, was the extensive Tribal land alienation which virtually made them landless without any sustainable sources of livelihood.

Meanwhile, majority of the government-sponsored welfare and developmental projects for the Adivasis were derailed mainly due to large scale corruption and the lack of sincerity of the political leadership and bureaucracy. Ironically, even those Adivasi leaders who were elevated as ministers under the banner of mainstream political parties have become epitomes of such corruption betraying their own suffering poverty-stricken Adivasis. These factors were brought out by a recent survey by the Kerala Institute of Local Administration (KILA). The average illiteracy rate of Adivasis was 33.5%, the average rate of unemployment hovers at around 9% and those without electricity and toilet facilities were to the tune of 61% and 52% respectively. The entire Tribal belt showed high infant mortality rate with maximum number of casualties in the Attapaddy belt which even attracted national and international attention and demolished many myths associated with the much trumpeted 'Kerala Model Development'. Some of these major socio-economic indicators of the Tribals are delineated in Table 3.1.

In fact, the above economic indicators of under-development and deprivation of Adivasis have reflected on the overall economy of these districts. As per the district-wise distribution of Gross State Domestic Product (GSDP) at constant prices,[9] for the year 2014-15, Wayanad district has the lowest income (₹ 8,87,882) in the State, whereas it was positioned 12 out of 14 districts in respect of per capita income (₹ 77,593) for the year 2014-15 at current constant prices (2011-12). Those figures (GSDP and per capita income) for Palakkad district were ₹ 32,46,376 (11th position) and ₹ 84,461 respectively.

Such factors, like the economic backwardness, unemployment, alienation of land, lack of development/infrastructure and basic amenities, have made the Adivasis the most vulnerable section which can be easily carried away by the motivated or orchestrated propaganda of Maoists and other radical groups. Thus, the Adivasi dominated areas of Wayanad district witnessed the early phase of the Maoist armed uprisings in 1968-70 and later in 1981, when the Adivasis and the landless peasants were organized for the attack on Police Stations and killing of landlords, branding them as class enemies.

Subsequently, the Left Wing Extremists (LWE) groups made organized efforts to mobilize these sections by floating

TABLE 3.1: Major Socio-Economic Indicators of Adivasis in Wayanad and Palakkad districts

Name of Panchayat/ district	Illiterates	School dropouts (below 18 years)	Without land/ houses	Without electricity	Without toilet facilities	Infant morta-lity (0-3 years)	Without employment (18-45yrs)
Pulpally/Wayanad	2464(31.32%)	111(3.88%)	2(0.11%)	1182(65%)	986(54%)	13	419(10.9%)
Thirunelly/Wayanad	4102(31.11%)	218(4.46%)	14(0.45%)	2308(74.07%)	1636(52.5%)	15	692(12.2%)
Mullenkolli/Waya	909(31.86%)	60(5.19%)	3(0.97%)	392(61.4%)	264(41.3%)	6	100(7.5%)
Agali/Palakkad	3556(30.28%)	32(0.85%)	517(15.4%)	1646(49.16%)	1712(51%)	28	927(1.33%)
Pudur/Palakkad	3910(40.38%)	27(0.75%)	308(11.6%)	1607(60.7%)	1740(66%)	29	465(10%)
Sholayur/Palakkad	3295(35.70%)	37(1.30%)	376(14.5%)	1424(54.9%)	1162(44.7%)	24	565(12%)

(Ref: Study report/2011-12 of Kerala Institute of Local Administration, Trichur.)

front/extension organizations espousing their cause especially the land related issues. Such bodies had come to lime light in Attapaddy Tribal belt during 1990s by taking up the issues of Adivasis especially the land alienation. The formation of autonomous Tribal organizations and their protracted struggles for the restoration of alienated Tribal land, to a great extent, had checkmated the strategy of Maoists and other radical groups to make further inroads into these sections. The Adivasis who had lost faith on major political parties have now estranged from these outfits which too have become the shadow of political parties. Obviously, the strategy of Maoists is to exploit this crisis of faith among Adivasis to their advantage.

OBJECTIVES AND HYPOTHESIS

The main objectives of this study are:

(a) to examine the support of Adivasis to the Maoist insurgency especially in States like Kerala where the movement is yet to take deep roots;

(b) to study the socio-economic and land related issues influencing the growth and expansion of Maoists;

(c) to assess the role of independent organizations of indigenous groups in countering the Maoist expansion, through specific case studies;

(d) to study the extent of political socialization of Tribals impacting the Maoist insurgency; and

(e) to arrive at conclusions as how the Maoist insurgency can be effectively contained especially in areas where the movement is in infant stage. In line with the above objectives, the following research questions were formulated to undertake the project:

1. Whether the support of Adivasis contributes to the growth of Maoist insurgency?
2. Whether the land related issues in the Adivasi areas help the growth of Maoists?
3. Whether the emergence of independent organizations of Adivasis is helpful in checkmating the spread of Maoist insurgency?
4. Whether the political socialization of Adivasis and their integration help to check the growth of Maoist groups?

RESEARCH DESIGN

The entire project was designed based on the above objectives and the scope of the study. Accordingly, the research design included initial desk research followed by detailed field survey. It was a combination of both primary and secondary survey/ sources. The secondary data was collected mainly through published books, research studies, and articles in the national and international print media, government reports and internet resources. These also included websites of the Census of India, Planning Commission of India, State Government of Kerala, Kerala Institute of Local Administration (KILA) etc. This data which enabled us to gain an insight into the socio-economic profile of the area of research was used to understand the background of the Maoist insurgency and helped to verify primary data collected through random sampling (500), special questionnaires and depth interviews.

DATA GATHERING INSTRUMENTS

The conventional data gathering instruments such as questionnaire and interview schedule were used on the basis of the inputs gathered from the study of literature. These included:

1. a 5-point scale 'Likert model' questionnaire covering the main hypotheses of the study with an open ended question eliciting views/suggestions from the samples to check the spread of Maoist insurgency among Adivasis/other marginalized sections;
2. special interview schedule for ex-Maoist leaders, leaders of autonomous Adivasi bodies, pro-left intellectuals and constitutional/legal experts; and
3. observation schedule for independent Adivasi organization with a self-assessment format.

Besides, structured interviews were conducted with elected representatives of Block/Panchayat bodies, officials attached to Panchayat, Tribal Development, and Health, Forest and educational institutions and Anganwadi workers.

PROCEDURAL STEPS

Methodology included both qualitative as well as quantitative approach. Qualitative information in terms of in-depth interviews (DIs) were conducted from selected 45 respondents comprising ex-Maoists, pro-Left intellectuals, Central/State Government officials, NGO functionaries/activists and the police. Data from Kerala Institute of Local Administration (KILA) as well as different State Government establishments were collected and analysed to observe implementation status of different schemes meant for Adivasis/the weaker sections in the sampled areas of study. The study of literature comprising several books, research papers, articles, documents and special write-ups by social scientists, academicians, social activists, police/security analysts and journalists, highlighting the genesis and spread of Maoist insurgency and the approach of indigenous population helped to collect useful data on the main research questions. As many of those studies are based on secondary data, attempts have been made to co-relate them with the primary data collected through field studies, responses from random samples and in-depth interviews. The literature relevant to the study has been critically reviewed. The information/data gathered from both primary and secondary sources were analysed using various statistical packages like SPSS and on the basis of that the reports have been prepared.

REVIEW OF LITERATURE

The relevant literature has been reviewed under five broad heads namely:

(a) the history of Maoist insurgency;
(b) its support or otherwise among Tribals;
(c) socio-economic and land related issues helping the growth of Maoists;
(d) the impact of political socialization and indigenous organizations over the movement; and
(e) the past, present and future trends of Maoist insurgency in Kerala.

Kujur Rajat provided a detailed overview of the history of India's Maoist organizations in "Naxal Movement in 2008: An Assessment". While 1970-2000 periods was marked by high intensity conflicts among different Naxalite groups, the formation of CPI (Maoist) in 2004 through the merger of two major Naxalite outfits that are committed to violent struggles was the driving force of their recent growth. Pratul Ahuja and Rajat Ganguly state that there is evidence that the Maoist insurgency has grown sufficiently powerful and is even challenging the legitimacy of the Indian State. They hold that the Naxalite groups maintain links with alien insurgent groups such as the Maoist extremists from Nepal and members of the erstwhile Liberation Tigers for Tamil Elam (LTTE) in Sri Lanka, especially for arms training and procuring of landmines and Improvised Explosive Devices (IEDs) ("The Fire Within: Naxalite Insurgency Violence in India").

The impact of Maoist insurgency on country's economy is a matter of serious concern. Ajit Kumar Singh notes that Maoist violence has interfered with India's major mineral export industry. Industrial investments in these mineral belts have slowed down due to lack of security, affecting access to rich supplies of coal, bauxite and iron ("India: Maoists Targeting Economy", published in *Eurasia Review News and Analysis*). Sujeet Kumar reported that the mining companies are reluctant to enter the Maoist infested regions until security conditions improve in. A number of Maoists training camps are known to be operating in the forests of Chhattisgarh ("Troops Closing in on Maoist Training Zone: Chhattisgarh Minister").

In an analytical study, Institute of Peace and Conflict Studies (IPCS) highlights that there are two major schools of thoughts in the Indian strategic community, interpreting Maoist insurgency. Those who interlink it with the developmental issues view the Maoist struggles as an offshoot of poverty and political disenfranchisement. Others hold it as a basic law and order issue which should be dealt with an iron hand by the State apparatus ("Left Extremism in India: Naxal Movement in Chhattisgarh and Odisha"). Prakash Singh (*The Naxalite Movement in India*), former Director General of the Border Security Force (BSF) who has ground level experience in combating the Maoists maintains that the root cause of Maoist insurgency is the serious issues of governance and corruption in our system. Retired Lt-Gen VR Raghavan,

Advisor, Delhi Policy Group identifies Maoism as a complex socio-politico-economic phenomenon with their main bases in rural areas spread over in many States (*The Naxal Threat: Causes, State Responses and Consequences*). Souvik Chatterjee (*Naxalism: A Threat to Indian Internal Security*) regards the Naxalite movement as one of the important components in the political spectrum in India which many idealists interpreted as the beginning of a new world.

Edward N Muller and Mitchell A Seligson (*Inequality and Insurgency*) highlight various social, economic, and political issues as the causative factors for Maoist insurgency. James D Fearon and David D Laitin ("Ethnicity, Insurgency, and Civil War"), identify social exploitation, illiteracy, unemployment, lack of economic gain, lack of representation, lack of judicial reforms, lack of land reforms and the caste related grievances as the major factors for the growth of the movement. According to George Kunnath, lack of social and economic development coupled with the lack of governance in the rural and Tribal regions for over a period of four decades have been exploited by Maoists. Jose Binoj while analysing the emergence and growth of the Naxalite movement in India, found that the negation of distributive justice was one of the major factors that led to the emergence of these militant organizations. Distributive justice will ensure social, economic and political justice ("Peace and Eco-Social Justice: Failed Distributive Justice, Violence and Militancy in India").

Edward Duyker highlights the Tribal participation in the Naxalite movement as manifested by Santals in West Bengal. The use of Tribal symbols, their customs and traditions helped to build up revolutionary fervour among cadres ("Tribal Guerrillas: The Santals of West Bengal and the Naxalite Movement"). DD Nag and RP Saxena, on the basis of their extensive study of Tribal dominated districts (Mandla,

Bilaspur, Durg and Balaghat) in undivided Madhya Pradesh highlighted the special features of Tribal economy which in many respects could not be preserved in the Planning process. Incidentally all these districts had turned into the citadels of the Maoists. Priyanka Vora and Siddhant Buxy in their article titled "Marginalization and Violence: The Story of Naxalism in India" find that the root of the problem lies in the marginalization of the poor forest dwellers by the government as the very land that they depend on for their sustenance is snatched away. It has been transferred to Multinational corporations in the name of development. According to Ramachandra Guha, the exclusion of Tribals from the mainstream of India's growth story is one of the key driving forces of the Maoist movement. The Expert Panel of the Planning Commission in their Report on the "Developmental Challenges in Extremist-Affected Areas" found that the main support and the recruits for the movement are mostly from lower castes and Tribal population. The social base of the movement, according to Bhatia consists overwhelmingly of landless, small peasants with marginal land-holdings and lesser extent middle class peasants. Gopala Rao N (1978) studied the process of transfer of land from the Tribals to the non-Tribals and the various factors influencing such transfers in Srikakulam district of Andhra Pradesh. He found that land has been alienated by some people to finance agricultural operations. Describing Naxalism as an agrarian and social problem, Uday Kumar feels that effective implementation of the government's rural schemes is vital for engaging the Tribals, who provide the support and manpower to the movement (*Defeating Naxalite: Ways and Means to Defeat Naxalism*).

The Bureau of Police Research and Development (BPR&D) sponsored research on the "Social, Economic and Political Dynamics in Extremist Affected Areas" had indicated the nexus between the politicians and extremists of the region.

The extremists remain an effective tool of garnering political support, especially during elections. Dean Joros (1973) presented his views on the relation between political socialisation of the Tribals and integration process or the effect of Tribal welfare programmes on the political socialisation process. He reveals that by analysing the political socialisation process of Tribals, a more complete evaluation of Tribal welfare programmes can be ensured. This view is also explained by PRG Mathur (1977). He points out that induction of political culture and integration into the mainstream of national life are part of one and the same process. And without achieving political socialisation, Tribals' integration into the national social life is impossible. Political socialisation must precede their integration into national life. Such a process will help to contain the influence of Maoists among Tribals.

Different strategies have been adopted to fight against the Maoists. Nilakantan and Singhal in their research paper ("The Economic Costs of Naxalite Violence and the Economic Benefits of a Unique Robust Security Response") highlight that Andhra Pradesh has been successful in containing Maoist insurgency by pursuing a strategy of targeted development and the deployment of a specialized police force. Deepak Aneel Boyini points out that enemy-centric measures based on reliable intelligence, a capable force, and a unified command followed by population centric aspects of winning hearts and minds, lead to success in countering Maoist insurgency ("Explaining Success and Failure: Counterinsurgency in Malaya and India"). PV Ramana stated that over the years, the Maoists have enhanced their lethal capabilities by improvising their weaponry and tactics ("The Maoist Movement in India"). Praveen Swami while analysing India's counterinsurgency architecture points out those studies have primarily focused on factors explaining success part of counterinsurgency and have applied these models to failed insurgencies without analysing the causes of failure. He cites the example of the British model of population control and isolation strategy in Malaya, which was great success, but a total failure in of Chhattisgarh ("For a Review of Counterinsurgency Doctrine").

In his study "The Political Economy of the Maoist Conflict in India: An Empirical Analysis", Joseph Flavian Gomes used sub-national micro data to identify the causes of civil conflicts like Maoist insurgency. Using data on 362 districts for 3 time periods, he found evidence as how land inequality is extremely important for the Maoist conflict. Another contributory factor was the exclusion of the low castes and Tribal people from the growth story of India. The study "Hearts and Mines: A District Level Analysis of the Maoist Conflict in India" by Kristian Hoelscher, Jason Miklian and Krishna Chaitanya Vadlamannati was aimed at addressing the lack of local level analysis and the lack of a robust data set by merging previous qualitative fieldwork. It unfolds the relationship between development works, violence, and natural resource extraction. Under certain conditions mining activity increases the likelihood of conflict; it is the presence of Scheduled Caste and Scheduled Tribe (SC/ST) communities that is the best predictor of violence. The effective implementation of development programmes like Mahatma Gandhi National Rural Employment Guarantee Programme (MNREGP) may be helpful to contain the violent activities in districts affected by the Maoist conflict.

As far as the literature on Maoist insurgency in Kerala, there are few rigorous empirical studies. Ms Luisa Steur's study "Adivasi Mobilization: 'Identity' versus 'Class' after the Kerala Model of Development?" highlights that the Naxalites, the underground Maoist party that was active in Kerala in late 1960s had strong base among Adiyas and Paniyas, the most economically backward Tribals in the State. Many of them still remember Anikkad Varghese, the Naxalite leader who took genuine interest in their issues and was killed by the police in 1970 while fighting for their cause. What attracted them to the movement were the Naxalite-led struggles of late 1960s which enabled them to get enhanced daily wages. Meanwhile, the emergence of independent Tribal bodies offered them opportunities to realize social justice more than what Communists and Maoists did. Naturally, the quality of life indicators for Tribals in Kerala were significantly higher than those of Tribals elsewhere in India. In 1991, the literacy rate for male and female Scheduled Tribes (STs) in Kerala was 74% and 51% respectively much higher than 24% and 18% for STs across India. Despite such advancement, the upper class/caste values dominated and marginalized the voice of Tribals giving some space for Maoists and other radical groups to open their fronts among these sections.

Dr R Rajeevan ("Towards Political Empowerment: Political Socialization and Political Participation of Tribal Community in Kerala") finds that the Naxalite movement was strengthened in the northern Kerala notably in Malabar area mainly due to the attitude and approach of mainstream political parties towards the Tribals and the marginalized. Almost all major political parties remained indifferent towards the crucial issues of Tribals. The Left political parties especially the Communist Party of India (Marxist) with which many Tribal people had early association saw the Tribal question within a class framework and were not prepared to view it as a problem specific to certain communities. This universalizing stance of the Leftists even on Tribal issues in Kerala was one of the major contributory factors for the spread of Maoist movement among the Tribals. They believed that the Maoists would politically empower them. Thus, they were enthusiastically attracted to Maoism. J Tharamangalam observes that Adivasis/Tribals were never part of the political parties and the hegemonic class discourse especially by the Left adversely affected their interests. Deepa Chandran maintains that the higher gap between the Tribal and non-Tribal population in Kerala in various socio-economic development indicators as compared to the rest of the country presents a situation of paradox within paradoxes. This paradox, to a great extent, had been exploited by Maoists. However, the increasing political mobilization of Tribal communities in Kerala has considerably influenced their approach towards Maoist groups.

R Rajeevan highlights that land alienation is one of the main issues of Tribals in northern Kerala particularly in Wayanad and Palakkad districts. More than 15% of the Tribals in the State are landless. The successive governments in the State remained indifferent in enforcing various legislations in respect of the restoration of Tribal land or its allotment to the landless Tribals. Since 2002, the rate of allotment of identified land to Tribals has drastically come down apparently to safeguard the interests of non-Tribal settlers. These factors are exploited by Maoists and more militant sections among Tribals. Ms Sreerekha ("Challenges before Kerala's Landless: The Story of Aralam Farm") holds that despite being the forerunner in taking steps to ensure distributive justice, the unsatisfactory implementation of the Transfer and Restoration of Alienated Land Act aggravated Tribal sufferings which, to a great extent could be exploited by Maoists. Chattukulam John holds that the socio-political and economic conditions needed to facilitate Tribal communities to enjoy the fruits of development were virtually absent in the State. Sreekumar and Parayil argue that the State projects for the benefit of larger society did not cover Tribals often dispossessing and displacing them. The programmes intended exclusively for their benefit had only marginalized and deprived them further. Thus, retired Justice of Supreme Court, VR Krishna Iyer laments: "They are the victims of social deprivation, dubious promises and dishonourable existence, who suffer as derelicts and driftwood."

Such general psyche among Adivasis was the main reason for the formation of autonomous Tribal organizations especially Adivasi Gothra Maha Sabha (AGMS). Describing AGMS as the first social movement in Kerala explicitly aimed at Tribal rights, Ms Steur expresses doubts as how far its indigenous identity would help the process of political mobilization of Tribals and other marginalized sections. Surely, the more modern, class based and anti-caste forms of Tribal politics can meet the challenges in the neo-liberal age. Rajeevan holds that it was the first Tribal movement in Kerala which showed the unity and spirit of the Tribals. Almost all Tribal groups participated in the land struggles launched by it. It revolutionized the Tribal mindset in Kerala and to a great extent checkmated the efforts of Maoists and radicals to make inroads among Tribals.

However, Maoists are engaged in working out alternate strategy to overcome such bottlenecks. Amartya Deb holds that the past experiences in the country show that when the Maoists have not been active in terms of violence, they have been using the time for improving their organisational strength by recruiting, recuperating, striking new alliances and looking for newer ways of raising funds and acquiring weapons. While there has been a weakening of the Naxalites in the Red Corridor, there has been substantial growth in places like Kerala (Manekshaw Paper No 57, 2015, "Naxals in Kerala: Their Networks, Resources, Legitimacy and Solutions for Curbing Future Growth"). An attempt has been made to define and explain the key words that constituted the main theme of the research.

MAOIST INSURGENCY

Bard gives the conceptual definition of an insurgency as "a struggle between a non-ruling group and the ruling authorities in which the non-ruling group consciously uses political resources (eg, organizational expertise, propaganda, and demonstrations) and violence to destroy, reformulate, or sustain the basis of legitimacy of one or more aspects of politics." This is the strategy formulated by Mao Tse-tung to capture political power through a combination of armed insurgency, mass mobilisation and strategic alliances – a process of protracted people's war. According to Bard, the three phases of the Maoist insurgency strategy are organization terrorism, guerrilla warfare, and mobile conventional warfare. The ultimate goal of this strategy is the displacement of the established regime.

The Communist Party of India (Maoist), an amalgamation of the People's War Group (PWG) of Andhra Pradesh and Maoist Communist Centre (MCC) of Bihar, is vigorously pursuing this strategy in India. One has to see their expansion and consolidation – they started from Naxalbari in the late 1960s; faced ideological differences, disunity and disintegration leading to the formation of different groups in the 1980s and 1990s and re-emerged as the vanguard of Maoism through merger and consolidation in 2004. Thus, the terms 'Naxalites', 'Left Wing Extremists' (LWE) denoting the whole lot of parties and groups upholding Maoism, Maoist thought and Maoists indicating, CPI (Maoist) have been alternatively used in this research.

ADIVASIS OR TRIBES

They constitute a major demographic section of the Indian population. The Imperial Gazetteer of India (1911) defines a tribe as "a collection of families bearing a common name, speaking a common dialect that occupy or profess to occupy a common territory and is usually not endogamous though originally it might have been so." Adivasis mean the original inhabitants. Article 366 of the Constitution describes Scheduled Tribes (STs). Empowered by Clause 1 of Article 342, the President of India will notify the list of STs in the States and Union Territories. These orders can be modified only through an Act of Parliament. There are over 500 tribes (with many communities falling in more than one State) as notified under Article 342. As per SC/ST Orders (Amendment) Act, 2002 (Act 10 of 2003), the list of STs in Kerala consists of 36 communities. The main Adivasi communities in the area of this study are Adiyan, Kattunaikkan, Kurichiyas, Paniyas, Vettakuruman, Kurumar, Malaarayas (all in Wayanad district) Irular, Kurumbar, Modugar (all in Palakkad district).

ADIVASI ORGANIZATIONS

Conceptually, these are the bodies formed among Adivasis mainly to take up their causes/issues. There are two types of organizations – one floated at the instance of political parties and the other formed by Adivasi leaders and independent in nature.

NOTES AND REFERENCES

1. "Dr Amartya Sen and the Kerala Model" by George Mathew, *The Hindu* dated January 9, 2001. www.thehindu.com/2001/01/09/stories/05092523.htm last accessed on October 15, 2016.
2. *Ibid*, Sl No 1, above.
3. Sree Narayana Guru (1856-1928) was a social reformer of Kerala who led a reform movement rejected castes, and promoted new values of spiritual freedom and social equality and worked for the spiritual and social uplift of the downtrodden.
4. Ayyankali (1863-1941) was a social reformer who worked for the advancement of those people in the then princely State of Travancore, British India, who were treated as untouchables.

5. Dr Palpu (1863-1950) was a relentless fighter for ensuring social justice and equality to the backward castes of Kerala especially Ezhavas.
6. Gautam Navlakha, "Day and Night in Maoist Heartland", *EPW*, Vol XIV, No 16, April 2010.
7. Dilip Simeon, "Permanent Spring", *Seminar*, No 607 (March 2010). (www.india.seminar.com last accessed on October 12, 2016).
8. In three-tier Panchayati Raj set up in India, Gram Panchayat is the lowest unit with population ranging from 30,000-40,000.
9. http://www.kerenvis.nic.in/Database/Economics_830.aspx last accessed on November 5, 2016.

4

Maoists and Adivasis

The support of the indigenous population notably in the backward and underdeveloped areas where landlordism and semi-feudal tendencies are powerful is crucial for the spread and consolidation of the Maoist movement. It is a debatable issue as whether those sections *suo motu* extend their support to this movement or are forced to align with the ultras under coercion or fear. In fact, no specific conclusion could be arrived at in such matters in view of the diversity of indigenous groups, their different ethno-cultural perceptions and perspectives and of course, the extent of their assimilation in the national mainstream. Moreover many extraneous factors such as nature of governance and distributive justice, role of enforcement agencies, developmental issues etc, influence their approach towards the Maoists. Our attempt is to unravel as how the support of Adivasis in Kerala contributed to the potential of the Maoist insurgency. For that purpose, the primary data collected through empirical survey, inputs gathered from individuals connected with the movement through scheduled interview and the secondary data from different sources have been analysed.

Majority of the respondents felt that Adivasi support was crucial for the movement during its different phases. Such responses were more from Wayanad district, where the Maoist insurgency made serious challenges during late 1960s. Even illiterate Adivasi women respondents of the area still remember Varghese, the Maoist leader who worked among Adivasis and landless peasants and was killed in 1970. However, overwhelming majority of them felt that sections of Adivasis were drawn to the early phase of the movement without understanding its ideology or anticipating its ramifications in the society. Neither they were aware of Maoist ideology, nor their strategy or tactics or larger designs.

More than 65% of the respondents opined that, despite organized attempts, the Maoists could not build up their support base among the Adivasis. They felt that Maoists were unable to effectively take up the issues of Adivasis; nor attract them to their ideologies.

An analysis of the historical/secondary data on the different phases of Maoist insurgency in Kerala supported those findings. The unique geographic and demographic features of Northern Kerala especially Kannur, Kozhikode Malappuram, Palakkad and Wayanad districts considerably influenced early Maoist armed uprisings of 1968-70. These districts that fall under the tri-junction of the Western Ghats and its adjoining areas with half a dozen mountains and criss-crossed by Kabini river and its tributaries constituted a contiguous zone of difficult terrain with thick Reserve Forests, conducive for any armed revolutionary movement. The presence of sizeable chunk of Adivasi population – illiterate, socially and economically backward and exploited for centuries by landlords and plantation lobby – provided a fertile ground for Maoists to build up their support base.

Thus, the ex-cadres of the Communist Party of India (Marxist) who were working among the Adivasis could easily mobilise them in their planned action against the landlords/

Police Stations during the first phase of Maoist insurgency in Kerala. Though such attacks were planned and led by petty bourgeoisie intelligentsia, the majority of the action squad members were Adivasis and landless peasants. Thus, Ms Steur[1] had rightly commented that the 'Adiya' and 'Paniya' tribes were the main base of the early Maoist insurgency of late1960s in Kerala. Others like Rajeevan[2], who made extensive study on the Adivasi paradigm in Kerala, felt that these sections neglected and betrayed by the mainstream political parties supported the early Maoist insurgency thinking that the Maoists would politically empower them.

However, they were not ideologically organized or adequately trained for armed struggle, as clearly manifested during the attack on Police Station at Tellicherry, Kannur district where only one-third of the mobilized cadres turned up on the day of attack. And moreover, those turned up were panic stricken on seeing heavy security deployment at the station. The lack of indoctrination coupled with lack of proper training on Maoist insurgency strategy incapacitated the cadres to withstand the strong police action and other repressive measures of the State. Bereft of proper leadership, the fear psychosis, so created among Adivasis, through a reign of terror by police, had forced them to dissociate with the movement.

During the post-Emergency phase, the Maoists in Kerala tried to woo Adivasis through cultural movement. The conceptual framework for the strategy was based on the hypothesis that revolutions should start with the attack on the moral-political order and traditional hierarchy and class statuses. As part of this strategy Janakeeya Samskarika Vedi (JSV) (People's Cultural Forum)[3] was formed in 1980 with the main task of creating a new democratic culture in the country by allying with all new forces of democratic revolution and struggles at various levels. The JSV activists and pro-Maoist intellectuals under the banner of the Depressed Classes Renaissance Front had organized campaign and activities in Adivasi hamlets and Dalit colonies to attract them to the Maoist movement.

The State witnessed the proliferation of a number of theatre, literary and cultural groups on the pattern of Jana Natya Mandali[4] and Revolutionary Writers Association (RWA)[5] in Andhra Pradesh. Serious attempts were made to incorporate Adivasi customs, traditions and cultural symbols in their street plays and other art forms. Wayanad district with major concentration of Adivasi population was at the centre stage. Wayanad district Samskarika Vedi with their street plays and dramatic presentation of Gorky's[6] immortal work *Mother* played a major role in this regard. The play Nadugaddika[7] staged by the Vedi in many places throughout the State had virtually revolutionized the conventional theatre; art and culture when majority of those associated with it were Adivasis themselves. Moreover the play, by using myths, folk traditions, symbols and superstitions among Adivasis had immortalized Varghese, the Maoist leader who was killed by the police in Wayanad during the early phase of the movement in the State. Similarly, progressive poets and writers such as of Kadamanitta, Sachithanandan, Balachandran Chullikkad, Civic Chandran etc, through their works tried to present before the civil society the bitter agonies, oppression and exploitation of Adivasis and other weaker sections and made a clarion call to fight against such injustices under the banner of progressive forces.

The strategy of disseminating Maoist ideology among the Adivasis and other marginalized sections, camouflaged under indigenous art or cultural events, had partially succeeded in the State when sections of Adivasis and Dalits had started associating with the various campaigns of Maoists such as 'public trials' of the corrupt bureaucrats and cruel landlords.

However, in the aftermath of the Kenichira action[8] in May 1981, the Adivasis and other pro-Maoist elements in Wayanad district had to face severe State repression leading to the steady erosion in the support base of Maoists among the Adivasis. With the drastic police action coupled with the enforcement of draconian legislations, the cultural activities came to a standstill.

By this period, modernist trends had set in Kerala. Globalization and liberalization have raised new challenges. This has led to the emergence of new social movements focusing on neo-colonial issues adversely affecting Adivasis, Dalits and the indigenous people. Those movements occupied the major space hitherto made use of by Maoists to build up their support base. One major development was the genesis of apolitical autonomous Adivasi organizations like Adivasi Gothra Maha Sabha (AGMS)[9] espousing the cause of Adivasis especially their land related issues. The formation of such bodies and their protracted struggles, to a great extent, has blunted the strategy of Maoists to make inroads into these sections. Added to this was the political mobilisation of Adivasis by mainstream parties which through their rosy promises and rhetoric created a chimera among these sections much against the slogans of violence and bloodshed by Maoists.

The fantasy so created by the political parties and autonomous Adivasi organizations has started vanishing from the mind of the majority of Adivasis. The betrayal and neglect of the community by the mainstream political parties have been fully exposed. Despite a plethora of developmental and welfare schemes exclusively meant for Adivasis, they continue to present a dismal picture. In fact, an illegal nexus of political intermediaries, business/contract men and bureaucrats have successively exploited the Adivasis for decades virtually uprooting them from their traditional homeland. The large scale alienation of Tribal land, steady exodus of non-Tribal communities towards the traditional Tribal hamlets in the uplands and the inter-related socio-economic issues have opened a vicious circle of maladies such as malnutrition, addiction to liquor, health hazards, and indebtedness. On an average 40 to 50 Adivasis, mainly women, are murdered in Attapadi alone every year. Attapaddi area[10] recorded the highest number of death of new born Adivasi babies, which caught country-wide attention. Their young are forced to work in far off places as household helps. The women are often made a target of sexual depredation. Thus, the number of unwed Adivasi mothers is on increase. In Wayanad district alone there are around 200 such unfortunate victims whose cases are totally neglected by the law enforcement agencies and the administration. Dominated by vote bank politics, the mainstream parties have conveniently ignored such issues and are keener to protect the interests of the powerful non-Tribal settlers' lobby.

In that process, the independent Adivasi bodies like AGMS which organized historic land struggles 1990s and 2000s have been relegated to the background. Ironically, even the founding leaders of such outfits could not resist the temptations made by political parties. Bereft of dynamic leaders or plan of action, these bodies have lost much their credibility and autonomous character. Having lost faith on mainstream political parties and indigenous Adivasi organizations, the Adivasi community in the State is at cross roads. The simmering discontentment and disappointment among Adivasis against the successive governments is a fertile ground for the Maoists to exploit their sentiments.

Leaders of other organizations such as Bhooparishkarana Samithi (Land Reforms Committee) Vanavakasa Samrakshana

Samithi (Forest Dwellers Protection Committee), Adijana Sabha (Adivasi Sabha), Attappadi Adivasi Sanghatana (Attapadi Adivasi Forum) etc, which are active among the Adivasis have expressed similar line of approach. They are also critical of the State Government's strategy to deploy Tribal people for anti-Maoist operations on the ground that by using Adivasis as human shields, they would unnecessarily attract the wrath of the ultras.

Obviously, the present strategy of Maoists is to exploit this situation to their advantage. Roopesh, an underground Kerala Maoist leader (now in detention) claimed that the Western Ghats Special Zonal Committee (WGSZC) was formed to target the scores of Tribals, Scheduled Caste people, landless poor farmers in the tri-junction of Kerala, Tamil Nadu and Karnataka who are subjected to extreme exploitation and oppression. Thus, issues that are closely intertwined with the life of Adivasis were taken up especially in the Adivasi dominated areas in Wayanad, Palakkad, Kozhikode, Malappuram and Kannur.

The Forest department and its personnel were targeted on the grounds of harassment of Adivasis on flimsy grounds and connivance with the timber mafia responsible for the devastation of reserved forests. Moreover, the department's network of field units and offices in the interior of the forests created impediments for the movement and guerrilla type activities of the Maoists. At the instance of the Western Ghats Special Zonal Committee (WGSZC), camp sheds of the Forest Department deep inside the forests in Palakkad, Malappuram and Wayanad were destroyed. Similarly, as part of the campaign to protect the environment and the natural flora and fauna closely interlinked with the life of Adivasis, a couple of stone crusher units and mining sites in other districts were attacked.

The Maoists have also launched campaigns and high voltage propaganda on the apathetic attitude of the successive governments to mitigate the hardship and sufferings of the Adivasis. For example, the recurring death of little children in the Tribal regions of Attappadi in Palakkad district due to abject poverty and malnutrition has been projected as governments' callous neglect of this community for decades. Pro-Maoist outfits such as Adivasi Land Reforms Committee and their leaders like M Geethanandan[11] described these deaths as genocide and have called for action against all those responsible for the situation. Responses from Adivasi settlements indicate that there are many takers for such allegation of genocide levelled against the authorities as the successive governments had never taken any effective step to end the encroachments by settler farmers of Adivasi lands but had effectively supported such activities with their silence.

Unfortunately, the approach of the mainstream parties and of course, the governments led by them, is that the majority of the Adivasis will not fall in the trap of the Maoists. Thus, their efforts to counter the Maoist move to make inroads into Adivasi community are half hearted, bereft of sincerity and commitment. Such steps like the free distribution of food kits each worth ₹ 100 in vulnerable Adivasi colonies every day, free supply of medicine and balanced diet to pregnant Adivasi women, better medical facilities in Adivasi hamlets, appointment of Tribal promoters to oversee the basic amenities/facilities in the colonies etc, failed to improve their overall condition.

Instead of launching specific projects and programmes to ameliorate the hardships and sufferings of the community, the emphasis of the governments is to deal with the Maoist insurgency as a typical law and order issue. Thus, the State Government, over the last couple of years, has been knocking at the doors of the Union Government to include 3 districts in

Kerala – Wayanad, Malappuram and Palakkad – under the anti-Naxalite Security Related Expenditure (SRE) scheme. Though funds under the scheme are basically meant to tackle Maoist threat, the entire scheme is designed for strengthening the law enforcement set up in Maoist infested areas. Perhaps, such strategies may lead to temporary success in the task of tackling Maoist threat. But the ultimate success lies in the formulation and implementation of sound developmental and welfare schemes for the Adivasis and the marginalized sections. The words of a Development Officer closely associated with a number of Adivasi related issues in Attappadi area for decades clearly reflected this reality:

> "The Government should be extra careful about the Adivasi issue in the context of the reports on Maoists' bid to get a foothold in the Tribal areas. In today's condition in the settlements, spreading roots among the Adivasis anywhere in Kerala wouldn't be very difficult for the Maoists. Police alone cannot do anything in such issues."[12]

NOTES AND REFERENCES

1. Steur, Luisa, 2009, Adivasi Mobilization: Identity versus class, After the Kerala Model development, Journal of South Asian Development 4: 1(2009) 25-44, Sage Publications, London.
2. Dr R Rajeevan, 2010, Towards Political Empowerment. Political socialization and Political participation of Tribal community in Kerala, Kalpaz Publications, New Delhi.
3. JSV was floated by Left Wing intellectuals of Kerala in late 1970s to promote LWE ideology among masses through various cultural/literary activities.
4. Jana Natya Mandali was the cultural front of PWG in Andhra Pradesh. Gaddar was the chief exponent of the movement who through his revolutionary ballad and folk art tried to spread Maoist ideology among masses.

5. Viplava Rachayitala Sangham (VIRASAM) or Revolutionary Writers Association (RWA) is a forum floated by Pro-Maoist writers of Andhra Pradesh led by Varavara Rao to promote Maoist Ideology.
6. Alexei Maximovich Peshkov (1868-1936), primarily known as Maxim Gorky was a Russian and Soviet writer, founder of the socialist realism literary method and a political activist. The *Mother* is one of his most famous works.
7. JSV's famous street play that artistically deploring many customs, superstitions and practices among the Adivasis and depicting the heroic role of Maoists in liberating them from the clutches of landlords.
8. Madathil Mathai, a non-Tribal settler of Kenichira in Wayanad district was killed in May 1981 by Maoists, branding him as class enemy. This action was in pursuance of the military line of CRC-CPML.
9. Formed at the instance of CK Janu in 1995 for fighting for Tribal rights. It is now inactive.
10. The first Tribal block in Kerala, which comes under Palakkad district.
11. Geethanandan, previously associated with Maoists in 1980s and 1990s, is one of the founder leaders of Adivasi Gothra Maha Sabha (AGMS).
12. Personal interview with Block Development Officer of Attappadi area (July 2013).

5

Socio-Economic Condition of Adivasis and Maoist Insurgency

The co-relation between socio-economic condition and the spread of Maoist insurgency is a debatable theme. The crucial question is whether the Maoist activities or their presence in some parts of India, but not in other parts, can be explained by differences in economic and social conditions? Truly speaking, no conclusive answers could be arrived at on such questions. Some backward districts known for their most depressive socio-economic conditions are free from the Maoist challenge, whereas some other areas with moderate socio-economic advancement are in the grip of Maoist insurgency. Thus, apart from socio-economic conditions, other factors such as topography, demography and political awareness influence the spread of Maoist ideas. But, the hard reality is that the social and economic deprivation experienced by a significant part of the Indian population acts as a catalyst for the genesis and spread of Maoist insurgency. Basically, these deprived lots comprise the Adivasis and the Dalits.

We have empirically examined these issues in the backdrop of the Maoist movement in Kerala. In this chapter, we will discuss as to what extent the social and economic deprivation of the Adivasis and the resultant frustration and helplessness influenced Maoist insurgency? The life of Adivasis and for that matter their socio-economic conditions are inextricably intertwined with '*Jal*, *Zameen* and *Jungle*' (water, land and forest). That is why the Maoist led struggles have been sometimes described as the fight to establish the right of Adivasis over these areas. On the basis of a 5 point Likert model questionnaire, the responses from 500 samples in respect of the socio-economic condition among Adivasis such as extent of possession of land, impact of land reforms, accessibility to basic amenities like safe drinking water, Health, Education, Road communication network, Public Distribution System were analysed. Their views on the approach of forest personnel towards the Adivasis were also ascertained.

Overwhelming majority of respondents felt that of the various socio-economic issues, the Adivasi land alienation has adversely affected them in all areas of their life. The deprivation of cultivable land has opened a vicious circle of maladies such as malnutrition, addiction to liquor, health hazards, and indebtedness and different forms of exploitation of Adivasis. Ms CK Janu, the Adivasi leader, who organized a series of agitations including the Muthanga land struggle in 2003 demanding restoration of alienated Tribal land has highlighted that "the Adivasis are now deprived of their traditional land, viable employment, and food or health facilities."[1]

The land reforms in Kerala, described by many as the most revolutionary piece of legislation since the formation of the State in 1950, have not helped to resolve the land related issues among Adivasis. Majority of respondents expressed their discontentment on the inordinate delay in getting title deeds etc, for the land that they occupy. The Adivasi land alienation is the main issue that has agitated the large majority of Adivasis in Northern Kerala. Thus, the issue to some extent has been exploited by Maoists and more militant sections among Adivasis. As the land related issues have attained new dimensions after emergence of market economy and the rise of crony capitalism, the Maoists try to exploit a number of issues such as the displacement of Adivasis from their homeland in the name of big projects or National Sanctuaries/Parks, mining and quarry activities in forest areas leading to environmental hazards, steady and systematic replacement of conventional crops by high yielding cash and other crops and the operations by forest, sand and spurious liquor mafia in Adivasi dominated areas. More than 70% of respondents felt that the Maoists with their weak organizational set up could attain limited success in exploiting such issues to their advantage.

A peep into the secondary data connected with the land related issues of Adivasis in the area of study supported our findings. Historically, the Adivasi deprivation and exploitation commenced since the 18th century when large scale migration of Adivasis to Kerala started from bordering forest areas of Karnataka and Tamil Nadu to work in the large scale plantations of Tea, Coffee, Rubber, Cardamom, Teak etc. The post-Independence phenomenon of steady migration of outsiders to the Adivasi dominated areas dispossessed the Adivasis of the bulk of their land. Devoid of cultivable land or better wages from manual labour, they were forced to borrow money from their landlords for livelihood. Inability to pay off debts landed them in bonded slavery. The Commissioner of Scheduled Castes and Scheduled Tribes commented in his report of 1965-66:

> "The survey on the economic conditions of Paniyars of Wayanad in Kerala conducted by the Bureau of Statistics and Economics of the Government of Kerala, throws light on the system of bonded labour prevalent in that area."[2]

Basically, the entire area was predominantly dominated by feudal landlord tendencies. In the case of Wayanad, the Rajas of Veda tribe ruled the region for many decades. When the reins of power came to the Travancore-Cochin Royal dynasty, they allotted large areas of land to upper caste Hindu families, who at the instance of the British converted bulk of these lands into tea and coffee plantations, besides other cash crops. Side by side, the British converted large tracts of land as Teak plantations to meet their commercial and infrastructure requirements. This led to the steady influx of Adivasis who worked in these plantations as slaves. After independence, the exodus of non-Adivasis was unabated. The decadal growth rate of population in the district during 1951-1961 was 62.5%. Those outsiders occupied large tracts of Tribal and forest land. Thus, by 1976, more than 60% of Adivasis became landless. Without land or other means of livelihood, majority of them worked like slaves in the plantations or the agricultural fields of the settlers.

A similar scenario prevailed in the Attapaddi Tribal belt in Palakkad district. The Zamorin of Calicut[3], with his Royal lineage had absolute possession of the land for many decades. He, in turn, distributed the entire land to three traditional landlords who in 1880s converted bulk of the land into Rubber, Tea and Cardamom plantations. Large areas were leased out to outsiders including the settlers from Tamil Nadu. This led to the extensive alienation of Tribal land and large scale illegal felling of trees.

In fact, the approach of the successive State Governments and the major political parties gave more leverage to the Maoists to exploit the issue to their advantage. One main criticism is that the governments were never sincere in restoring the alienated Adivasi land, nor its distribution among the Adivasis. Even the enactment of The Kerala Scheduled Tribes

(Restriction of Transfer of Land and Restoration of Alienated Land) Act, 1975, has been interpreted by many as political response to Maoist uprisings of late 1960s in the State, with the aim to wean away the Adivasis and the peasants from the influence of Maoists. Thus, Ms Sreerekha[4] commented that despite being the forerunner in taking steps to ensure distributive justice, the unsatisfactory implementation of the "Transfer and Restoration of Alienated Land Act" shows the State apathy towards Tribal sufferings. Similarly, the 1996 amendment to 1975 Act legalizing all transactions on Adivasi land during 1960-1986 was a retrograde step aimed at helping the settlers' lobby. This had given an opportunity to the pro-Maoist Porattom to come to lime light in 1996 by taking Palakkad District Collector as hostage demanding the scrapping of the above amendment.

Another inter-related issue is the lack of basic amenities such as power, drinking water or communication facilitis in the majority of the government-sponsored Adivasi resettlement colonies in Wayanad and Palakkad districts. In fact, after the Muthanga struggle, rehabilitation colonies were set up in these districts for resettling Adivasis and the landless poor. As part of this programme, the Kerala government had launched a Tribal Resettlement and Development Mission (TRDM) which would allot one acre to every landless Adivasi family and provide financial assistance until they were completely self-reliant in their new environment. A couple of centres like Aralam in Kannur and Sugandhagiri in Wayanad were started with much fanfare for resettling large number of Adivasis on the above lines. However, in the absence of any development activities or the basic amenities, the majority of resettlement colonies are in a state of degeneration. The bulk of the resettled Adivasis had left the centres whereas the others are languishing there in absolute poverty. Ironically, such centres have become milch cows for the politicians and bureaucrats in the name of Adivasi development. Sociologist TY Vinod Krishnan points out how the politicians, thinking of ways to eat up public money in the name of Tribal uplift, are being hypocritical about this.' Even the Paniyar tribe, constituting 23% of the total Adivasi population in the State, does not have 10 graduates. Now the government is planning to establish an Adivasi university! A former Chief Minister of the State has laid the foundation for a flat complex (apartment block) for rehabilitation of Adivasis, when thousands of Adivasis have no shelter or proper hutments in many places in Wayanad and Palakkad districts!

The Maoists always try to exploit the Adivasi land alienation and related socio-economic issues by identifying with the indigenous people or their organizations. They had extended full support to Muthanga struggle of 2003[5] spearheaded by Adivasi Gothra Maha Sabha (AGMS), an autonomous Adivasi organization. Similarly, the pro-Maoist outfits tried to intervene in the Chengara land struggle[6] in Pathanamthitta district (August 2007–October 2009), demanding distribution of excess land belonging to Harrison Malayalam Plantations Ltd to landless Adivasis and Dalits. The Maoists propagate that the tangible solution to tackle the Adivasi land issues is the takeover of large tracts of forestland with major business houses like the Tatas, Goenkas, Birlas/ Gwalior Rayons, etc, in the name of maintaining plantations and other allied activities.

Majority of the respondents felt that deprivation in respect of basic amenities and infrastructural facilities in Adivasi areas is equally glaring. As regards to Health and drinking water facilities, overwhelming majority of respondents held that these facilities are inadequate. The government health schemes in the area failed to take off properly. On the ground, the death of new born babies of Adivasis was a clear indication of these lacunae. A study undertaken by Kerala Institute of Local Administration (KILA)[7] in 2012 revealed that there were 81 cases of such deaths of infants (0-3 years) during the period 2010-2012. In 2012-13, Attappadi had garnered national attention following the death of 63 Adivasi children. In the wake of large number of infant deaths the then, central and State Governments had announced a special package of ₹ 400 crore for Tribal welfare in Attapadi. But the irony was that such funds were not properly used; death of the new-borns continued in the Adivasi areas with 30 deaths in 2014; 14 in 2015; 9 in 2016 and 10 in 2017 (July).[8] Thus, KA Ramu, convenor of 'Thampu' an Adivasi organization in Attapaddi rightly commented: "The nutrition schemes do not reach the children. Despite the huge fund flow, malnutrition among children still persists."[9]

Despite some exaggeration, the seriousness of the issue had well reflected in the words of the Prime Minister Narendra Modi during his hurricane election tour in Kerala in May 2016. The Prime Minister had equated the poverty and malnutrition deaths among Adivasis and Tribals in Kerala to that of south Saharan countries like Somalia where Infant Mortality Rate (IMR) was 85 in 2015,[10] whereas IMR in Attapaddy region, as per a study by National Institute of Nutrition in 2013 was 66 compared to 12 in the rest of Kerala.

Lack of adequate medical facilities in the close proximity of Adivasi hamlets coupled with the malnutrition and neglect of pregnant mothers were the main causative factors for such tragedies. Though the successive governments have declared that the issue would be tackled on war footing, the ground level implementation of various schemes and the utilization of funds are far from satisfactory. The militant Tribal organizations and pro-Maoist outfits try to exploit these issues without any major success.

The deficiency of drinking water and inter-related issues are more acute in the Adivasi belt of Palakkad. Despite a number of governmental schemes for providing drinking water for Adivasi hamlets, over 60% of Adivasi families of Attapaddy area are facing shortage of drinking water for six months or more. One of the priorities of the 45 US million dollar cost projects of Attappadi Hill Area Development Society (AHADS),[11] launched in 2000, was to improve such facilities in the area through massive ecology restoration programmes. However, these schemes had failed in its real mission due to over-emphasis in institutionalization and inter-related projects such as housing and community development. The centuries old water supply system with semi-broken pipelines and storage tanks had virtually defeated the mission of uninterrupted drinking water supply to Adivasi hamlets.

While scarcity of drinking water has agitated the minds of the majority of Adivasis, the Maoists along with other activist groups could open a front at the nearby Plachimada village, predominantly an Adivasi area with over a thousand families in Palakkad district, mostly landless and eking out a living as agriculture labourers. The Plachimada struggle, started in 2002 against the entry of the Multinational giant Coco Cola has developed as one of the epoch making struggles in modern India for the preservation of water sources against the plunder by the Multinationals. Though the company has winded up its operations in 2005, in the wake of intense agitations by the local people, many inter-related issues such as compensation to all the Plachimada victims, special packages/projects to supplement farming and drinking water needs of the region remain unresolved. The Plachimada Struggle Committee comprising Dalits and Tribals continue their campaigns/agitations highlighting these demands. The Maoist/pro-Maoist elements of Western Zone Special Committee try to exploit these issues to their advantage by declaring solidarity with the

Plachimada Struggle Solidarity Committee and various civil society movements who are in the forefront of these campaigns/agitations.

On the question of Maoists' efforts to exploit the issues of poverty among Adivasis especially the deficiencies in Public Distribution System (PDS), over 50% of the respondents felt that Maoists do exploit such issues. Two issues that came to the fore are the malpractices by ration shop owners and the distribution of sub-standard ration items. Even Anganwadis are facing such problems. While many ration dealers siphon off the ration to the local traders, section of Adivasis belonging to Below Poverty category sell off their ration items to traders to earn money for personal needs. Such practices lead to a vicious circle of extreme poverty in many Adivasi hutments, malnutrition and health hazards especially to Adivasi women and children and addiction of many Adivasis to drugs and spurious liquor. Majority of the respondents felt that though such malpractices are rampant, the government or its agencies failed to take effective steps to curb these irregularities.

There is marginal improvement in educational facilities in Adivasi areas especially in the case of new educational institutions. However, over 60% of respondents held that there is shortage of teachers and supporting staff in these institutions. Moreover, the professional calibre of majority of these personnel is below par. Another disturbing trend is that educational avenues are not properly made use of by the Adivasis. The school drop-out rate of Adivasis (below 18 years) was 4-5% in Wayanad district and 0.75-1.30% in the Adivasi areas in Palakkad district. The number of Adivasi students going for higher education continues to remain low mainly because of inadequate hostel and other facilities. Isolated cases of humiliation and maltreatment of Adivasi students in such institutions and hostels by the student organizations of mainstream political parties have been fanned out by student bodies with left radical proclivities. The Maoists and pro-Maoist outfits have taken up such issues to create support base among the educated sections in Adivasi community.

Almost same line of thinking prevails among majority of respondents in respect of road communication facilities in the Adivasi area. One common concern among Adivasis is that they remain cut off from the mainstream largely due to poor transportation and communication facilities. Colonization in remote far flung areas as part of rehabilitation of landless Adivasis has aggravated the situation. Though substantial funds have been pumped into this sector, the overall improvement in their communication facilities is marginal. This is largely attributed to the corruption and malpractices and development works based on political lines or influence. The political intermediaries or those heading Local Self Government (LSG) decide the construction of new roads or the maintenance of roads without considering the requirements of local population or the overall improvement. As illegal nexus exist among such functionaries, contractors and LSG officials, the quality of maintenance works remain poor. The Maoists who undertake clandestine movements and activities are not much concerned over such maladies in the communication front.

The area of study covers vast areas of forest with a number of Adivasi hamlets in their immediate proximity. Majority of the respondents felt that section of forest personnel are hand in glove with the settlers and the plantation lobby in illegal activities such as encroachment of forest land and felling of trees from the forests. On the other hand, they constantly harass the Adivasis especially their women-folk whenever they step into forest for collecting minor forest produce such as medicinal herbs or fire wood. This has created discontentment among Adivasis. Thus, issues such as non-implementation of Forest (Rights) Act, 2006, eviction of Adivasis from forest land, denial of access to Adivasis on minor forest produce, high-handed behaviour of forest officials towards Adivasis etc, have been disseminated and propagated by Maoists and their front organizations to build up their pockets among these sections. However, these campaigns have not created much impact in the Adivasi belt: thanks to the 'neo-liberal impact' of the new generation of Adivasis who never consider forest as their traditional abode or source of livelihood.

The study report by Kerala Institute of Local Administration (KILA) also revealed that other indicators which determine the socio-economic status of the people remain comparatively low among Adivasis. The average illiteracy rate of Adivasis in the area is 33.5% and the rate of unemployment is around 9%. Those without electricity and toilet facilities are 61% and 52% respectively.[12] Taking cue of these factors, it is evident that the Adivasis were the most backward and exploited lot when Maoist insurgency struck Kerala in late 1960s.

The findings of the study are in consonance with that of earlier researchers. Ms Luisa Steur who found improvement in various socio-economic indicators of Adivasis during the heydays of Kerala Model Development experience identified that for many centuries the Adivasis worked as slaves for upper caste households. Others like Deepa Chandran[13], Sreekumar[14] and Parayil[15] also identified higher gap between the Adivasi and non-Adivasi population in Kerala in various socio-economic and development indicators. This was largely due to wrong policy decisions at governmental level and serious bottlenecks in their implementation. Unless the government and policy makers take corrective measures, the Adivasis devoid of '*Jal, Zameen* and *Jungle*' in their own traditional area will be attracted by the slogans of Maoists.

NOTES AND REFERENCES

1. Personal interview with Ms CK Janu, leading Adivasi leader in Kerala (July/2013).
2. From the report (1965-66) of the Commissioner of Scheduled Castes and Scheduled Tribes in Kerala.
3. Zamorin is the hereditary Royal title used by the Hindu rulers of Calicut/Malabar. They ruled for 6 centuries between 12th and 18th century based at Calicut.
4. Sreerekha, MS, 2010, The Story behind Kerala's Landless: The story of Aralam Farm, Economic and Political Daily (Special Article), 45(21), pp 52-62.
5. The Muthanga struggle of 2003 was organized by AGMS by forcibly occupying forest land of the wildlife sanctuary at Muthanga, Wayanad district demanding restoration of alienated Tribal land.
6. 300 families – mostly Dalits and Adivasis – entered Harrison Malayalam Plantations Rubber Estates at Chengara in Pathanamthitta district during August 2007, set up tents and refused to move out until they were given 5 acres of cultivable land (for each family). The agitation was withdrawn in October 2009, following an agreement between the agitators and the Kerala government.
7. Kerala Institute of Local Administration (KILA) is State Government's agency under Local Self Government Department, Kerala which conducted a number of studies on Tribal issues.
8. On the basis of figures compiled by Integrated Tribal Development Project (ITP) in 2017.
9. Personal interview by the author (Agali/August 2016).
10. World Bank Report, 2015.
11. AHADS, an institution under Rural Department of Kerala was formed in 1995 with the main aim to accelerate development of Adivasis with an initial financial aid of ₹ 219 crore from Japan International Co-operation Agency (JICA).
12. From the report of KILA, 2012-13.
13. Chandran, Deepa, 2012, The Paradox within Paradoxes: Emerging

signs of change in the unappealing Tribal scenario in Kerala, Centre for the Study of Regional Development, JNU, New (Developing Country Studies, ISSN2224-607X, Vol 2, No 6, 2012.

14. Sreekumar TT, 2006, "Interrogating Development: New Social Movements, Democracy and Indigenous Peoples Struggles in Kerala" in *Kerala: Paradoxes of Public Action and Development*, Editor: Tharamangalam, J, New Delhi, Orient Longman (with G Parayil), pp 56-80.
15. *Ibid*, Sl 12.

6

Adivasi Organizations/NGOs versus Maoist Groups

The emergence of a number of indigenous movements during the last quarter of 20th century was a major trend in many South Asian countries. We also witnessed such movements in many Indian States, sometimes posing serious challenge to the unity and integrity of the nation. On many instances, the Maoist groups – exploiting the situation to build up their base among these sections – have declared solidarity and support to such struggles interpreting them as manifestations of the indigenous and marginalized sections to uphold their independent identity, culture and sub-nationalist aspirations. The support extended by Maoist groups to Khalistan movement in Punjab or the secessionist forces like Jammu Kashmir Liberation Front (JKLF) in Kashmir or the insurgent outfits such as the United Liberation Front of Assam (ULFA) in late 1980s were their major strategic moves in this direction. Many activist groups and Non-Governmental Organizations (NGOs), also stepped into such areas targeting Adivasis and the marginalized with the declared objective of their upliftment and welfare.

In this chapter, an attempt has been made to empirically examine as how such movements and organizations could impact the growth and expansion of Maoist insurgency.

Majority of the respondents felt that apolitical Adivasi organizations having decisive influence among the Adivasis can effectively counter the spread of Maoist ideology. But, organizations floated by political parties and functioned as their appendages with partisan interests failed to play any decisive role in such matters.

On the ground, such trends were clear. The mobilization of Adivasis on political lines was a major agenda of the major political parties in Kerala. Thus, the erstwhile Jan Sangh formed Adivasi Sangham as early as in 1969; the Communist Party of India floated Kerala Girivargha Sangham; the Communist Party of India (Marxist) made use of Karshaka Sangham to mobilize Adivasis and the Indian National Congress was instrumental for forming Kerala Adivasi Samajam. The organized activities of Vanavasi Kalyan Parishad of Rashtriya Swayamsevak Sangh (RSS) among Adivasis gave an impetus for the formation of Wayanad Adivasi Swayam Sevak Sangham (WASSS) in 1963 which in 1969 came under the control of the Jan Sangh as Wayanad Adivasi Sangham. The Sangham's various campaigns and agitations for the restoration of Tribal land, mainly targeting non-Tribal settlers sharpened the differences between Adivasis and settlers. Meanwhile, the CPM with their hegemonic class approach stepped in by floating Kerala State Karshaka Thozilali Union (KSKTU) which took up the issues of Adivasis from time to time.

The Adivasi belt of Palakkad and Wayanad districts noted for the socio-economic backwardness with a mosaic of ethnic and environmental issues witnessed the proliferation of NGOs during the last 4 decades. However, more than 70% of respondents held that the NGOs working among Adivasis have limited role in checking Maoist influence as majority of them are guided by their own agenda or the directions of the donor bodies. No doubt some pioneer NGOs like 'Solidarity'[1] had made some contributions in field of literacy and education among Adivasis, but they gradually withdrew from the scene.

Later, majority of these NGOs were formed on religious or caste community lines having their own independent agenda. For example, Wayanad Social Service Society (WSSS), one of the major NGOs having wide spectrum of activities among Adivasis operate under the Social Service wing of the Catholic Diocese of Mananthavadi, Wayanad district. They have taken up micro projects like drinking water, nursery schools, Mother and Child Health programmes, plant nursery and sponsorship programmes for the all round development of Adivasis. The Shreyas Social Service Centre (SSSC), another prominent NGO, formed by the Malankara Catholic Diocese, Sultanbatterry Wayanad district in 1974 is active in around 135 Adivasi hamlets. Besides Adivasis, their target groups are small and marginal farmers, agricultural labourers, rural women and Tribals. The Jesuits of the Catholic Church in 1996 formed Tudi; a socio-cultural movement aims at achieving their sustainable development, education and social empowerment through the promotion of indigenous tradition and culture. On the other hand, two outfits namely Wayanad Adivasi Sangham (WAS) and Adivasi Sangham functioning under the tutelage of Sangh Parivar bodies are engaged in various activities to preserve the cultural and ethnic identity of Adivasis in an attempt to bring them closer to Hinduism.

The prominent secular NGOs/activist groups in Wayanad district include:

(a) Fedina, formed in 1987, mainly working among the Adivasis in Sulthan Bathery Thaluk aiming to promote the right and responsibility among the Adivasis through their awareness programmes and also by imparting non-formal education to the Adivasis;

(b) High Land Development Agency (HILDA) which came into existence in 1993 tries to promote the ideals of self reliance among Adivasis through people centred development initiatives and community participation in development process;

(c) Kanavu, formed in 1993 which runs a Gurukulam model school in the district is engaged in ambitious programmes such as imparting education to Adivasi children who are the school dropouts and who are unable to follow the curriculum in regular schools; teaching them traditional skills, occupations, Tribal rituals, stories and songs with the help of elders, eminent poets, writers, activists and educationists; and

(d) Uravu formed in 1996, has been working for empowering the marginalised groups, women, traditional artisans and Adivasis by promoting small and cottage industries based on natural resources especially bamboo and imparting training to Adivasi people in bamboo cultivation, bamboo processing, establishing micro enterprises, marketing of bamboo based products.

A similar scenario exists in Attapaddy Tribal belt in Palakkad district, where almost all major religious/community groups have floated NGOs with their own agenda. However, three prominent independent NGOs which are active among the Adivasis are:

(a) 'Sarang', which is essentially an organization revolving around a teacher couple who have strong ideological faith in organic farming, succeeded in regenerating forest through local action primarily by protection against fire and by gap filling using local species identified by the Tribals.

(b) Prakriti Samrakshana Samithi whose main aim was afforestation in Bommiampady hamlet in 1985 through participative afforestation.

(c) 'Nature' formed in 1985 has a plethora of activities such as community health care, participative watershed management and organic agriculture. With the help of four committees namely housing committee, water supply committee, agricultural development committee and women's committee, they have targeted four Adivasi hamlets for systematic development. Trained Adivasi animators are working for the NGO in those hamlets.

Another category of NGOs which depend on government grants and funds are keen to project government line on developmental matters instead of adopting a realistic approach on Adivasi issues. Such NGOs lacked credibility among Adivasis and are unable to counter the propaganda/activities of Maoists or other radical groups. Thus, despite a plethora of governmental and Non-Governmental Organizations in the Adivasi belt of these districts, majority of Adivasis are victims of poverty, deprivation and exploitation. Such trends have given an impetus for Maoists and radical groups for repeated 'NGO bashing' branding them as agents of imperialist forces or political parties. Basheer Madala, who had researched into the plight of Adivasis in Attapaddy area, has succinctly described the situation as:

> "The more the number of government and non-governmental agencies and departments in Scheduled Tribe areas, the worse will be the plight of Adivasis and other marginalized."[2]

But, apolitical outfits like Adivasi Gothra Maha Sabha (AGMS) presented an entirely different picture. A case study of the organization revealed such trends. The Adivasis who constitute around 2% of Kerala population are treated as outliers or peripheral communities for many decades by the mainstream political parties. However, the genesis of coalition politics in Kerala during late 1960s with two evenly balanced political fronts – the Indian National Congress (INC) led United Democratic Front (UDF) and the Communist Party of India (Marxist) led Left Democratic Front (LDF) – compelled these fronts to have their vote banks among Adivasis who can influence the electoral outcome of at least one dozen Assembly constituencies mainly in Wayanad, Palakkad and Idukki districts.

Thus, dominated by vote bank politics, the mainstream political parties conveniently played the shrewd game of appeasing both the settlers and Adivasis. Barring a couple of regional political parties known for their overriding sympathies with the settlers, other mainstream parties tactfully discussed and debated the main issues of Adivasis such as restoration of alienated Tribal land and redistribution among Adivasis, abolition of bonded labour or slavery and implementation of minimum wages for the Adivasi workers. But, the hard reality was that none of these parties were sincere in safeguarding the interests of Adivasis. Dr Rajeevan who studied these issues commented:

> "The Congress showed little interest in the parochial issues related to the Tribals. The Left parties particularly the Communist Party of India (Marxist), with which many Tribal people had earlier association, saw the Tribal question within a class framework and were not prepared to view it as a problem specific to certain communities. This universalizing stance of the Leftists even on Tribal issues in Kerala was one of the reasons for the emergence of new Tribal organizations."[3]

Over the years, convinced by such realities and worried over their identity and existence, resurgence among many of these indigenous groups was noticed leading to the formation of a number of autonomous organizations. The Mala Araya Maha Sabha (Idukki), Girijan Sevak Samiti (Attappadi/Palakkad), All Kerala Tribal Workers' Union (Pathanamthitta), Adivasi Vikasana Pravarthaka Samiti, Adivasi Federation, Adivasi Aikkya Samiti (all in Wayanad) and Adivasi Vimochana Munnani (Kannur) were some such outfits. However, these micro level outfits could not create much impact in espousing the Tribal cause. Thus, efforts to rally different Adivasi organizations on a common platform gained momentum since early 1990s.

One of the milestones in this direction was the Tribal meet held in October 1992 at Mananthavadi (Wayanad district), in which representatives of Tribal organizations from Kerala, Tamil Nadu and Karnataka attended. Ms CK Janu, the Adivasi leader from Wayanad took initiative for this meet which deliberated upon the problems of Tribals in India and worked out an action plan for strengthening the unity of various Tribal organizations. The above conclave, the first major effort to mobilize Adivasis without any political patronage evoked protests from mainstream parties like the BJP and the CPM. This meet along with a similar one held in Coorg (Karnataka) during 1993 laid the foundation stone of AGMS.

This apolitical movement vigorously took up two key issues namely Tribal land alienation and the implementation of the Kerala Scheduled Tribes (Restriction of Transfer and Restoration of Alienated Land) Act, 1975 which have been agitating the Adivasis since long. Accordingly, under the banner of Adivasi Samyuktha Samara Samiti (ADSS) and allied organizations, agitations including forcible occupation of Revenue land were organized at 3 centres in Wayanad district during 1994-95. The strong-arm measures of the police in handling the peaceful ADSS struggle by destroying the hutments and crops of Adivasis in the occupied land evoked wide spread public protest. The Samiti's awareness rally from the Adivasi heartland of Wayanad to Thiruvananthapuram, the State capital and the novel mass *satyagraha* by Adivasi women and children by erecting temporary huts in front of Kerala Secretariat during February 1996 forced the State Government to open the dialogue with the agitators. But the talks failed and struggle by Adivasi outfits continued.

The issue of Tribal land alienation took a controversial turn in September 1996 when the CPM led government passed the Kerala Scheduled Tribe Amendment Bill that legitimized the Adivasi land transactions from 1966 to 1986 giving leverage to the settlers. This evoked widespread protest from various Adivasi organizations which resorted to a series of agitations throughout the State. The pro-Maoist 'Ayyankali Pada' created sensation by detaining Palakkad District Collector during October 1996. The storm of protest could be calmed down by the enactment of the Kerala Restriction on Transfer and Restoration of Lands to Scheduled Tribes Bill of 1999 which made null and void of the 1996 Amendment Bill. Ms Janu, who was in the forefront of all these campaigns and agitations emerged as the most popular leader of the Adivasi movement in Kerala. Her leadership coupled with the growing awareness among Adivasis on their plight as a result of various struggles, led to the formation of Adivasi Gothra Maha Sabha (AGMS) in 2001.

Disenchantment with the policies and programmes of political parties notably the Left towards the Adivasis was the main factor for the genesis of the organization. This was clear from the background of its founder leaders. For example Ms CK Janu, the founder leader of AGMS from Wayanad district joined politics at the instance of her relative, PK Kalan, a district level CPM leader. Janu belonging to poor Adiya tribe came to lime light through the Kerala Karshaka Sangham, the front body of the CPM active among farmers and Adivasis. Later, as CPM candidate she was elected to the local Panchayat body and was in the forefront of the party in various campaigns and agitations. She left CPM because she had been dissatisfied with the style of functioning of the party. In her own words:

> "I left CPM because I became dissatisfied with the manner how the Adivasis were simply rounded up by party leaders to participate in agitations and party programmes and shout slogans that they hardly understood and that the party never intended to implement. I was also frustrated by the approach of the party leadership to strangulate autonomous Adivasi movements purely from vote bank politics. I was convinced that by making hollow promises, the party or local leaders like us can never win over the hearts of the poor Adivasis."[4]

The story of M Geethanandan, another founder leader of AGMS was almost on similar lines. Hailing from a poor Dalit family of Tellicherry in Kannur district, a citadel of the CPM, he started his political career as a CPM activist. Later, he left the party and joined the Communist Party Marxist-Leninist (CPML) and was in the forefront of the activities of Central Reorganizing Committee (CRC)-CPML in Kerala. As a prominent organizer of CRC's Depressed Classes Renaissance Front, he along with other Maoist activists made serious attempts to mobilize Adivasis and Dalits. By playing the role of a Cultural ambassador of Adivasis, he tried to popularize their customs, traditions and culture through various art-cultural programmes under the banner of Janakeeya Samskareeya Vedi (JSV) the cultural wing of CRC floated in Kerala during late 1970s. After the dissolution of JSV, he was associated with other social reform movements especially of Adivasis and Dalits. Such activities and campaigns helped him in rallying Adivasis under AGMS.

The main aim of the organization was to mobilize all sections of Adivasis from the level of their hamlets and villages and fight for their rights, liberation and empowerment through various campaigns and struggles. As part of this, AGMS made serious efforts to enrol members from 33 clans of Adivasis. More emphasis was given to recruit the young as volunteers who, after basic training and orientation, were directed to function among Adivasis for preserving their cultural identity and diversity. The 'Ooru Sabhas' (Adivasi representative council) were restructured in such a way that they should impose strict code of conduct among members against consumption of illicit liquor, use of drugs and other social evils. As an apex body of different Adivasi groups, AGMS tried to ensure the tradition, language and culture of different Gothras (clans) while working for the larger interests of the whole community.

The AGMS could successfully build up an organizational set up with clear hierarchically organized channels for the enrolment and representation of all Tribals in the State. Except for the top structure of the organization, lower level units followed the Tribal pattern. Ooru Sabhas which are the basic units are constituted by enrolling members from 25 or more families of a Tribal settlement. Above the Ooru Sabhas, there are other bodies such as Panchayat Gothra Sabha Council, District Gothra Sabha and the State presidium. Adequate attention was given to ensure due representation to women and different tribes so as to contain inter-clan differences and conflicts.

In this regard, the main endeavour of the organization was to develop Ooru Sabhas into self-governing institutions for the promotion of the socio-economic development of the Adivasi community. For that purpose, attempts were made to ensure participation of the members of the Ooru Sabhas in the decision making process of Adivasi Gram Panchayat in Tribal areas; identify the Scheduled Tribe areas; involve them in the formulation of development projects and ensure their presence with government bodies at various levels. These efforts have created resurgence within the Adivasi community with a clear psyche that they have the potential to fight for their genuine issues and demands.

Over the years, the organization could broaden its support base through a series of campaigns and agitations which included:

(a) Interception of the Mobile van of Kerala Civil Supplies Corporation in Wayanad district in 2001 and distribution of food items to the Adivasis and the local people in the wake of starvation deaths in Adivasi hamlets.

(b) 48 days historic *satyagraha* in front of Kerala Secretariat, Trivandrum, by setting up shelters/ hutments, in 2001 demanding distribution of 5 acres of land to Adivasis with less than one acre of land and inclusion of Adivasi areas under 5th Schedule of the Constitution.

(c) Forcible occupation of State land near Muthanga Wildlife Sanctuary[5] in Wayanad district during 2003 and declaring Muthanga Forest Area as Adivasi Self-Rule Area under 5th Schedule.

(d) Agitations demanding restoration of alienated Tribal land and distribution among Adivasis by opening 'New Samara Bhoomis' (agitation fronts) at various centres in 2013.

(e) Solidarity and support to the 'Chengara land struggle'[6] (2007-09).

Through such struggles and campaigns focusing on the major issues of Adivasis, AGMS could achieve unity of various clans within the community. Their different mode of agitations such as setting up of huts on the premises of government offices/ urban areas and prolonged mass Satyagraha by men, women and children in their traditional attire had caught the attention of the media, intelligentsia and the general masses. By and large, these campaigns were peaceful except the Muthanga agitation that led to police action resulting in the death of one Tribal and one police personnel. Describing their struggles as the new face of Civil Disobedience, the leaders highlighted that the Adivasis would not fall into the trap of radical groups or political parties or organizations encouraging the cult of violence.

In this backdrop, it is of considerable interest to us to analyse as how AGMS countered the Maoist strategy of winning over the support of Adivasis. In fact, the various Maoist groups adopted different strategies to make inroads into Adivasis, particularly in Wayanad, Palakkad, Malappuram and Idukki districts. They propagated that the major political parties and the successive governments, influenced by landlord-petty bourgeois axis failed to implement radical land reforms to protect the interests of Adivasis, Dalits and other marginalized sections. Thus, outfits like CPML, CPML (Liberation) and CPML (Red Flag), as a tactical move, extended full support to AGMS during the Muthanga agitation and declared solidarity to other agitations and campaigns focusing on issues like Adivasi land alienation/restoration of Tribal land, starvation deaths among Adivasis, and implementation of Tribal Rights Act etc. It was on the same issue of 1996 Amendment Bill that Ayyankali Pada (Maoist group) detained Palakkad District Collector for hours during October 1996.

Similarly the past history of Adivasi participation in the 'Naxalite actions' in Kerala during late 1960s gave much inspiration to Maoist groups to look upon these sections for building up their support base. Their strategy of annihilation of class enemies especially the landlords known for brutalities and inhuman treatment against Adivasis and landless peasants created good-will among sections of Adivasis towards the Maoist groups which found the sad socio-economic plight of the community as a favourable factor for exploitation.

Fully convinced of the strategies and larger designs of Maoists and their extension outfits, AGMS' endeavour was to checkmate the spread of the outfit among the Adivasis. Firstly, the growing trends of indigenism effectively disseminated by international and national level bodies such as the National Trust for Adivasi Self Rule[7] and South Zone Adivasi Forum influenced the approach of many Adivasi leaders in favour of the formation of independent indigenous movements. Their pioneering efforts in this direction could evoke considerable support from Adivasis. The attempts to form mass based indigenous bodies had also sparked controversy when Maoist groups and Left parties branded such leaders as agents of NGOs and neo-colonial forces working against the genuine interests of Adivasis. Even mainstream parties joined in the chorus of slanderous campaign to discredit them in order to safeguard their vote bank among these sections.

Secondly, the bitter legacy of the past when Adivasis became the sad victims of police atrocities and excesses after every action or operation by Maoists especially in Northern Kerala continued to haunt them and their representative bodies. This fear psychosis, to a great extent, prevented large sections of Adivasis from associating with Maoists or other radical groups. The third aspect was the general approach among their leaders that the problems/issues of Adivasis could be resolved through peaceful means and not by violent protracted struggles pursued by some of the Left Wing Extremist groups.

More than the rhetoric, the AGMS could achieve significant gains on certain sensitive issues such as restoration of alienated Adivasi land and its distribution among landless Adivasis. Its 48th day strike by fasting forced the Kerala government to enter into an agreement with the outfit and decided to grant five acres of land to each Tribal family. Accordingly, the land distribution programme was organized with much fanfare in Idukki district during April 2002. More than that, it was at the instance of AGMS that Adivasi land alienation was brought to the centre stage of State polity. Following their various campaigns and struggles, the State machinery had initiated steps to resolve the vexed issue of restoration and redistribution of Tribal land. As per a letter issued by the State to National Human Rights Commission (NHRC) in April 2002, 1,308 acres of land were allotted to 568 Adivasi families, which accounted only 2.2% of the identified land for allotment. On the other hand, AGMS leaders claimed that around 25,000 persons were allotted land/ house sites because of their efforts.

But conscious efforts were made by the Maoists and the mainstream political parties to belittle the achievements of AGMS. One major criticism was that the outfit made compromises with the State Government and accepted the offer of alternate land, rather than alienated land. This according to the detractors has helped land grabbers' interests and betrayed Adivasis' deeper sentimental bond to their ancestral land. The AGMS, to some extent, could overcome such criticism through their forcible occupation of forest land near Muthanga Wildlife Sanctuary in Wayanad district which they claimed as a Tribal ancestral land where their ancient temples were in existence. The 'Muthanga struggle' was a landmark event in the history of all land related struggles in Kerala. This struggle demonstrated the potential of Adivasis and the marginalized sections to organize themselves and to launch successful agitations in support of their genuine demands. Most importantly, it revolutionized the Adivasi mind-set of Kerala on its own checkmating the strategies of Maoists to exploit the Adivasi sentiments on land issues. The 'Muthanga episode' gave inspiration for Dalits and other backward sections to launch similar struggles such as the historic land struggles in Chengara in Pathanamthitta district of Kerala.

The Muthanga struggle and the positive support received by AGMS from the civil society had emboldened its leaders to float the Rashtriya Maha Sabha (RMS)[8] with the support of Dalit/backward organizations. However, this experiment had proved to be counter-productive as major chunk of Dalits in the State who are under the dominating influence of mainstream political parties showed lukewarm approach towards autonomous Adivasi Dalit body like RMS. The poor performance of candidates fielded by the RMS in a couple of Lok Sabha seats in 2009 Polls was reflective of the above trend. This had also demonstrated that AGMS was unable to occupy any major space in Kerala politics.

The entry of AGMS into politics had eclipsed its image as an apolitical organization sincerely fighting for Adivasi cause. This had also sharpened the inter-clan differences and created impediments for the outfit to emerge as the sole representative body of the Adivasi community in the State. Moreover, the existence of different Adivasi clans in the State with different socio-economic settings always acted as major stumbling block for the community to attain monolithic indigenous status. For example, Kurichiyas, the landowning Adivasis are well placed at the social and economic ladder whereas the large majority of Kattunaikkans and Adiyas are at the bottom of the ladder. The detractors of AGMS could highlight such disparities and differences to undermine the leadership role of the founder leader Ms Janu, who belonged to Adiya clan.

Once the status of the indigenous identity of AGMS was at stake and when its prominent leaders came under criticism from within the community, the task of political parties to break the outfit has become easier. Some of its founder leaders like Ms CK Janu, who had been attracted to the world of parliamentary politics in 2009, became an easy target of mainstream parties. Thus Janu who floated Janandhipathiya Rashtriya Sabha (JRS) has aligned with the National Democratic Alliance (NDA) and unsuccessfully contested from Wayanad Lok Sabha seat in 2014 polls. That marked the death knell of AGMS.

The Adivasi issues in Kerala continue to revolve around their land alienation and sustenance for life. The land related issues in Adivasi areas have become more complex due to the presence of huge plantations by major industrial groups like Tata, Harrisons, Birla etc, and the emergence of powerful politically-backed settlers lobby. Majority of the land legislations and reforms in the State had only marginal impact in resolving the land related issues in the Adivasi areas. This was largely due to certain provisions in such legislations excluding plantations, lands occupied by religious bodies, educational institutions etc, from the prescribed ceiling. Added to this was the large scale corruption and malpractices in respect of various funds for the development and welfare of Adivasis. Even, the Adivasi representatives of major political parties have become epitomes of such corruption and irregularities. The voice of Adivasis – their sufferings and neglect – falls in wilderness. Thus the Maoists have been seriously trying to re-open their front in the Adivasi belt of Kerala. Even attempts are going on to form Revolutionary Peoples' Committees (RPC), full fledged organizational set up of Maoists in Adivasi-dominated belt of the tri-junction of Kerala, Karnataka and Tamil Nadu in the Western Ghats. The assessment of the Maoists is that it is the right time to spread their message and ideologies among the Adivasis.

NOTES AND REFERENCES

1. A Wayanad based NGO, started by Jos Sebastian floated with inspiration from Liberation Theology and engaged in Frisian Literacy campaign etc, among Adivasis.
2. Personal interview (July 2013) with Basheer Madala, an independent columnist and author of titles on Adivasis, born and brought up in Attappady Tribal belt.
3. Dr R Rajeevan, 2010, Towards Political Empowerment: Political Socialization and Political Participation of Tribal Community in Kerala, Kalpaz Publications, New Delhi.
4. Personal interview with Ms CK Janu (July/2013).
5. The Muthanga struggle of 2003 was organized by AGMS by forcibly occupying forest land of the wildlife sanctuary at Muthanga, Wayanad district demanding restoration of alienated Tribal land.
6. 300 families – mostly Dalits and Adivasis – entered Harrison Malayalam Plantations Rubber Estates at Chengara in Pathanamthitta district during August 2007, set up tents and refused to move out until they were given 5 acres of cultivable land (for each family). The agitation was withdrawn in October 2009, following an agreement between the agitators and the Kerala government.

7. National Trust for Adivasi Self Rule is a Delhi based organization which has been demanding separate law for self-governance of Scheduled (Tribe) areas. At the instance of the body, the Union Government appointed a Committee headed by Dileep Singh Bhuria, MP, which submitted its report in 1995.
8. RMS was floated with the main aim to bring Dalit-Adivasi organizations on a common platform and to emerge as political force; which could not be materialized.

7

Maoist Insurgency and Political Mobilization of Adivasis

The extent of political mobilization or socialization of the marginalized and under privileged sections through effective mechanisms is one of the major indicators in determining the success or quality of democracy. In almost all democracies, there are a plethora of provisions such as reservation of seats, decentralization etc, which are basically meant to ensure due representation of these sections in various democratic institutions. The more the political socialization, the greater will be their assimilation in the national mainstream. Such assimilation creates a feeling of participation in development and governance, which is a prerequisite for stability and unity of a nation. On the other hand, when the feeling of neglect and discrimination develops among the outlier or peripheral communities like Adivasis and Dalits due to confluence of socio-economic and political factors, naturally unrest and instability arise. Such trends can be easily exploited by the vested interests to their advantage.

The political parties which are the pillars of democracy play a crucial role in the political mobilization of various cross sections of the society especially the marginalized sections. One of the questions examined by us was the extent of political mobilization of Adivasis by the political parties and its impact over the Maoist movement. Overwhelming majority of respondents felt that the political parties tried to mobilize the Adivasis with an eye on their vote bank and were never sincere in ameliorating their problems or sufferings. Among sizeable section of Adivasis there is strong erosion of faith on the mainstream political parties. Even the Adivasis elected to local bodies have such impressions over political parties and their leaders. In many Adivasi hamlets their women-folk who are ignorant of party politics lamented that the so called leaders with different coloured flags could be seen only during elections. The elected members to local bodies never attend their genuine problems, but are keen to regularly meet Tribal block officials or other functionaries of the local bodies.

Ironically, majority of the Adivasi leaders who are elected to various bodies under the banner of mainstream political parties betray the cause of the community by totally ignoring the genuine grievances and concerns of their brethren. On many occasions, they become mere puppets in the hands of the powerful leaders of these parties which tactfully use them for perpetrating large scale corruption and malpractices with the help of the bureaucrats who control them from behind the curtain. For example, a young Adivasi lady who was elevated as State Minister in the Congress led coalition government in Kerala in the recent past had an ignominious exit because of scams and scandals, personal nepotism and lack of governance capabilities. Virtually, she could not do anything constructive for the Adivasi community which had high hope and expectations on her elevation as Minister. Such issues especially the manipulative politics of political parties to use Adivasi leaders as pawns in their political checker board breed frustration and anger within the community especially among the younger generation, which, to some extent, were exploited by Maoists and other militant sections to their advantage.

Many respondents felt that such illegal nexus between local politicians, contractors and officials is the main reason for various maladies of the area and the sad plight of Adivasis. In a number of instances, many developmental projects such as construction of roads for Adivasi hamlets; laying of pipes for drinking water supply and better facilities for Primary Health centres etc, find place in official records solely to claim funds under Tribal sub-plan and other schemes! A couple of hamlets, here and there, are provided with better facilities for 'show-casing' them to senior politicians or bureaucrats whenever they visit the area.

A case study of Attapadi Adivasi belt in Palakkad district which witnessed series of infant casualties over the last few years due to malnutrition of pregnant Adivasi women revealed as how political parties and successive governments neglected this area for decades. The 745 square kilometres Attappadi area with an Adivasi population of around 10,000 was the first Tribal Block in Kerala. In the immediate post-Independence period, more than 90% of the area constituted deep reserve forests. After around 15 years, the forest cover had come down to 82%, followed by steady depletion of forest area which is now around 20%.

In fact, the enactment of The Kerala Private Forests (Vesting and assignment) Act, 1967, restricting the land-holding to a maximum of 15 acres per landlord led to widespread sale of private forest land at throw away prices by half a dozen landlords who owned lion's share of land in Attapaddi. The new owners mainly comprising of contractors, timber merchants and saw mill owners had virtually finished the forests through the extensive felling of trees. While the governments failed to check the menace, majority of the political leaders had collusion with such groups. Thus, the process of deforestation continued unabated till 1980 when Silent valley[1] controversy caught the attention of environmentalists and nature lovers even at international level.

The destruction of forests not only created serious environmental and ecological problems such as shrinking water sources, climatic changes etc, but also adversely affected the life of Adivasis. They had to abandon the cultivation of traditional crops like ragi, corn, millets and pulses. The goat and cattle farming had become extinct and the collection of minor forest produce such as honey and medicinal herbs had become impossible. Unemployment and poverty had become the facets of the Adivasi population.

The changed demography of the area had adversely affected the life and sustenance of the majority of Adivasis with the settlers pushing them out of their land and traditional livelihood. The percentage of Adivasi population in the area had come down from 91% to 41% during the last 50 years. During the same period the non-Adivasi population increased from 9% to 59%. According to a survey report,[2] the settlers who migrated from Central Kerala, Tamil Nadu and Karnataka had encroached 10,472 acres of Adivasi land in Attapadi Block. The worst sufferers were the Irula tribe who lost 8,996.14 acres; followed by the Mudugas 1,083.17 acres and the Kurumbas, 26 acres.

Ironically, the influential political leaders of the area encouraged the large scale influx of non-Tribals and also managed to grab large tracts of forest or Adivasi land. Naturally, they became the strong supporters of the settlers' lobby. Moreover, a number of political leaders especially those espousing the case of settlers managed to procure large land-holdings at throw away prices and converted them into plantations by using the workforce of Adivasis even denying minimum wages.

Thus, despite series of agitations and campaigns by various Adivasi organizations over the last three decades, the State has been unable to tackle the basic issue of the restoration of the alienated Adivasi land and its distribution among the landless Adivasis. No doubt, the restoration of alienated land is a complex issue, but the main hurdle in working out a solution by protecting the interests of Adivasis is the lack of sincerity and commitment on the part of mainstream political parties. While a couple of regional parties openly bat for the cause of the settlers, other major parties and their leaders have sympathies with the settlers and not the Adivasis!

In 1999, the State Government identified land in the remote areas of Sholayar Panchayat for distribution among landless Adivasis. However, large majority of Adivasis, despite accepting the title deed of the land, did not move to the above barren land bereft of any basic amenities or infrastructure. Above all, out of 2523 land dispute cases in Attapadi area, only 13 cases totalling 44.77 acres have been settled so far. Now, one can better imagine as how sincere and committed is the State and political masters in resolving the vexed issue of the restoration of the alienated Adivasi land in Kerala!

The story of the development of the Adivasi areas was equally horrendous. The political masters and bureaucrats were the key players. It was almost after two decades of independence, new projects and schemes meant for the development of the area were envisaged. The State Government had declared Attappadi as the first Tribal Block in the State in 1975 with the main aim to ensure all round development of Adivasis so as to bring them to the national mainstream. With this announcement, the Centre and the State had pumped substantial funds for the construction of roads, houses, bridges and other basic infrastructures.

An illegal nexus of contractors, political middlemen and bureaucrats had virtually torpedoed the major projects and schemes and siphoned off the lion's share of such funds. By late 1980s, series of stories of corruption and scams on the utilization of funds had surfaced which virtually turned Attapaddi into a fertile land for organized corruption. Besides the various schemes launched by the Centre and the State, a number of funding agencies and NGOs had stepped in with various projects and schemes in the areas of afforestation, water conservation, education, health and literacy among Adivasis. Their organized activities alien to the indigenous culture and customs had virtually derailed the traditional life style of sections of the local population.

Ironically, some of the policy decisions of the governments – though claimed to be with good intentions – boomeranged against the overall interests of the indigenous people. One such decision was the total prohibition imposed in the area with the effect from April 1995. All the arrack and toddy shops were closed down and the toddy tapped from Attappadi area was sent outside in bulk. The worst victims of the decision were the Adivasis. The large majority of the Adivasis who traditionally used liquor during extreme winter and for their rituals and customary practices had started brewing illicit liquor in their hamlets. Soon the majority of Adivasi hamlets in the interior areas had turned into dens manufacturing and selling country liquor. The organized liquor mafia operating from outside the area used them for their illicit liquor business. With their connivance, Ganja cultivation had started in the interior forest areas. Such activities had opened a saga of operations by enforcement agencies with frequent raid and harassment of Adivasis. When Adivasis became the victims of such operations, the illicit liquor mafia and enforcement agencies had flourished with the backing of local political leaders.

Another decision was the ban on cattle rearing in Attappadi on the ground that extensive use of hilly terrain for such purposes had adversely affected the fragile ecology and the flora-fauna of the area. This decision was taken as part of one of the most ambitious developmental programme namely Attappadi Wasteland Comprehensive Environmental Conservation Project with a financial assistance of US $ 2.19 billion from the Japan Bank for International Co-operation launched in 1995 under the aegis of the Attappadi Hill Area Development Society (AHADS).[3]

No doubt, the above project had undertaken a number of schemes such as eco-restoration through planting of trees, construction of bunds, rain water harvesting etc, skill development and income generating programmes for Adivasis and restructuring of Adivasi hamlets with better houses, community centres etc. However, by discouraging traditional vocations such as cattle-goat farming and agriculture among Adivasis and settlers in the name of eco-restoration and by creating lakhs of man-days for these sections, the above project had ultimately alienated large chunk of Adivasi population from their traditional sources of livelihood. More than that some of the programmes or schemes initiated under the project were dropped half way or had become unviable in the changing socio-economic scenario. Its adverse impact continues to adversely affect sizeable section of Adivasis and its latest manifestation was the series of infant deaths in Attapaddi area. The irony is that even the additional funds sanctioned by the Centre and the State to meet such tragedies on war-footing were not properly used.

The case of Attappadi is not an isolated one. Wherever, there are areas with major chunk of Adivasi population, an illegal nexus between politicians and bureaucrats come up in the name of the development. They play the crucial role in formulating the policies and programmes for the indigenous people without considering the ground level realities or their larger interests. On many occasions, they are guided by extraneous factors and quantum of funds. Seldom have they paid any heed to the voice or views of the target groups or their representatives. Many of them have developed a general psyche that Adivasis should confine to their hamlets and have nothing to do with policy matters or decisions!

Fed-up with such psyche and culture, the younger elements in the Adivasi community are distancing themselves from major political parties. This political alienation and the growing trend of mistrust against the political parties have been exploited by Maoists. Branding the mainstream political parties in the State as feudal, aristocratic, casteist, communal or male chauvinist, the Maoists propagate that these parties either singly or together try to suppress people's struggles. They highlight that the Adivasis or the marginalized sections would never get any justice from these parties which represent the landlord bourgeois – caste-communal forces. To this effect, they cite the issues like the delay in the restoration of alienated Adivasi land, the socio-economic backwardness of Adivasis etc.

Thus, their propaganda goes to the effect that the only alternative before the people is to mobilize themselves against the political establishment that includes industrial and business groups, leaders from various parties, corporations, dominant religious and caste groups and media etc. On the ground, the Maoists declare support and solidarity with such people's struggles. This is part of Maoist strategy to demolish the institutions like the political establishment through orchestrated campaigns and propaganda thereby destroying its credibility and acceptance among the people.

That is why Dr Rajeevan and J Tharamangalam[4] had rightly observed that the major political parties remained indifferent towards the Adivasis. The approach of the Left especially the Communist Party of India (Marxist) interpreting the 'Adivasi question' within class framework and not problem specific to certain communities led to the emergence of autonomous Adivasi organizations and pro-Maoist outfits among them. In fact, such findings give Maoists more confidence to target Adivasis in their attempt to strengthen their mass base.

NOTES AND REFERENCES

1. Silent valley is the reserved Forest Range in Western Ghats known for its rich bio-diversity and rare species of flora and fauna. The move to construct Hydro-electric project in that area causing destruction to Silent valley was later abandoned due to strong resistance by various environmental groups.
2. From the Survey report of RDO, Palakkad, 2010.
3. AHADS, an institution under Rural Department of Kerala was formed in 1995 with the main aim to accelerate development of Adivasis with an initial financial aid of ₹ 219 crore from Japan International Co-operation Agency (JICA).
4. The Perils of Social Development without Economic Growth: The Development Debacle of Kerala, India by Joseph Tharamangalam.

8

Looking Ahead

In the backdrop of the renewed efforts by the Maoists to take rebirth in Kerala especially in the Adivasi dominated areas of the Northern districts, we have examined in detail some crucial issues such as the Adivasi paradigm that influences the spread of Maoist insurgency, the co-relation between the socio-economic factors especially the land related issues and the growth of Maoist movement and the impact of indigenous outfits and political mobilization of indigenous population in countering the insurgency. Various research tools have been applied to collect empirical data from a wide spectrum of samples. The views of personalities closely connected with the above themes of study, elicited during personal interview, were also analysed to reach specific conclusions.[1]

On the issue of Adivasi support to the Maoist insurgency, it was overwhelmingly felt that the Adivasis support the Maoists due to compulsions by circumstances. On many occasions, they were herded together under the movement through force, coercion or intimidation. This had clearly echoed in the words of Ms CK Janu, who was active in the Adivasi front for over three decades:

> "During the initial phase of Maoist movement in Kerala in late 1960s and early 1970s, many sections of illiterate and oppressed Adivasis participated in Maoist-inspired activities. But they were totally ignorant of the Maoist ideology or strategy. Early Maoist leaders could win over their support by taking up the issues such as their low wages and continued exploitation by the landlords."[2]

In fact, lack of ideological indoctrination coupled with weak organizational set-up and failure to actively take up Adivasi issues created impediments for the Maoists to build up their support base among Adivasis. Thus, the Adivasis who participated in the Maoist-inspired struggles or operations dissociated from the movement especially under pressure from police or other agencies. K Venu, one of the leading ideologue of Maoists of the yester years succinctly put their limitations as:

> "The Maoists in Dandakaranya region built up their strong bases by exploiting the issues of Adivasis. But in Kerala, they could neither exploit such issues nor make any serious efforts to bring them under their influence. Though the Maoist armed guerrilla struggles started in the State with a big bang in 1970s, they failed to come out with any concrete agenda on many vexed issues of Adivasis such as their special rights, land rights or rights over forest resources. Instead, the Maoists are playing a proxy war against the corporate lobby or the neo-colonial policies of the governments by using Adivasis in their occasional campaigns or struggles."[3]

Drawing lessons from the past, the present strategy of Maoists is to create awareness among Adivasis about the apathetic attitude of the successive governments and mainstream political parties in ameliorating their long pending grievances and demands such as restoration of alienated Adivasi land or special forest rights. The newly formed Western Ghats Special Zonal Committee (WGSZC), through clandestine net working in Adivasi dominated areas of the tri-junction of Kerala, Karnataka and Tamil Nadu, is engaged in this task. Local residents revealed that three dalams (armed squads) named after three nearby rivers namely Kabini, Bhavani and Nadukani, comprising of members from the above three States, have been visiting the selective Adivasi hamlets of the area since the last three years with the main aim to recruit members from the community.

The Maoists have taken up a number of issues such as legal and illegal quarrying and mining, Resort expansion in forest areas, unemployment, agrarian crisis and excesses against Adivasis by forest and police personnel with the propaganda that Adivasis would never get justice from the State and its establishments in such matters. The younger elements in the community frustrated due to unemployment and uncertainty in life – to some extent are influenced by such propaganda and campaign.

In fact, the failure of the State and its agencies in ensuring systematic development of Adivasi areas or resolving their burning issues provides the Maoists a launch pad for increased activities among the Adivasis and other weaker sections through organized propaganda. Justice (late) VR Krishna Iyer who had long innings in the Supreme Court and dealt with a plethora of cases involving Tribals and other marginalized sections rightly commented:

> "Tribals from ancient times had certain community rights commonly enjoyed even in forests and jungles. But alas, today, the Tribals are deluded of these jungle rights. They have no homes or places of shelter. They have no means of livelihood because their free spaces are given away on commercial terms to foreign interest. De facto discarded as

> flotsam and jetsam by the State and de jure proffered jungle slices which do not exist, these Tribal communities have not been a trace of what belonged to them. No wonder that Maoists are expanding their invasionary jurisdiction far from being eliminated."[4]

Ms K Ajitha, who participated in the first Maoist action in Kerala (1968) as a teenager and presently a leading social activist, expressed similar views:

> "Maoist insurgency could not be ruled out in Kerala as governments have always neglected the demands of the Adivasis and the marginalized over the last several years. Discontent is brewing among these sections."[5]

Naturally the root cause of the mounting discontentment among Adivasis was due to a mosaic of socio-economic factors. We examined in detail the co-relation between these factors and the growth of Maoist insurgency in the State. Data on a number of socio-economic and welfare indicators of Adivasis such as possession of land, impact of land reforms, accessibility to basic amenities like safe drinking water, health, education, road communication network, Public Distribution System etc were collected from 500 samples on the basis of a special questionnaire.[6] Majority of the respondents felt that deprivation in respect of basic amenities and infrastructural facilities foment discontentment among Adivasis, which to some extent, has been exploited by the Maoists. Thus, instances like malnutrition and starvation deaths do occur in Adivasi hamlets; steady alienation of Adivasi land continues; the number of unwed mothers increases and the exodus of non-Tribals to Adivasi areas continue unabated.

But of all the socio-economic issues confronting the Adivasi community in Kerala, the Adivasi land alienation is the root cause of all such issues, which to a great extent, could be exploited by the Maoists. The words of K Venu clearly reflected this trend:

> "If we analyse the spread of Maoism, we can see that Maoists could build up their influence in backward and under-developed areas. As ours is an agrarian economy, the land and land related activities play a decisive role in the socio-economic advancement of the large majority of people and their overall development. Wherever land resources were effectively distributed and properly harnessed for the larger interests of masses, the socio-economic disparities have drastically come down. That is why it is well argued that wherever land reforms have taken place, there are no major Maoist activities."[7]

Though Kerala has a unique status in respect of the successful implementation of land reforms, the Adivasis were not much benefitted out of these reforms. Instead of the actual tillers or farm workers getting the ownership right of land, members of intermediary communities/castes, as tenants became owners of land. Majority of the new owners were eager to expand their land-holdings through legal and illegal means. The Adivasis became their easy targets. The result was the large scale alienation of Adivasi land. Another lacuna was the exemption of plantations from the provisions of the Land Ceiling Act, which facilitated the landlords and major groups to retain their land-holdings. Many plantation groups illegally occupied Adivasi and forest land with the connivance of the revenue authorities leading to sharp decline of forest and Adivasi lands in many places.

Above all, the successive governments were half-hearted or indifferent in checking the large scale alienation of Adivasi land or the restoration of the alienated land from the powerful settlers' lobby. The various legislations enacted by the governments in this regard were sabotaged or kept in cold storage at the instance of the powerful settlers' lobby in the State. Thus, there is no wonder that a legal luminary like Justice (late) VR Krishna Iyer expressed his great anguish and concern as:

> "The social disease of alienation of Adivasi land-holding for years is yet to be cured. In 1975, the Kerala Legislature unanimously enacted the Kerala Scheduled Tribe (Restriction of Transfer of Lands and Restoration of Alienated Land) Act. Had this Act been implemented with social passion, the Tribal land alienation problem should have been resolved. Unfortunately due to political compulsions and obviously to safeguard the interests of non-Tribal settlers in the Tribal land, the Act could not be effectively implemented by the successive State Governments. Thus Adivasi protest against unjust privation appears in one form or the other."[8]

The Maoists, from the very beginning could exploit such issues to their advantage. Thus, the ideologues in CPML in late 1960s identified landlordism as the principal contradiction. Their strategy was that the landlordism which is the main base of imperialism/capitalism should be demolished. Thus, the party meticulously followed the strategy of the 'annihilation of landlords' branding them as class enemies. This had created favourable response from the Adivasis and the landless poor during the initial phase of the Maoist movement in Kerala. Later, pro-Maoist groups like Porattom resorted to extensive campaign and propaganda on the issue of Adivasi land alienation and apathetic attitude of successive governments in doing justice to Adivasis through the restoration and redistribution of alienated lands. Despite such organized moves, the Maoists were unable to make much headway among the Adivasis.

It was overwhelmingly felt that the emergence of indigenous Adivasi movements such as the Adivasi Gothra Maha Sabha (AGMS) and political mobilization of Adivasis by mainstream parties, to a great extent, had checkmated the moves of Maoists to woo the Adivasis to their camp. The AGMS, through a series of struggles on the issue of the restoration of alienated Adivasi land could effectively build up their support base among Adivasis. Moreover, at the instance of AGMS, the Adivasi issues have started getting some attention from the governments, enabling the organization to boost up its image and credibility among the large chunk of Adivasis. Thus, Civic Chandran, an erstwhile Maoist, now associated with ultra left social movements has rightly commented:

> "Despite the active association of many ex-Maoist activists with AGMS, the outfit could successfully resist the attempts of Maoist groups to hijack it during the crucial phase of their land related struggles at 'Muthanga' in Wayanad district. The autonomous line of AGMS in many respects influenced the historic land struggles at Chengara when the Sadhu Jana Vimochana Samithi which spearheaded the movement outrightly rejected the offer by various Maoist groups to participate in the struggle. The urge of indigenous groups to stand on their own foot counter-poses Maoist strategy to make inroads into the community."[9]

The organized efforts by various political parties to retain Adivasis as traditional vote banks by exploiting their backwardness and ignorance created major impediments for outfits like AGMS. One disgusting trend was that Adivasis were never allowed to voice their independent views. Their elected representatives in local self-government bodies are forced to function either as silent spectators or as mere dummies of powerful lobbies. Thus, practically, the much hailed decentralization of democratic institutions for the active participation of Adivasis and the under-privileged sections in decision making process remained as a myth!

Fully aware of these realities, AGMS since its inception had distanced from all political parties. Thus, AGMS had to face stiff resistance from parties as they feared that autonomous bodies would erode their vote banks among the Adivasis. These parties adopted different strategies to discredit the movement through slandering campaign attributing their links with Maoists and extremists or foreign agencies. Attempts were made to woo prominent leaders by offering positions in their parties. Ms CK Janu, who has been at the centre of Adivasi politics since that last few decades has revealed such bitter realities as early as in 2013:

> "Over the last many decades, the Adivasis, cut off from outside world were treated by mainstream parties as solid vote banks as a result of which the ethnic harmony has been shattered. Inter-clan differences and conflicts became common. New political equations were drawn dividing the Adivasis on class, clan and caste lines. Yet, their development continued to remain as a myth. The Maoists and other radical groups exploited the situation. The major political parties played hide and seek game in such complex scenario; new slogans of assimilation and development filled the air. But, the Adivasi voice was never heard; nor allowed to be heard; nor their members were allowed to come up in the social or political ladder. Whoever tried to rise up fighting against all odds and hazards were cunningly absorbed by mainstream parties offering loaves of political

> power. They were emulated as symbols of integrated Adivasi politics! Yet, there was no real salvation for the community."[10]

Ironically, Ms Janu herself has become the best example of the Adivasi dilemma. In the Lok Sabha elections of 2004, when the Tribal land issue was in the forefront of the political discourse, she unsuccessfully contested from Idukki under the banner of Rashtriya Maha Sabha (RMS), a conglomeration of various Adivasi-Dalit organizations. In 2006, she again contested as an independent from Mananthavadi in Wayanad. Ms Janu, bereft of the support of any political party failed to cut much ice with the voters. In 2016, she floated her own party namely Janadhipathya Rashtriya Sabha (JRS); became an ally of the National Democratic Alliance (NDA) and once again unsuccessfully contested from Sultan Battery assembly seat.

That was the transition of an Adivasi leader, who for many decades functioned as the vanguard of an apolitical indigenous organization, but ultimately landed on the lap of a political front ruling the nation. With her entry into electoral politics, AGMS has lost much of its steam. The story of Ms Janu and for that matter the AGMS explains that in a political system with parties vigorously pursuing vote bank politics, the survival of apolitical organizations is a great challenge. Perhaps, such challenges, on many instances, become a launching pad for the Maoists and other radical groups to build up their organization highlighting the maladies of democracy and its established institutions.

NOTES AND REFERENCES

1. The prominent personalities who were interviewed as part of the research included Justice (retired) VR Krishna Iyer of the Supreme Court, K Venu, ex-Maoist leader and an ideologue of the Maoist

movement in India, Ms K Ajitha, who participated in the first Maoist action in Kerala during 1968; Gro Vasu, another pioneer leader of Naxalite movement in Kerala and a member of the action squad who attacked Pulpally Police Station in 1968; Civic Chandran, erstwhile Maoist leader who was active in the cultural front; Ms CK Janu, the Adivasi leader who was instrumental for the formation of Adivasi Gothra Maha Sabha (AGMS) and led historic struggles on Adivasi land issues in Kerala, M Geethanandan, ex-Maoist activist and one of the founder members of the Adivasi Gothra Maha Sabha (AGMS) and Jacob Lazer of People's Union for Civil Liberties (PUCL), Kerala.

2. Personal interview with Ms CK Janu at her house at Thirunelli (July 2013).
3. Personal interview with K Venu at his house in Trichur (July 2013).
4. Personal interview with Justice (retired) VR Krishna Iyer at his house in Ernakulam (June 2013).
5. Personal interview with Ms K Ajitha at her house in Calicut (June 2013).
6. Copy of the special questionnaire in Annexure A.
7. *Ibid*, Sl No 3.
8. *Ibid*, Sl No 4.
9. Personal interview with Civic Chandran at his house on the outskirts of Trichur (June 2013).
10. *Ibid*, Sl No 2.

9

Kerala - The Current Scenario

The Left Wing Extremists (LWE) especially the CPI (Maoist) who totally negate 'democracy' and focus on capturing political power through protracted armed struggle based on guerrilla warfare, no doubt, are delighted over the current scenario in the State. The Maoists and other radical groups, as part of their strategy to undermine democracy and the State power, exploit the degeneration of political institutions and the devaluation of political ethos and values, which have now become the facet of the State politics. Ironically almost all major political parties in the State are in the vortex of such controversies, scandals and scams that have now rocked the State with major ripples in the areas of governance, development and law and order.

The Indian National Congress (INC), which occupied major political space in the State since the formation of Kerala in 1956, riding high on the halo of the freedom struggle, has been virtually devastated in the 'tsunami' of scandals and scams. Just like the United Progressive Alliance (UPA) government at the Centre, the INC led United Democratic Front (UDF) government which was in power in Kerala during 2011-16 was immersed in series of allegations of corruption, malpractices, scams and sexual escapades. The then Congress Chief Minister Oommen Chandy, half a dozen of his cabinet colleagues and a number of MLAs were involved in these scams and scandals. The Bar Licences Bribery case, solar scam, Pattoor land case and civil supplies corruption etc, were some of the major scams. The Bar bribery case cost Finance Minister KM Mani his job, while another Congress Minister, K Babu, *suo motu* stepped down but withdrew resignation under pressure. The octogenarian Mani, the chieftain of the regional party, Kerala Congress, who had the blessings of the powerful Catholic Church hierarchy for many decades, has now lost much of his clout among the church leaders with his ignominious ouster from the State cabinet. Moreover, a section of the party rank and file formed another regional outfit 'Janadhipathiya Kerala Congress' (Democratic Kerala Congress) eroding the support base of the parent party in its citadels.

But, the worst of it all were the numerous decisions taken by the cabinet in the fag end of their tenure helping big plantations, real estate lobby and big business by way of transferring land/estates or sanctioning projects in contravention of the provisions of Kerala Land Reforms Act, Kerala Conservation of Paddy Field and Wetland Act etc. These decisions that invited severe criticism by a section of Congress leaders including VM Sudheeran, Kerala Pradesh Congress Committee (KPCC) President considerably tarnished the image of Congress. Similarly, the overt and covert means and methods adopted by the Congress/UDF to come out of such controversies and scams by scuttling the due process of law by influencing august institutions such as bureaucracy, law enforcement or even judiciary have not been appreciated by the large segments of right thinking people. The general feeling among sections of the masses that the Congress has been succumbing to the 'pressure politics' of regional parties like the Indian Union Muslim League (IUML) and the Kerala Congress (KC) jeopardizing the genuine interests of the majority community in the State caused more damage to Congress/UDF.

The above trends have clearly reflected in 2016 Assembly polls when the ruling UDF was ousted from power. In the 140 member State Assembly, the Communist Party of India/ Marxist(CPI-M) led Left Democratic Front (LDF) won a clear mandate by winning 91 seats with a vote share of 43.54%, as against 47 seats of the UDF with a vote share of 38.6%, a decline over 7% as compared to 2011 polls. But the BJP/NDA has emerged as a third force in the bipolar politics, which has been the norm in the State for decades. The alliance won one seat with a vote share of over 15%. This signalled the creation of a new political space, which could be a precursor to a major shift, in the State's politics.

As the main opposition in the State, the problems of the UDF have been compounded. Oommen Chandy, tainted Chief Minister, owning the moral responsibility for the Front's defeat, took a stand not to hold any position in the UDF set up, albeit he would be in the forefront of all its campaigns. This was a tactical move to salvage his group ('A' faction) whose leaders were in the thick of major scams. The mantle of the Opposition leader fell on Ramesh Chennithala, the former State Home Minister, who was also keen to safeguard the interests of the rival group ('I' faction). Thus, there was no let off in the group-oriented activities in the party that adversely reflected in its functioning in the State Assembly and outside.

VM Sudheeran who was anointed as the KPCC President, at the instance of the Party High Command and was untouchable to the major factions in the State has ultimately vacated his position due to the belligerence of prominent State leaders. MM Hassan, a protégé of Oommen Chandy has been appointed as the new President, pending the ongoing exercise of the party organizational elections which have been deadlocked due to the hectic moves of rival groups to get their loyalists inducted to the party committees at various levels. The main reason for the unending schism and group differences in the party is that the writ of a weak Party High Command headed by Rahul Gandhi seldom created any impact on the style of functioning and approach of senior State leaders especially Oommen Chandy.

The Justice G Sivarajan Commission's Report placed in the State Assembly at its special session in November 2017 came as a thunderbolt that has virtually shaken the edifice of Congress party in Kerala. The above Commission was appointed by the UDF government headed by Oommen Chandy on October 23, 2013, after allegations of corruption in the multi-crore solar panel deal rocked the State. The main allegation was that the fraudulent solar energy company 'Team Solar', used the services of a woman Saritha S Nair to create political contacts with links even to the Chief Minister's office, duped several influential people to the tune of ₹70 million, by offering to make them business partners, or by offering to install solar power units for them, after receiving advance payments for the same. The Commission has indicted Oommen Chandy along with his personal office staff holding that all had 'assisted' accused Saritha S Nair in 'cheating' customers. Chandy has been accused of receiving an amount of ₹2.16 core as commission and of sexually exploiting Saritha S Nair on multiple occasions at his official residence, Cliff House, Kerala. The report also included the details of the controversial letter written by Saritha on July 19, 2013, in which she had levelled serious sexual and corruption charges against a dozen Congress leaders including former State and Union Ministers, sitting MPs/MLAs/ex-MLAs and two senior IPS officers. Jose K Mani, MP, the son of controversial State Finance Minister KM Mani of Kerala Congress also figured in the list.

Another set of Congress leaders came under the scanner of the Commission for sabotaging the investigation of the case. It found that the former Home and Vigilance Minister Thiruvanchoor Radhakrishnan had made all efforts to ensure that Chandy was extricated from criminal liability by influencing the investigation agencies. The Commission has named a few senior police officers including two former police chiefs who played in the hands of the Minister/leaders, whereas the head of the Special Investigation Team (SIT) adopted dubious methods to sabotage the investigation of the case. Another lacunae pointed out by the Commission was that the SIT did not probe the alleged involvement of other ministers, government officers, central minister, MLAs and police officers in the investigation of solar cases.

In fact, sex scams and corruption cases were not new to Kerala politics. There were a number of such cases like the Suryanelli case (related to the abduction and sexual exploitation of a minor girl hailing from Suryanelli in Idukki district by several persons in 1996), ice-cream parlour sex racket case (involving a sex racket operated from an ice-cream parlour in Kozhikode during 1997) etc, in which senior political leaders like PK Kunhalikutty (former State Industries Minister and presently MP/IUML, in Lok Sabha) were involved. High libido among politicians of all hues in the State and the scandals orchestrated by the electronic media, have caused much embarrassment to almost all parties. The latest scam related to AK Saseendran, the sole Nationalist Congress Party (NCP) nominee in the ruling Left Democratic Front (LDF) government, who lost his ministerial berth during September 2017 for his alleged phone sex with a woman, as claimed by a channel which aired an audio clip. Saseendran episode has caused considerable embarrassment to the State Government. As rightly commented by Dutch psychologist Joris Lammers, "a direct, causal link between the experiences of power and moral hypocrisy" leads to increased number of sex scams among the political leaders in Kerala.

The solar scam is perhaps the best example in this regard. The arrogance of the unchallenged power filled some Congress leaders with enough confidence to abuse vulnerable women as well to satisfy their carnal desires with impunity. Justice G Sivarajan has taken a serious note of the issue. The Commission has recommended to the State Government to seriously consider the applicability of the provisions of the Prevention of Corruption (PC) Act against whom corruption, illegal gratification and sexual favours have been alleged. Further inquiry by a competent authority was necessary to uphold the discipline of the police force, the Commission said, coming down on what it called 'dubious methods' of the previous Special Investigation Team (SIT) to extricate Oommen Chandy from criminal liability. Accepting the recommendations of the Commission, the Chief Minister assured that the government would initiate legal proceedings under the Prevention of Corruption Act and other Indian Penal Code (IPC) sections, against all persons who are found by the Commission as having indulged in corruption and other criminal offences. An order has been issued forming a SIT team to probe various aspects of the solar scam based on the findings and recommendations of the Commission. If the State Government seriously go ahead with the due process of law, the Congress party in the State would have tough time in the days ahead.

However, pro-Left Wing extremist intellectuals and the State BJP leaders allege that UDF and LDF are playing adjustment politics and ultimately nothing will happen to the accused of these scams and scandals, as it is natural that birds of the same feather flock together. The ongoing rhetoric by the LDF on solar scam or other corruption cases during UDF regime is just a ploy by LDF to fool the public and divert the attention from its own failures. Aggrieved over the decision of the LDF government to initiate legal proceedings against those Congress leaders named by the Commission in the solar scam, a young Congress MLA has come out that that the party has been made to pay for its own folly of letting top CPM leaders off the hook in the sensational TP Chandrashekharan murder case. It is public knowledge that while the UDF government arrested all those who were involved in the gruesome murder of the Marxist dissident, it simply did not bother to track down the conspirators who allegedly included senior leaders of CPI(M). Such stories of 'adjustment politics' between the CPI(M) and their political opponents are not new to the State. One such story was that the top CPI(M) leadership in the State tried to save Congress ally, PK Kunhalikutty (of IUML) in the infamous ice cream parlour sex scandal. The main allegation was that a senior lawyer and former Advocate General MK Damodaran had provided legal advice to the 2006-11 LDF government to spare Kunhalikutty from the case after accepting bribe from him. The issue had created sharp differences between hardliners and the neo-liberalists in CPI(M) during the 20th Party Congress held in Kozhikode during February 2006.

The ground reality is that the Communist parties, notably the CPI(M) has considerably lost their revolutionary or proletarian sheen and they have downgraded to the status of any bourgeois party. Virtually, the neo-liberal tendencies have influenced the large majority of the rank and file. Though the party organization has emphasised 'rectification campaign' at all levels to defeat such unhealthy trends and un-Communist tendencies, such programmes have virtually failed as manifest by the mounting instances of indiscipline, moral decay and corruption and malpractices. As the popular dictum goes that power corrupts and absolute power absolutely, such trends emerge more ominous whenever the party or the party-led fronts are in power. Perhaps, the best example is the case of West Bengal where more than three decades of CPI(M) rule had virtually alienated the party from the large chunk of the people because of such omissions and commissions.

The State of Kerala is another State where Communist parties were in power for long period. Perhaps it is the first State in the world where a Communist party was voted to power in 1957 through democratic process. Influenced by the legacy of great anti-colonial struggles during the pre-independence period and proletarian ideologies, the first Communist government in Kerala headed by the veteran Communist leader, EMS Namboothiripad could initiate a number of progressive and radical reforms; majority of which could not be implemented in their letter and spirit due to the 'liberation struggle' by the major communities in the State leading to the dismissal of the government in 1956 under Article 356 of the Constitution.

Compelled by political exigencies or the dominating parliamentary ambitions, the Communist parties had made major ideological compromises that on many occasions led to internal differences and contradictions resulting in major split in the parties. In late 1940s and early 1950s, influenced by the Communist Party of Soviet Union (CPSU) and the Chinese Communist Party (CCP), these differences were mainly on the question of armed struggles or 'peaceful transition'/approach towards national bourgeoisie, leading to the split in the undivided Communist party with the formation of Soviet-backed Communist Party of India (CPI) and China-supported Communist Party of India (Marxist) in 1964. Recently, the Kerala CPM was in the vortex of such a controversy when the party supremo and the present Chief Minister Pinarayi Vijayan, while addressing a party conclave in Kozhikode on January 3, 2018 has openly praised North Korean leader Kim Jong-un for putting up a 'tough' resistance against the 'imperialist' United States of America better than the Communist-ruled China. On the other hand Party's State Secretary Kodiyeri Balakrishnan, while addressing a party convention in Alappuzha district alleged that an axis of countries like US, Japan, Australia and India has taken shape for attacking China from all sides. The pro-China and pro-North Korea gestures of the Party have evoked criticism from sections of the party rank and file in the State.

Meanwhile at domestic front, the 'alliance politics' had become the hallmark of the CPM which entered into electoral alliance/understanding with parties or groups which are ideologically opposed to the very concept of Marxism-Leninism. In fact, Kerala has been a political laboratory of such alliances since 1967, when both the CPM and the CPI forged a grand alliance of seven parties which swept the 1967 Assembly polls. It was for the first time that the Communists in Kerala aligned with the Indian Union Muslim League (IUML), which as its very name suggests has been branded by many as a communal outfit. Thus, the tall claims of the Communists that all those parties and groups espousing communal, parochial or sectarian ideologies are untouchable to them, have been exposed. Such opportunist political alliances coupled with the CPM's deviation from its strategy of building up revolutionary mass struggles gave an impetus to the detractors of the Party in Kerala to embrace the path of Charu Majumdar and Kanu Sanyal as early as in late 1960s when the Maoist (Naxalite) movement started with a big bang in the Darjeeling district of West Bengal. The CPM was the main target of attack of the various Left Wing Extremist groups that had emerged in Kerala during 1970s and 1980s.

There was wide dichotomy on the professed ideology of the CPI(M) and its actual practice on the ground. Moreover, there was no consistency on the part of CPM in working out electoral or political alliances. Though the Party outwardly projected uncompromising stand against communal and fundamentalist parties, they on many instances, worked out alliances or adjustments with such parties solely for the sake of capturing political power. Thus, in 1980s, the party had welcomed the All India Muslim League (AIML), a breakaway faction of IUML to the Left Democratic Front (LDF). However, the AIML which was opposed to the line of the CPM on the Shah Bano case deserted the LDF and returned to their parent party (IUML). But during late 1980s, the State CPM opposed tooth and nail of the attempts of a section of Party leaders headed by firebrand leader MV Raghavan to broaden the LDF set up by accommodating parties like IUML and Kerala Congress (a regional party predominantly of the Christians of the Central Travancore). These differences ultimately led to another split in the Party with the formation of the Communist Marxist Party (CMP) which ironically became a partner of the INC led United Democratic Front (UDF). On the other hand, the CPM, in due course, had no reservations to enter into electoral alliances or understanding with such parties including Kerala Congress groups or the Indian National League (INL) whose founding father was none else but late Ibrahim Sulaiman Sait, MP, a key figure associated with Organization of Islamic Conference (OIC), All India Muslim Personal Law Board (AIMPLB), All India Milli Council and All India Babri Masjid Action Committee (AIBAC) etc.

But the most leading controversy that had shaken the ideological foundation of CPM in Kerala was the party's tactical line of aligning with Peoples Democratic Party (PDP) of ICS Abdul Nasser Madani, during 2009 Lok Sabha polls with a view to break the impregnable fortresses of the IUML in Malappuram district. As part of this tactics, Ponnani, a LS seat traditionally contested and lost by the CPI under the banner of

LDF was taken over by the CPM which fielded an independent candidate, Hussein Randathani (who had the blessings of Madani) against ET Mohammed Basheer of IUML/UDF. During the electioneering in the constituency in April 2009, Pinarayi Vijayan, the then State Secretary of the CPM along with other party comrades shared open platform with Madani, who then was released from Coimbatore jail after years of incarceration as under trial prisoner in connection with Coimbatore serial bomb blasts case. Even the well-wishers of the Left had winced at the spectacle of the prominent CPM leader sharing platform with Madani, who all along had the image of a religious fundamentalist with extreme radical ideologies. While LDF partners like the CPI and Janata Dal had expressed their displeasure on this issue, the octogenarian CPM leader VS Achuthanandan, former Chief Minister used it as a potential propaganda weapon to attack Pinarayi Vijayan in the Party and outside. Not only had that Pinarayi-Madani sponsored candidate been defeated by over 80,000 votes, but the 'Pennant episode' had also exposed the true face of CPM in the State politics.

In this backdrop, let us make introspection as to what extent the present CPI(M) led government in Kerala could uphold true Communist ideology or the proletarian philosophy, while ensuring the development of the State and the welfare of the people. In 2016 assembly polls, the poll slogan of the party was "LDF will come, everything will be alright" which was their solemn promise to the voters that they would set right the system and polity once voted to power. The new Chief Minister, time and again reiterated his government's commitment to bring all culprits involved in various scams, scandals, corruption and malpractices before law. For that purpose a cabinet sub-Committee was constituted to examine all the 'controversial and illegal' decisions taken by the UDF regime; the State Vigilance set-up was reconstituted and revamped and Special Investigation teams were formed to expedite the pending investigation of major scams and corruption cases. Ironically, more than rhetoric, nothing concrete or specific has come up so far even in sensational cases such as Bar Licences Bribery case or Pattoor land case in which senior UDF leaders are involved.

Meanwhile, the LDF government faced a major embarrassment when the State Industries and Sports Minister, EP Jayarajan (Central Committee member of CPM) and a protégé of Pinarayi Vijayan (State Chief Minister) was involved in a controversy of appointing his close relative as the Managing Director of Kerala State Industries Enterprises Ltd (KSIE) flouting all norms and procedures. The appointee was the son of another Central Committee member and Kannur MP, Ms PK Sreemathy. The appointment was scrapped after widespread criticism, whereas the Minister has resigned in October 2017 hardly after 4-months of the formation of the new government, adversely affecting its image. Another relative of Jayarajan/Sreemathy too resigned from the post of General Manager of Kerala Clays and Ceramics Ltd in the wake of the controversy. These were clear instances of nepotism and favouritism which showed the dichotomy of the party in what they profess and practice in real politics.

In fact, Jayarajan has courted many controversies during his political life spanning over four decades. As Kannur district secretary he constructed a palatial house at Pappinniserri using mechanised laterite bricks, leading to opposition from the rank and file of the party's trade union front for depriving the labour to the workers. In another instance, he took bonds worth ₹2 crore from lottery baron Santiago Martin for party mouthpiece *Deshabhimani*, at a time when VS Achuthanandan, the then Chief Minister of CPM had declared a war against lotteries of other States. The party was forced to remove him from *Deshabhimani* General Manager's post, but later reinstated after settling the bond controversy by paying ₹2 crore to Santiago Martin. There were allegations against him related to financial irregularities in the conduct of Football tournament, in Kannur district in memory of EK Nayanar, former CPM Chief Minister. He was also at the centre of controversy during CPM plenum in Palakkad district in 2016, when *Deshabhimani* published an advertisement of controversial businessman VM Radhakrishnan who was facing corruption cases. Jayarajan as the architect of Vismay Water Theme Park and Mangrove Park in Kannur district attracted the wrath of environmentalists and sections of local population facing acute water shortage in the area. The Mangrove Park, however, could not take off because of court intervention.

The Jayarajan episode was not an exception to the degeneration of Communist culture and ethos and the value based polity on which the senior leaders used to make mountain sermons to the cadres as well as to the public. The present Chief Minister, Pinarayi Vijayan is involved in the SNC-Lavalin scandal that related to a hydroelectric infrastructure contract between the Kerala government and Canadian company SNC-Lavalin in 1995 which resulted in an alleged net loss to the tune of US $62 million to the State exchequer. The contract was signed when Vijayan was the State Power Minister. It was the first ever corruption-related prosecution of a Politburo member of CPM. Though the Central Bureau of Investigation (CBI) Special Court and the Kerala High Court in August 2017 has exonerated Vijayan, the legal battle on the issue is in the offing in the Supreme Court of India. More than the legal battle, his detractors in the party and outside including VS Achuthanandan used Lavalin case as a political weapon to create stumbling blocks in the political career of Vijayan. Any decision or strictures against him by the

Apex Court would open another saga of anti-Pinarayi crusade by the UDF as well as his opponents within the party.

The growing trend of neo-liberal influences among the rank and file is a serious challenge confronting the party in Kerala. The latest example is the release of a 'self-glorifying' music album of P Jayarajan, CPM's strongman in Kannur district. Such tendencies to promote 'personality cult' in the party clearly manifest the failure of the much trumpeted 'rectification exercises'. More deplorable are the episodes of party leaders involving in sexual escapades or mafia-like operations. The party's Secretaries in Kannur and Ernakulam districts, who had long innings in the party organization were expelled/downgraded from the party in 2015/16 on specific charges of sexual demeanour/misbehaviour towards women comrades or their relatives. Ironically, the women members had to approach the central leadership against the attempts by section of State leaders to bury such issues under the carpet giving lenient action to the involved leaders. Similarly, allegations of corruption and unholy linkages with Multinational Groups and their agents had come up against Elamaram Kareem, former State Industries Minister and prominent Trade Union leader, who started his career as casual labourer, but recently elevated to the Central Committee of the party. He has often been criticised in party circles for his close connections pro-capitalist lobby both in the State and abroad and his keenness to bring in bigger projects that demanded huge investments, even endangering ecology and environment.

Such pro-capitalist/neo-liberal strategies have considerably influenced the CPM leadership in Kerala in the selection of candidates during the 2014 Lok Sabha and the last Assembly polls. No doubt, the strategy paid rich dividends to the party in the electoral battle, but evoked new issues adversely affecting the image of the party/government. A comedian from Malayalam silver screen pitted against veteran Congress leader from Chalakudy LS seat won the elections, but was subsequently involved in a series of controversies due to his 'filmy dialogues' on gender issues/dignity of women and the rape of young Malayalam actress. Another silver screen actor elected as MLA, in party's ticket from Kollam district too has courted such controversies through his open statements apparently deviating from the official line of the party. Similarly, a couple of CPM-backed independents elected to the State Assembly caused more damage to the image of the government when more and more stories of their involvement in encroachment of government land, holding of surplus land and launching of new parks or projects causing environmental hazards etc, were brought out by the electronic and print media.

Added to this were the controversies evoked by a few legislators of the LDF partners. Thomas Chandy, the nominee of the Nationalist Congress Party (NCP) who was inducted into State cabinet as the State Transport Minister after the ignominious exit of AK Saseendran in the sex scandal, opened a Pandora's Box of allegations on his involvement in encroachment and reclamation of portion of Punnamada Lake in Kuttanadu in Alleppey district and the construction of huge tourist complexes violating the provisions of Kerala Wetland Conservation Act etc. Ultimately, Chandy has resigned after prolonging the issue for almost three months. The dilly-dallying of the Chief Minister to take prompt decision on the issue, the polemics between CPM and CPI on the controversy and certainly the sweeping references made by the Kerala High Court on sensitive issues like the collective responsibility of the cabinet etc, caused unprecedented damage to the image of the government. Similarly, the sole MLA of a splinter Kerala Congress group with filmy background, known for his lascivious style of life and filmy connections caused embarrassment to the government through his involvement in 'Saritha controversy' and open statements defending the accused actor in young actress rape case.

The neo-liberal policies have also influenced the style of functioning of the LDF government. The Communist leaders who were generally averse to pro-capitalist scholars or economists during 1980s and '90s have now become more open to such sections; seeking their professionalism and expertise in matters of policy formulation and governance. Pinarayi Vijayan has now half a dozen advisors including Gita Gopinath, John Zwaanstra Professor of International Studies and of Economics at Harvard University, whose neo-liberal economic policies, on many accounts, are in conflict with the declared economic policies of CPM. Though her appointment created differences within the party, Pinarayi Vijayan with the backing of neo-liberal lobby, stuck to his decision. Though the government has tried to improve the overall governance and administration with the help of such advisors and bureaucracy, no tangible progress could be achieved in these fronts.

On the other hand, the Pinarayi government's move to clean the Aegean stable of State bureaucracy including the senior IAS lobby led to a showdown between the government and the bureaucracy. Everything started with the appointment of Jacob Thomas, IPS as State Vigilance Director with unbridled powers to continue his anti-corruption crusade in the State even targeting corrupt IAS officers. In his over-enthusiasm, the new Director and the team targeted top 'babus' including additional chief secretaries, for their alleged corrupt practices. K Padma Kumar, Managing Director, Malabar Cements Limited, was arrested in a corruption case; an FIR was filed against Additional Chief Secretary Paul Antony in the nepotism row that forced the minister EP Jayarajan to quit; Additional Chief Secretary Tom Jose was grilled in connection with a disproportionate corruption case and the official residence of a couple of senior IAS officers like KM Abraham were raided. Besides, the anti-corruption watchdog had initiated the probe against some top bureaucrats in corruption cases that apparently annoyed the influential IAS-IPS lobby, which was successful in foisting allegations of malpractices/irregularities against Jacob Thomas, while working as Port Director, Kerala and in procuring 151 acres of land in Coorg district of Tamil Nadu in his wife's name. The Lokayukta, Kerala ordered a preliminary inquiry into these allegations, whereas, a Judge of the Kerala High Court hearing a set of Vigilance cases, made verbal observations such as 'Vigilance Raj' apparently targeting Jacob Thomas. The Chief Minister, who defended the officer throughout the trials and tribulations, was forced to yield to the pressure tactics of the IAS-IPS lobby and sections of the party comrades. Thus, Jacob Thomas was removed from the post of the Director, Vigilance and Anti-Corruption Bureau.

Basically, the elevation of Jacob Thomas, who was sidelined by the previous UDF government due to certain controversial decisions in the course of the investigation of sensational vigilance cases, by the LDF government as the Vigilance Director was to boost up the image of the government in the anti-corruption crusade. The euphoria created by him through his catchy slogans in fighting corruption, registration of cases against big guns in different fields and the much publicised raid of the premises of top bureaucrats could be easily cashed in by the LDF government to their advantage. But, on the ground, there was no palpable progress in the investigation of a number of sensational cases in which senior UDF ministers/leaders were involved. Moreover, the Vigilance wing's pursuit of cases against top bureaucrats of the State, including the then finance secretary KM Abraham, additional chief secretary and Kerala IAS Association President Tom Jose and Industries Secretary Paul

Antony, has lost much of the steam midway, thereby creating an impression that LDF government is not sincere in fighting corruption at the higher level of bureaucracy. On the other hand, by antagonizing the IAS-IPS lobby, the government has faced serious setback in tax collection, timely utilization of Central funds and implementation of developmental projects. Above all, the unceremonious ouster of the Vigilance Director created strong impression among larger section of the masses that he was shunted out as he became unacceptable to the CPI(M) leadership for initiating cases against party leaders including EP Jayarajan.

Of the various issues, the lapses in policing have caused the greatest harm to the image of the LDF government. In fact the politicisation of the force had begun soon after the LDF assumed power. The chief minister sent a message by showing the door to DGP, TP Senkumar in May 2016, alleging dereliction of duty with regard to the investigation of two high profile cases – Puttingal temple fireworks tragedy on April 9, 2017 and the rape and murder of Dalit student Jisha on April 28, 2017. However, the Supreme Court order to reinstate him as the Police Chief was a major setback to the State Government especially the CM who was in charge of Home portfolio. Moreover, Senkumar, through his open tirade tried to create an impression that he was removed from that post as he had taken stern action in many cases related to political murders including that of TP Chandrasekharan (dissident CPM leader from Kannur district) in which CPM leaders and workers were involved. 'Senkumar episode' created differences among the senior echelons of the force; a section of them batting in his favour, while others opposing his calculated moves to discredit the force. The appointment of Tomin Thachenkerry, IPS, Additional Director General of Police (ADGP) who is involved in a number of controversies and scandals, at Police Headquarters with key assignments led to open confrontation between him and Senkumar creating a growing feeling among the general public that everything is not right in the home department.

Though Loknath Behera, the successor of Senkumar tried to revamp the force through a thorough reshuffle of officers of all ranks, no improvement in policing was noticed. On the contrary, the situation has turned worse, with the sudden rise in crimes, especially against women and children, and the failure of the police in bringing the culprits to book. The high-handedness of police in dealing with the public resentment and protest on police inaction has been construed as the failure of the government to exercise proper control over the police. One such example was the handling of Jishnu Pranoy case. Images of the mother of the young engineering student who committed suicide due to the alleged harassment of the private management, being dragged by police had become etched in the public mind. The images of half a dozen police personnel remaining as mute spectators of the attack on young couples by moral policing activists of Shiv Sena in the heart of Cochin city went viral in the social media, making the police the laughing stock of all. The opposition parties, ostensibly to make political mileage out of such police excesses organized State-wide *hartal* and other protest programmes demanding that the Chief Minister should relinquish Home portfolio.

The deterioration of law and order naturally led to steady increase in political murders. According to police statistics, 12 RSS or BJP workers and four CPM workers have been killed due to suspected political rivalry during the first year of LDF regime in Kerala. Kannur district the citadel of CPI(M) accounted for almost 50% of these political killings. In fact, Kerala has a long history of political violence. Police records of political murders between 2000 and 2017 impugn both the left and right wing fronts. In the last 17 years, 85 CPM workers, 65

RSS or BJP workers, 11 workers of Congress and IUML each have been killed – mostly by their political rivals including CPM and RSS or BJP. With the emergence of Muslim radical organizations and their political outfits like the Socialist Democratic Party of India (SDPI), such parties are involved in the killing of their political rivals. For example, SDPI members were accused of murdering Nazirudeen, an IUML man from Kuttiyadi, Kozhikode district in July 2016. One notable feature was that the graph of political killings showed an upward trend during the LDF rule in the State. In 2000, for instance, when the LDF was in power, Kannur recorded nine deaths in a single year. In 2008, again under LDF rule, 12 persons were killed – five each from the CPI(M) and the RSS-BJP and 2 from other parties. According to National Crime Record Bureau (NCRB) data, while Kannur contributed to 50% of political murders in the State during the two LDF terms between 2000 and 2016, it accounted for 20-30% of the political murders committed during the UDF regimes in this period. Overall, Kannur contributed to 36% of all political murders in Kerala between 2000 and 2015.

The increasing trend of political violence in Kannur district is due to a confluence of factors – historical, social and political. Historically, Kannur has the legacy of warrior culture where the local chieftains excelled in martial art (Kalarippayattu), settled their disputes through open fights. The ballads here are full of such heroic stories of chieftains and their womenfolk. The district witnessed one of the longest and bloodiest resistances to the British in India. The revolt led by Pazhassi Raja kept a large part of the district in a state of war from 1792 to 1806. Many places in the district like Kayyur, Koothali, Karivellur, Kavumbaim, Korom, Onchiyam, Munayamkunnu, Thilenkery and Padikunnu had the legacy of violent anti-colonial struggles. This was followed by prolonged rivalry among the landlords, who maintained their own gangs equipped with arms and martial training. The early Communist movement which adopted the strategy of revolutionary armed struggles built up the party in these areas through violent actions. Thus, with the formation of Kerala in 1956, Kannur district became stronghold of the Communists notably the CPI(M) with revolutionary fervour. Again, it was in Kannur district where the Left Wing Extremists (Naxalites) executed their 'first armed action' in 1967.

Over the years, the CPM was trying to protect Kannur as their exclusive preserve by maintaining iron control over villages. The party has taken control of around 40 such villages in the district where the party cadres do not allow the rival parties to enter these villages let alone allowing them to exercise their democratic rights. Political clashes erupted when other parties tried to make inroads into such bastions. The first of such challenge came from RSS/erstwhile Jan Sangh when they started setting up shakhas/units in areas that were considered as the impregnable fortresses of CPI(M). The organized attempt of the party to resist the RSS gradually attained communal colour and led to a major communal riot at Thalasserry in 1971, which is the epicentre of the current political violence in Kannur. Many of the present generation leaders of CPI(M) including Pinarayi Vijayan had come to the centre stage of State politics by playing a crucial role in 1971 riot. These leaders still believe that the threat of RSS/BJP or other political rivals can be effectively countered through the politics of violence. Even, their own cadres who deserted the party on ideological or other grounds were not spared. Thus, the political killings and violence in the district continue unabated casting a shadow on the peace and tranquillity of the State.

However, the current wave of political killings in the State especially in Kannur district have developed into a national issue when the BJP/Sangh Parivar bodies took it as a major agenda with a view to making further inroads into Kerala politics. As part of their strategy of galvanizing national opinion, attempts were made to prevent the official visit of Pinarayi Vijayan, CM, to States like Madhya Pradesh, Karnataka etc, whereas Sangh Parivar bodies organized protest marches to the Central office of CPI(M) in Delhi as also in other State capitals. The CPI(M) too held a march to the BJP headquarters, Delhi to protest against the alleged saffron terror in Kerala, in which senior leaders including Sitaram Yechury (General Secretary) participated. Meanwhile, the State unit of BJP organized two weeks long Jana Raksha Yatra (people's protection march) to highlight the 'CPI(M) violence and jihadi terror'. The Yatra which commenced from Payyannur on October 3, after passing through all the districts, ended in Thiruvananthapuram on 17 October 2017. A host of senior BJP/RSS leaders including Amit Shah (National President, BJP), Arun Jaitley (Union Finance Minister), Uttar Pradesh Chief Minister Yogi Adityanath etc, participated in the yatra at different places. The CPM leadership, describing the Yatra a total flop accused the BJP of being responsible for the growing violence in Kerala, saying that the BJP never manages to expand social base without "murderous attacks and communal polarization".

Another major issue intertwined with law and order is the threat of Islamic radicalization and the emergence of nascent Islamic terror out fits like the Islamic State of Iraq and Syria (ISIS). Initial reports of security agencies indicate that around two dozen Muslim youth from Kerala, inspired by the ideology of the Islamic State have infiltrated into the IS controlled areas in Afghanistan, Syria and Iraq as Islamic fighters. The message sent by some of these youth via the Telegram app or audio clips indicated that a few of them were killed while fighting for IS. Majority of those who joined the IS were from Kannur,

Kasergode, Kozhikode and Malappuram districts where the Muslim radical groups like the National Development Front (NDF), Popular Front of India (PFI) and SDPI have sizeable presence. Indications are that the above outfits operate from behind the curtain in the talent-spotting of potential Muslim youth for infiltration into IS strongholds. In some instances, the converts to Islam were indoctrinated and recruited to IS. Thus, the issue of 'Love Jihad' has developed as a major controversy in the State. The Hadiya case of the conversion of an educated Hindu girl of Kottayam district into Islam and her subsequent marriage with Muslim youth allegedly having links with IS has caught national attention when the Kerala High Court nullified their marriage. The Apex Court, on a petition challenged by the aggrieved husband and impleaded by the girl's parents and others, took the personal testimony of the girl before directing her to continue her studies in a medical institution in Tamil Nadu under foolproof security by police. However, the Court is yet to decide the crucial issue of the validity of their marriage and husband's prayer to allow her to join him.

Another issue closely connected with law and order is land related movements and struggles. The State occupies only 1% of the total land area of India, whereas its population of 3.33 crore (2011 census) is 3% of the total population of India. In view of the high density of population in Kerala, land has become dearer to all sections. The illegal occupation of government/forest land by major business groups and powerful sections in the society has become rampant. Thus, with the political patronage large areas of Reserve forests or adjacent government lands had been encroached by them mainly in Idukki, Wayanad and Palakkad districts and the coastal belt of the State. For example, Tata group had 1,37,431 acres of land in Kannan Devan Hills in Idukki district, besides illegally occupied vast stretches of forest land. According to the report of a High Level Committee constituted by the State Government, Harrisons' group has a total of 7,6769.80 acres of disputed land in Wayanad, Thrissur, Kottayam, Pathanamthitta, Kollam and Idukki Districts. Thomas Chandy, recently resigned from the State cabinet, has allegedly occupied large areas of land in the coastal belt of Alappuzha district violating the provisions of Kerala State Wetland Conservation Act etc. Besides, politicians and settlers in collusion with the revenue officials have encroached on vast areas of land in Idukki and Wayanad districts.

Though the successive governments in Kerala has legislated and implemented land reforms of a radical nature, much could not be done to end such illegalities or irregularities. For example, in 1971, the Kerala government introduced the Kannan Devan Hills (Resumption of Lands) Act with a view to distributing unutilised land that was held by the group to poor farmers, agricultural labourers, tribal people and others. However, in view of unending litigations and administrative procedures, the successive governments could not do much in taking over the land. The eviction drive in 2007 initiated by the Left Democratic Front government after creating much euphoria ran into roadblocks of all kind including the intervention of the Judiciary. Same is the case with the recent 'operation eviction of encroachers' in Munnar (Idukki district), where the present government, notably the CPI(M) was not seen supporting the officers responsible for the eviction. Instead, this has led to a tiff between the CPM and CPI, the second major party in the LDF.

One major fall out of such bottlenecks was the systematic marginalization of the subaltern sections especially the Dalits and Adivasis in Kerala. In Idukki and Wayanad districts, the land identified for the Adivasis was immediately grabbed by land sharks using Adivasis as a shield. According to Adivasi organizations, 45,000 tribal families in the State do not have even a strip of land. The case of landless Dalits was equally deplorable. The landlessness of dalits (9.8% of State's total population) and Adivasis (1.15% of total population) has virtually incapacitated them to participate in the much discussed 'Kerala Model Development' as a result of which their socioeconomic conditions continue to remain precarious. This has given them impetus to participate in land struggles organized under the banner of their own apolitical outfits. The Muthanga and Chengara struggles were two landmark events in this direction. In the case of Muthanga, people mainly Adivasis laid siege to the wildlife sanctuary at Muthanga in Wayanad District in February 2003 demanding to implement the State Government agreement of 2001 on the distribution of land to landless Adivasis. The drama unfolded, after the forcible occupation of the forest land, led to police firing causing the death of an Adivasi activist and a policeman. In Chengara (Pathanamthitta district) the Sadhu Jana Vimochana Samyuktha Vedi (SJVSV), an apolitical collective of landless Dalits, Adivasis and other marginalized sections spearheaded the land struggle for 790 days during 2007-08 demanding permanent ownership of agricultural land through transfer of ownership from the Harrison Company to the Dalits and Adivasis. The State has been witnessing more and more land related struggles, which really have become a matter of concern for all political parties.

In the backdrop of a myriad of socioeconomic and developmental issues, changes in the political scenario are in the offing. The era of bi-polar politics with Congress led UDF and the CPI(M) led LDF as the key players have come to an end with BJP/NDA occupying some political space in the State. The Congress which is slowly getting decimated in many States find it a herculean task to keep their partners together under the banner of the UDF. The 'solar scam' has added the dilemma of the party. A faction of Kerala Congress led by KM Mani, having 2 MPs (one each in Lok Sabha and Rajya Sabha) and 6 MLAs in the present State Assembly has left the front and now keeping a neutral stand. Similarly, Kerala Janata Dal (United) led by MP Veerendra Kumar, is not contented with the present state of affairs in the UDF. Same is the case with Revolutionary Socialist Party (RSP) in which a section of leaders are keen to mend their ties with the Left. The Indian Union Muslim League (IUML) with 3 MPs (2 in LS and 1 in RS) and 18 MLAs in the present assembly which has always succeeded to get a pound of flesh from the UDF, has virtually no other greener political pastures, albeit UDF. However, internal issues have started creating fissures in the party with the election of PK Kunhalikutty, who hitherto had decisive say in the State politics, to Lok Sabha in the bye-election from Malappuram PC, caused due to the death of E Ahmed. The faction opposed to Kunhalikutty is gradually gaining ground in the party. Meanwhile, the new political outfit SDPI has started eating the vote bank of IUML especially of the youth sections. In the recent (October 2017) bye-elections held to Vengara Assembly constituency, an impregnable fortress of IUML, the SDPI came in third position capturing around 9,000 votes, when there was a sharp decline of around 15,000 votes to the winning IUML candidate as compared to 2016 assembly polls. In fact, such distressing political signals from the UDF camp prompted senior Congress leader, AK Antony to make an open appeal to the Left parties like CPI(M) to join hands with Congress to work out a broad political front against BJP/NDA at national level.

However, the Kerala unit of CPI(M) which defeated the move of the West Bengal unit of the party to work out broad understanding with Congress in order to face the fascist threat from BJP/NDA is averse to any sort of understanding with Congress at national level or in the home turf. The assessment of the party is that any sort of understanding with a degenerated faction-ridden Congress in Kerala would be suicidal and there is no political exigency for the party to go for such an alliance or understanding. But, LDF too has internal squabbles or differences, mainly between the CPI(M) and the CPI, which time and again have come to the fore on many issues such as eviction of encroachers in Munnar, students agitation in Kerala Law Academy and of course, the stand on tainted Minister Thomas Chandy. On Thomas Chandy issue, CPI Ministers abstained from a crucial cabinet meeting protesting against the dilly-dallying of the Chief Minister in taking a decision on the matter. Such differences between the two parties continue in many districts especially in Idukki where the ongoing eviction drive of illegal encroachers of land at the instance of State Revenue Minister (CPI) led to open diatribe between the leaders of these parties shattering the coalition spirit of LDF. However, the Congress strategy of making political capital out of the ongoing schism between CPI(M) and CPI, failed to take off as the State Secretary of CPI categorically stated that no politician with an iota of common sense would align with the State unit of Congress, a degenerated party with two dozen leaders immersed in shameless scandals.

Despite such bickering and inter and intra party squabbles in the UDF and the LDF, the BJP/NDA could not make much headway in the State politics. Even, the tempo built up by the party in 2016 Assembly polls through its maiden victory of winning one seat in the assembly and the impressive performance in one dozen Assembly constituencies cannot be maintained, despite the best efforts of the Central leaders to prop up the party in Kerala. The dearth of charismatic leaders coupled with factionalism and group rivalries adversely affect the onward match of the party in Kerala politics. Added to this is the vicious and vituperative campaign and statements by certain party leaders and the fringe elements creating doubts, panic and concern by sections of people especially the minorities like Christians. Perhaps, such activities deterred veteran leader KM Mani and his party (Kerala Congress) associating with NDA set up in Kerala. Apparently, to overcome such hurdles, the Central leadership of the party, elevated an ex-IAS officer, Alphons Kannamthanam as Union Minister, sidelining hot aspirants from the State party. Such individual-oriented tactics to broaden the mass base of the party among the minorities or highly sectarian line of approach under the command of Sangh Parivar organizations would have limited impact in influencing the psyche of the people in the State in favour of BJP/NDA. What is needed is a genuine process of social engineering of the different sections of the people coupled with generous gestures from the Centre for the all-round development of the State.

10

Conclusion

The Maoist insurgency or the Left Wing Extremism (LWE) with its geographical spread, organizational network and violence potential is the most serious challenge confronting the nation in the present millennium. With around 25,000 regular cadres and over 40,000 supporters, the Maoists have their presence in almost one-third of the land mass of the country, nicknamed as the Red Corridor stretching from the Nepal border to India's South West coast. Their sophisticated weaponry and explosives coupled with ingenious guerrilla or jungle warfare techniques such as ambushes, encounters and macabre killings make them the most dreaded insurgent outfit.

Over the last four decades, the country has been engaged in serious fight against the Maoists in their main citadels. Its counter-Maoist strategy was a combination of both enemy centric and population centric measures with more emphasis on the military aspect. No doubt, there were successes and failures for the State in its confrontation with the Maoists. Time and again, it was established that proper mapping of the threat bringing out its support-base and the socio-economic factors contributing to their growth and consolidation is necessary to formulate sound counter-Maoist strategy and tactics.

As the factors influencing the Maoist insurgency are highly disparate and vary from State to State, any national or sub-national study of the problem has the inherent weakness of not properly reflecting the true picture of the threat. For example, if caste-based landlordism and interconnected socio-economic issues are main causative factors for the genesis and spread of the movement in States like Bihar, the great saga of oppression and exploitation of the Adivasis and Dalits and denial of justice to these sections by State super structures created fertile ground for Maoists in States like Jharkhand, Chhattisgarh etc. Thus, universalizing of the Maoist insurgency on many occasions will lead to defective formulation of enemy centric or population centric operational strategies. On the other hand micro level studies in many respects will help to unfold the ground level realities enabling policy makers to frame comprehensive action plan to meet the challenge.

This study is an attempt on the above stated lines. Certain crucial themes that were inextricably intertwined with the genesis, growth and consolidation of Maoist insurgency such as the extent of support of Adivasis to Maoists, the socio-economic and developmental issues impacting the movement, the political mobilization of Adivasis and the role of indigenous outfits in countering the movement, were empirically examined. Both qualitative and quantitative methods are used for undertaking the study in the Adivasi dominated areas of the Northern districts of Kerala which witnessed Maoist violence as early as in 1968.

FINDINGS

The ideological differences in Communist Party of India (Marxist) on its strategy of using parliamentary forum for establishing proletarian regime sow the seeds of Maoist movement in Kerala. Those cadres opposed to the party line of forming united front of parties and participating in elections to capture political power, but actively involved in the various struggles of farmers and impoverished workers became the pioneer leaders of the movement. Their association with the Communist parties and grass root level workers like landless peasants, Adivasis and Dalits facilitated them to unfurl the flag of Maoist insurgency in Kerala just on the lines of the armed uprisings in the Naxalbari village during 1967. Influenced and indoctrinated by Charu Majumdar's revolutionary line of the annihilation of class enemies, the pioneer Maoists in Kerala too targeted landlords and a couple of Police Stations.

While the leadership of the movement remained with petty bourgeois intellectuals, the majority of the foot soldiers in the action squads were the poor, illiterate and exploited sections of Adivasis and other marginalized groups. They were totally ignorant of Maoist ideology or strategy. Lack of indoctrination and training of the cadres on Maoist strategy resulted in their large scale desertion from the movement under pressure from the State and the police. Despite the erosion of support, the Maoists – during different phases of their growth – continued to target Adivasis and the landless poor to broaden their support base in the State. During the current phase of the movement in Kerala, the Maoists continue to pursue the above strategy. The main targets of the Western Ghats Special Zonal Committee (WGSZC) of Maoists presently operating in the tri-junction of Kerala, Tamil Nadu and Karnataka are the scores of Adivasis, Dalits and landless poor farmers who are subjected to extreme exploitation and oppression.

The Maoists adopt different strategies to woo the Adivasis. During the initial phase when they identified the feudal landlordism as the principal contradiction and annihilation of class enemies as the main strategy, they tried to mobilize

Adivasis through systematic propaganda based on the brutal oppression and exploitation of Adivasis by the landlords, even denying the minimum wages for their subsistence. In the immediate post-Emergency phase, the Maoists and their extension outfits successfully imbibed many of the cultural symbols, myths, customs and traditions of Adivasis in the street plays and other art-forms in order to glorify their struggles to emancipate Adivasis and other weaker sections from the clutches of feudal landlords. When the Adivasi land alienation had created big bangs in the State during 1990s, the different Maoist groups tried to hijack the issue by propagating that the mainstream parties and the successive governments in the State were never sincere in safeguarding the interests of Adivasis. The pro-Maoist outfit 'Porattom' could sensationalize the issue, by taking Palakkad District Collector as hostage in 1996.

The emergence of the indigenous Adivasi organizations like the Adivasi Gothra Maha Sabha (AGMS) to the centre stage of Adivasi land issues through their protracted struggles had considerably blunted the moves of Maoists to make inroads into the Adivasi community. Such bodies were successful in creating awareness among Adivasis on the futility of depending upon political parties or Maoists in safeguarding their cultural identity or genuine interests. The Maoists, as a tactical move extended their full support to various land struggles such as the historic Muthanga struggle in 2003, undertaken by Adivasi outfits. Once these apolitical Adivasi organizations have been tactically absorbed by mainstream political parties by accommodating their prominent leaders in their parties, the Maoists have initiated renewed efforts to occupy major space among the Adivasis especially in the tri-junction areas. Issues such as legal and illegal quarrying and mining, Resort expansion in forest areas, unemployment, agrarian crisis and excesses against Adivasis by forest and police personnel etc, have been exploited by them to woo the Adivasis.

The Maoist strategy, to certain extent, has been appealing to some sections of Adivasis in view of the prevailing socio-economic milieu in the Adivasi belt. Higher gap exists between the Adivasi and non-Adivasi population in various socio-economic and developmental indicators such as possession of land, accessibility to basic amenities like safe drinking water, electricity, health and educational facilities, road communication network, Public Distribution System etc. However, the Adivasi land alienation and the undue delay in the restoration of alienated land and its redistribution among the Adivasis was the most potential issue that has been exploited by Maoists to their advantage.

The land reforms in Kerala which were started as early as in 1957 by the first Communist government in the State were unique in many respects. But, the Adivasis were not much benefited out of these reforms. While the large majority of the tenants belonging to intermediary communities and castes obtained the ownership right of land, the bulk of Adivasis who toiled in these lands for decades continued to remain as tillers or farm workers. The new landowning class eager to expand their land-holdings adopted legal and illegal means to procure agriculture land. The Adivasis became their easy targets. The result was the large scale alienation of Adivasi land. Meanwhile, the powerful plantation lobby illegally occupied Adivasi and forest land with the connivance of the revenue authorities leading to sharp decline of forest and Adivasi lands in many places. Ironically, the successive governments were halfhearted or indifferent in checking the large scale alienation of Adivasi land or the restoration of alienated land from the powerful settlers' lobby. The various legislations enacted by the governments in this regard were sabotaged or kept in cold storage at the instance of this lobby.

Such bottlenecks in protecting the interests of Adivasis have been construed as reflections on the political ethos and approach of main stream political parties. The vote bank politics has cast a shadow over the process of political mobilization of Adivasis as a result of which the mundane idea of bringing them to the national mainstream continues to be distant dream. Clear signals to this effect are visible in the community. The younger elements are distancing themselves from major political parties. This political alienation and the growing trend of mistrust against the political parties have been exploited by Maoists. They highlight that these parties representing the landlord bourgeois – caste-communal interests can never protect the interests of the Adivasis or the marginalized sections. Thus, according to them, the only alternative before them is to mobilize themselves against the political establishment that includes industrial and business groups, leaders from various parties, corporations, dominant religious and caste groups and media etc. On the ground, the Maoists declare support and solidarity with such movements or struggles.

The new Maoist leadership in Kerala is convinced that without the support of Adivasis and the other marginalized sections; they cannot make any impact in the highly politicised Kerala society. They feel that strategies like the annihilation of class enemies or blood-chilling encounters or killings have become redundant as such actions did not suit the political sensibility of Kerala. This was largely due to the changing psyche of the major chunk of Kerala population due to a confluence of socio-economic and political factors. The Gulf bonanza of 1970s and 1980s has created a neo-rich class whose material-oriented outlook and petty-bourgeois sentiments act as strong deterrents against the class or armed struggles. The globalization and liberalization have opened wider horizons to the new generation who have forsaken 'isms' or ideologies, but are guided by epicurean thoughts and ideas full of colourful dreams. Their thoughts, perceptions and concerns on issues relating to environment and ecology, bio-diversity, gender equality, transgender sex, cultural identity of indigenous population etc, are entirely different from the Maoists or the conventional establishments. Attracting such neo-liberalists to the Marxist-Leninist-Maoist ideologies definitely is a herculean task.

Thus, the Maoists have now moved back to the strategic defence stage mainly focusing on Adivasis and Dalits, land and dignity issues, women, pollution and environment and of course the exploitation of natural resources notably the forests. More emphasis is on unarmed propaganda and agitations than organized violence of armed encounters. But, they are equally conscious on the need of cadres maintaining revolutionary fervour necessary for any Maoist outfit committed to the path of armed revolution.

RECOMMENDATIONS

Even though Kerala was once a fertile land for violent Maoist/ Naxal activity in the 1960s and '70s, the State could checkmate the growth of the movement in the following decades. However, any attempt to describe the State as 'post-Naxalite' or 'post-Maoist' would be a misnomer considering the ground level realities and the incipient challenges that we face from such groups. It is now an established fact that the Maoists have been seriously trying to open their operational base in the tri-junction bordering Kerala, Tamil Nadu and Karnataka by exploiting the discontentment and frustration among the sections of Adivasis, Dalits and impoverished workers and peasants. Neither the Kerala Model Development nor the agenda of planned development by the successive governments could ameliorate their problems and grievances.

The encounter killing of Kuppu Devaraj, a senior Maoist leader and Advocate Ajitha a woman cadre from Tamil Nadu in the Nilambur forests in Malappuram district during November 2016 is an indication to the larger designs of the ultras to open a war front in the area mainly with the backing of the indigenous population. Significantly, the Maoists in 1970s and 1980s had successfully worked out such strategy by opening up fronts in the border areas of Odisha-Andhra Pradesh-Madhya Pradesh and Jharkhand-Bihar-Odisha-West Bengal, which subsequently had turned into impregnable fortresses of the Maoists.

On the other hand, organized moves by the State and its agencies to create an impression that the Maoist insurgency has attained mammoth dimensions and the existing law and order architecture or logistics are inadequate to meet the challenge, are equally deplorable. In this regard, we need an introspection as how justifiable is the recent demand by the State to include three districts in Kerala namely Wayanad, Malappuram and Palakkad under the anti-Maoist Security Related Expenditure (SRE) scheme. The nature and gravity of violence perpetrated by the ultras is the sole criterion for inclusion of districts under the above scheme.

The critical question is whether any of the above Kerala districts has witnessed such high intensity violence on the behest of Maoists? The answer, no doubt, is No. Obviously there is increasing demand for the inclusion of more and more districts as Maoist-affected anticipating liberal funding from the Centre. That is why some ex-Maoists described the State's move as a ploy to get more funds from the Central Government in the name of hunting Maoists. In fact, the SRE scheme is mainly meant for the training and operational needs of the police and security forces and not for the development or the welfare of the people in the affected areas. But the ground level reality is that funds are required for the all-round development and welfare of the marginalized sections of those districts prone to Maoist influence.

1. The State and its agencies need to develop better understanding of the problem in order to formulate right strategies and policies to combat the Maoist threat. There is no consensus among the mainstream parties or the policy makers on the exact nature of the movement or the strategy in tackling the challenge. Some sections interpret the Maoist threat as a serious law and order or internal security issue that should be strongly dealt with by using extreme measures, whereas others consider it a socio-economic political movement that should be tackled with a more holistic and humanitarian approach focusing on development, poverty eradication and better governance.
2. Ironically, much dichotomy exists in such matters in the case of the Communist Parties which like the Maoists were initially moulded in the ideological framework of Marxism and Leninism. For example, the CPI(M) and CPI – the two key partners of the ruling Left Democratic Front (LDF) in Kerala were at loggerheads on the issue of killing of Kuppu Devaraj and Advocate Ajitha in Nilambur Forests during the police operations against the ultras in November 2016. The CPI leadership which openly describes the Maoist insurgency as socio-political movement is adamant against encounter killing or police excesses against the Maoists, whereas the stand of CPI(M) is that police cannot remain as silent spectators during

the organized depredations by banned outfits like Maoists which are trying to wage war against the State, jeopardizing the safety and security of the citizens.

3. The ground level reality that the large areas of the State and the major chunk of the population are 'Maoist-free' should not be ignored when the State formulates its anti-Maoist strategy. Thus, instead of focusing on enemy centric measures such as reinforced police-security apparatus and logistics, the emphasis should be on people centric projects and programmes like planned development, better governance, public perception management and protection of rights and privileges of the indigenous communities especially those sections vulnerable to Maoist ideology or influence.

4. The State should make all round efforts to wean away the vulnerable sections such as Adivasis, Dalits and the marginalized especially of the tri-junction bordering Kerala, Tamil Nadu and Karnataka from the influence of the Maoists. There should be a sincere introspection from the part of the State and its agencies as why the Adivasis, Dalits and other peripheral communities are discriminated and excluded from the development paradigm? That is mainly because of the weakness of the State machinery.

5. The weakness in the norms of administration and governance should be overcome with stringent corrective mechanisms mainly at the behest of the political executives. The first and foremost task is to demolish the illegal nexus of bureaucrats, political intermediaries and the middlemen who are instrumental for siphoning off the lion's share of the funds earmarked for a variety of welfare and developmental schemes of the Adivasis, Dalits and the under-privileged. To deal

with such aberrations and malpractices, mechanisms like the augmentation of Vigilance set up in such areas/ fields, social auditing of local projects and formation of watch dog committees comprising persons of known integrity and reputation etc, should be explored.

6. Among the various socio-economic problems of the Adivasis and the Dalits that are being exploited by the Maoists, restoration of alienated Adivasi land and proper resettlement and rehabilitation of Adivasis assume paramount importance. The State should demonstrate more political will and sincerity in overcoming the hurdles and resolving the issues to the satisfaction of the Adivasis so that Maoists and other radical groups will not get any opportunity to exploit the same to their advantage.
7. Mere resettlement or rehabilitation of Adivasis by restoring their land rights in areas alien to their traditional way of life or culture will not suffice. This should be followed by effective schemes for better education and skills development that would facilitate the rehabilitated indigenous people to explore labour in secondary or tertiary sectors. Such a duel economy model alone will help the Adivasis and other marginalized sections to come out of the vicious circle of poverty, indebtedness and social isolation.
8. As the Maoists do not uphold constitution and their long term strategy is to establish power through armed struggle, the State has every right to exercise its power and resources against the Maoists. But, that should be in accordance with the constitutional and legal provisions. The Encounter or extra-judicial killings, 'witch-hunting' of people who are Human Rights activists, intellectuals, lawyers etc, in the name of anti-

Maoist operations, should be avoided. In the recent past when such untoward incidents took place in Kerala, the civil society has raised a stink casting aspersions on the manner the State Government and the police deal with the 'Maoist issue'. The militarization of the Adivasi areas in the State will further alienate Adivasis from mainstream society, much to the advantage of Maoists to exploit them. On the other hand, the emphasis should be more on winning the confidence of the local population.

9. As rightly pointed out by Richard Clutterbuck*, the marriage between an un-corrupt police force and an alert and co-operative public is the healthiest guard against terrorism. Thus, the police or specialized wings such as the Thunderbolts engaged in anti-Maoist operations in Kerala, instead of terrorizing the Adivasis and the local population should strive to establish cordial relations with them. Perhaps, the best example, in this regard was the success of 'Greyhounds' – the Special Task Force of Andhra Police in their anti-Maoist operations in Andhra. They could penetrate into the dreaded Maoist outfit and target a number of prominent leaders of the movement with the help of a network of informers, built up through a process of assimilation with the local population and utilizing the potential of the surrendered cadres and supporters.

10. The reality that the Maoism has strong ideological base that promises an egalitarian society free of exploitation and oppression should not be ignored, while we work out strategies to counter the threat. This ideology is like

---

* Richard Clutterbuck (1917-1998) was a pioneer in the study of political violence especially terrorism and its impact in society. In his lifetime he was both a professional soldier and Academic.

opium for the exploited and the under-privileged sections like Adivasis who weave colourful dreams and aspirations on its dangerous halo. Ill-informed people are more vulnerable to Maoist ideology and propaganda. Creation of awareness and better education are the answers to overcome the challenge. Thus, educational curriculum and Schooling methods need to be improved by integration of Adivasi values and infrastructure development.

11. The State should ensure dignity and natural justice to the vulnerable sections like Adivasis and Dalits. The effective implementation of various protective legislations such as Protection of Civil Rights, Scheduled Caste and Scheduled Tribe (Prevention of Atrocities) Act, Panchayats (Extension of Scheduled Areas) Act (PESA), 1996; The Scheduled Tribes and other Traditional Forest Dwellers Act, 2006 and the National Rehabilitation and Resettlement Policy and so on will help to contain the social humiliation, indignity and injustice that the Adivasis, Dalits and the rural poor are subjected to. The government should properly monitor the concerned agencies so that these legislations would be implemented in letter and spirit without yielding to the coercive or pressure tactics by extraneous forces.

12. Revamping of the administrative set up in Adivasi blocks and Panchayats with sizeable Adivasi-Dalit population and effective decentralization to ensure the constructive participation of three tier Panchayat bodies in the planning and execution of development projects. The functioning of certain departments such as Tribal Welfare, Health, Sanitation, Water Supply, Forest, Rural development, Public distribution,

Irrigation and education should be streamlined with an effective mechanism to regularly monitor and evaluate their performance.

13. The cynical approach of civil society and their representative bodies, towards Adivasis or their issues needs to be rectified. While striving to safeguard the indigenous identity of Adivasis, they should also try to bring these sections close to national mainstream. Very often marginalization of these communities and the resultant discontentment and distress among these sections has been exploited by Maoists and other militant groups.

Annexure 1

Special Questionnaire for Survey

Questions	S/A	A	N/O	D	S/D
	(1)	(2)	(3)	(4)	(5)

1. Do the Adivasis strongly support Maoists?
2. Do the Maoists enjoy as much support among the Adivasis as in 1970s?
3. Do the Maoists have influence in the district?
4. Do you believe that Maoists are keen to take up the cause of Adivasis?
5. Do you believe that the land reforms helped to check Maoist influence among the Adivasis?
6. Do you believe the government health schemes for the Adivasis are effective?
7. Do you agree that drinking water facilities for the Adivasis are adequate?
8. Do you believe that the poverty among Adivasis due to lapses in PDS help Maoists to get their support?
9. Do you believe that educational facilities for the Adivasis are adequate?
10. Do you believe that road and transport facilities for the Adivasis are adequate?

11. Do you believe that behaviour of forest officials breeds resentment among Adivasis in the district?
12. Do you believe the Adivasi organizations are effective in checking Maoist infiuence among Adivasis?
13. Do you believe that Adivasi Gothra Maha Sabha (AGMS) of CK Janu is successful in mobilizing the Adivasis?
14. Do you believe the local activities of political parties help to check the influence of Maoists among the Adivasis?
15. Do you believe that Tribal NGOs help to check the influence of Maoists among Adivasis?

Name (optional), Age, Sex, Education, Occupation, Community

Open question: What are your suggestions to check the influence of Maoists among Adivasis?

(S/A – Strongly Agree; A – Agree; N/O – No Opinion; D – Disagree and S/D – Strongly Disagree.)

Annexure 2

Personal Interview of Ex-Maoists, Civil Rights Activists and Adivasi Leaders

(i) K VENU – IDEOLOGUE OF MAOIST MOVEMENT

K Venu, one of the pioneers of Maoist movement in Kerala is a prominent social thinker and political critic who interpret society and politics on the large canvass of science and philosophy. While doing research in Zoology during 1960s, he stepped into the world of Communism and soon became a protagonist of Communist Party of India (Marxist-Leninist). As the founder and editor of *Maoist* magazine, he effectively disseminated the ideology of the party attracting progressive intellectuals, writers, middle class intelligentsia and students to the Maoist (Naxalite) movement. While playing active role as an ideologue and think-tank of the party, he was arrested and jailed for around 4 years.

On his release, he played a key role in the regrouping efforts of the party that ultimately landed him in the jail in the aftermath of the National Emergency (1975-77). While in jail, he scripted two works *The Perspective on Indian Revolution* and *The Philosophical Problems of Revolution* which highlighted the Indian situation and ideological issues connected with armed revolution, while analysing the philosophical foundations of Marxism and its development into Maoism and Cultural

Revolution. His other works included: *Universe and Man* (1970), *Realization of Freedom* (1984), *An Introduction to Kerala Studies* (1987); *The Concept of Democracy by a Communist* (1992); *Rethinking by a Democrat* (2003) and *Indian Democracy – Problems and Possibilities* (2010).

Through his book *The Concept of Democracy by a Communist*, he ventilated the internal contradictions and ideological differences within Marxism and Maoist movement. Explaining the deficiency of the Marxist concept of society, he argued that a Communist party can never be a democratic party. On the other hand, different practices of Communist idea ultimately ended up in some form of party dictatorship denying individual freedom or a broader form of civil society. Moreover, he held that Communist dictatorships were historically retrograde developments as compared with parliamentary democracy.

His theoretical concepts and ideological deviations intensified the schism and polemics in the Maoist movement which finally led to his resignation from the All India Secretary post. Later he joined the dissident Communist party led by veteran Communist leader Ms KR Gouri and unsuccessfully contested to Kerala Legislative Assembly in 1996. Venu who is now in the forefront of various social movements regularly contributes articles and commentaries to vernacular dailies and periodicals, on various contemporary issues).

What attracted you to Maoist ideology and how you emerged as one of the pioneer leaders of CPI-ML movement in Kerala?

In fact, I inherited the legacy of Left ideology from my family which had strong pro-Left proclivities. While I was a research student, I, with a scientific bent of mind, took interest in contributing articles on various socio-political issues, to vernacular publications. Through such literary pursuits, I came into contact with late P Govinda Pillai, CPM leader who was then attached to their party publication (*Deshabhimani*).

Though Pillai suggested to me to join their Publication wing, I was keener to complete the research.

Meanwhile, West Bengal witnessed the first spark of the Naxalite movement; a lot of literature on their ideology and strategy had come up. Initially reading such literature, I was attracted to their revolutionary ideas much different from that of established Communist parties in the country. Inspired by these ideas and literature, I ventured a publication namely *Maoist* upholding Naxalite ideology and its relevance in Indian scenario. A lot of intellectuals, progressive writers and students who evinced interest on this publication contacted me.

Frankly speaking, I had no intention to join the movement, but to continue the dissemination of revolutionary ideas to more and more sections through *Maoist* and other publications. But what changed my mind was the killing of Anikkad Varghese, popularly known as 'Naxal Varghese' by police in the forests of Wayanad district, Kerala during 1970, after Naxalite-inspired actions in the State. With strong sympathies with Varghese and other Maoist comrades in the State, I started another publication *Inquilab* which soon became the vanguard of the revolutionary movement in Kerala. I came into contact with a number of early Maoist leaders like Ambady Sankarankutty, Kunnikkal Narayanan etc, who suggested me to use my local address for communication/contact with pioneer Naxalite leaders including Charu.

With the increased contacts with pioneer Naxalite leaders, a section of cadres from Northern Kerala suggested to me to personally meet Charu Majumdar in Calcutta and seek his instructions to streamline the activities of the Maoists in Kerala. I was also keen to meet Majumdar who was then in underground.

The meeting with Majumdar was really adventurous; for the first time I came to know about the functioning of the underground apparatus of the party with a network of contacts, link men and bodyguards who ensured fool proof protection to their senior Maoist leaders in UG. I still remember that after reaching Calcutta, at least four persons contacted me at different locations before taking me to Majumdar's well-secured hideout.

During meeting with Majumdar, the situation in Kerala was discussed with particular reference to the existence of different Maoist groups. The main difference at that time was on the question of principal contradiction. Reiterating that feudal landlordism was the main problem that the entire country faced, Majumdar justified the 'annihilation theory' including the killing of landlords as part of the Indian revolution.

On return to Kerala, I enlightened the cadres about Majumdar's commitment to 'annihilation theory' and the directions for Kerala. But the differences continued on this strategy. Meanwhile, a section of cadres inspired by Naxalite actions elsewhere in the country liquidated a couple of landlords. They carried out such actions without proper planning. Basically, feudal-landlord exploitation in the State was not as much acute or intense as in Naxalbari or Srikakulam. The early Maoists in the State could not take up any serious socio-economic issues of the Adivasis or the landless poor as their counterparts done in other States. For example apart from land related issues, the Maoists in Dandakaranya region organized a series of struggles to end the naked exploitation of Adivasis engaged in Tendu leaf collection. Such strategies helped Maoists to make inroads among these sections. But, in Kerala the Adivasis who were in the forefront of the early phase of the movement were neither indoctrinated on Marxist-Leninist ideology nor imparted the basic lessons of 'guerrilla warfare'. Thus, they could not withstand the strong police action.

Meanwhile, the police smelt about my Calcutta visit and my participation in a couple of meetings organized by local units. That was enough for police to arrest me. I spent about 4 years in jail; much of the time I spent in studying Marxism, Leninism and Maoism which gave me more insight on Maoist ideology and its contemporary relevance in the Indian situation. Accordingly, we prepared a detailed document which was sent from jail to the cadres seeking their views on rebuilding the movement. When I was released from jail in 1975, party committees were formed at various levels. I was elevated as the Secretary of CPI-ML.

The declaration of National Emergency in 1975 was a serious challenge when the State imposed all restrictions on individual freedom and expression. Even genuine cultural and literary activities were banned under one pretext or other. As a revolutionary movement, we decided to challenge the authoritarian powers of the State; the Police Stations representing the State power were attacked and landlords and class enemies playing second fiddle to the State were eliminated.

As part of this strategy, I led a team of cadres and attacked Kayanna Police Station. Our main aim was to challenge the State power and loot arms from the police. We had no plan to execute any police personnel; but when they used force against us, we retaliated leading to the death of two police personnel. We got only two Rifles during the operation. But what followed was most repressive police action; Rajan, an engineering college student from Calicut who was taken into custody by police in connection with the Police Station attack was killed during cruel police torture. Except the fact that he was associated with progressive art-cultural activities in the college, he had no role in Police Station attack or in the movement.

Why did you become disillusioned with the movement after more than two decades of active association with it?

My second jail term after Kayanna Police Station attack was a turning point in my life. Immediately after the operation, I went underground and evaded police over six months. The police arrested me in the middle of 1976 and I was in the jail for over 3 years. This incarceration gave me enough time to go deep into the philosophical and conceptual elements of Marxism-Leninism, starting from the historical foundation of Hegel's 'dialectical materialism'. My new insights into the whole ideology with deep commitment to Maoist perspective gave me enough confidence to write the book *The Philosophical Problems of Revolution*. At that time, my conviction was that Communism was the highest form of democracy.

However, on further analysis of the Marxist-Leninist movement on the larger canvas of class-caste relations, I developed serious doubts on the Marxist-Leninist-Maoist ideologies working in a democratic society. Serious questions on the 'principal contradiction' in the Indian context also haunted me. Based on my new insights, I published a thesis which was discussed at a meeting of the leaders. A section of the comrades vehemently opposed my thoughts describing them as 'bourgeois-deviations'.

But majority of comrades in Kerala had general consensus on our positions on issues like mass organizations, mass struggles and economic programmes. Drawing lessons from the past struggles, we identified that the main errors in the CPML movement were of developing mass organizations, mass struggles and economic programmes. We argued that armed struggles could be initiated only after uncovering and sharpening contradictions by intervening in ongoing mass and Trade Union struggles and developing them into political struggles. A section of leaders opposed to our position holding that it deviated from

1970 line of Charu Majumdar which categorically asserted that economic or partial struggles should not be a precondition for initiating armed struggle for political power.

Thus, we took initiative for the formation of new outfit, the Central Reorganizing Committee of CPML (CRC-CPML) in 1979. The CRC upheld the proletarian revolutionary line of Charu Majumdar and declared that armed struggle is the main form of struggle and all other forms of struggle should be complimentary to it. The CRC soon became the vanguard of revolutionary movement in Kerala. But ideological differences and strategic issues cropped up in the party. While we reiterated the importance of mass organizations and mass struggles in developing armed struggle, the others especially the Andhra State Committee overemphasized the military aspect. Firmly committed to this approach, the Andhra cadres launched a series of armed attacks that became suicidal leading to the killing and arrest of a large number of comrades.

Another major issue of difference was on CRC's position on parallel political power and its concept on political power. Upholding the new style of militant mass struggle on the slogan "to rebel against injustice is right", the CRC hailed 'people's trial' as rudimentary or embryonic form of parallel political power. Moreover the 'Janakeeya Samskarika Vedi' (JSV/ People's Cultural Forum) floated by pro-CRC elements in Kerala during 1980 was working in the direction of creating a new democratic culture by allying with all new forces of democratic revolution and struggles at various levels. Describing CRC's position on 'public trial' as erroneous, the opponents maintained that such actions arising out of the momentarily organized will of the masses on some partial issues and not protected by any revolutionary armed force were total negation of Mao's well established concepts on liberation of base areas and seizure of political power. The proponents of this line pushed ahead the military line; Madathil Mathai, a non-Tribal settler at Kenichira in Wayanad district was identified as 'people's enemy' and eliminated during May 1981. The CRC and JSV were plunged into another serious crisis.

The above differences continued in the party till the first All India Conference in 1982. Our document "Towards a New Phase of Spring Thunder" picked up some real errors in Charu Majumdar's positions and CPML's strategy and tactics in counterpoising of mass organizations and mass struggles to guerrilla struggle; lack of agrarian programme and one-sided stress on secret nature of work. We felt that class struggles cannot be developed by merely propagating revolutionary politics; on the contrary higher forms of class struggles need to be built up by actively taking up day to day problems of the people using open, secret and mass activities. It was also felt that the party was not implementing a well thought out and well defined line in the military front. Unless the State machinery is challenged in a very wide scale, simultaneously from many parts, all over the country, it is even impossible to think of building up any liberated zones by resorting to any military line. We came out with another document "To Work Out a Military Line" which was also questioned by the hardliners branding it as contrary to the very concept of Mao's people's war.

Since the early 1980s, the country witnessed a number of armed conflicts by nationalist forces and organized moves by the State to suppress them by using military power. We identified the situation as one of neo-colonialism distinct from imperialism and the armed struggles by such groups as class struggles of the neo-colonial era. During the period 1984-87, such struggles in Punjab, Gorkhaland, Kashmir and the North East had attained national dimensions. Thus, the 'nationality question' focusing on the armed struggles by different nationalities vis-a-vis the approach of the party had developed into a major issue. Our stand was that in situation where nationalist forces were already engaged in armed struggles, the party could intervene only by initiating armed struggle of its own. Accordingly, we had decided to initiate armed struggle in Punjab and prepare for such struggles in Kerala and Maharashtra. A party plenum convened in 1985 could not arrive at a general consensus on such strategic issues. We reiterated the line in the Second All India Conference of the party (1987) in which a strong lobby led by KN Ramachandran and others opposed our stand alleging that the party was trying to establish comradeship with secessionist-separatist movements like Khalistan. As both the camps failed to arrive at a compromise, a split was inevitable; those opposing our line formed CPML (Red Flag) in 1988.

All these developments disheartened me; I was convinced that the formation of a united all India revolutionary Communist movement was no more feasible. The emergence of the extremist outfit was a historical process and I could elicit rich ideological experience from that process. The developments in international Communist movement had also considerably influenced me. Since 1984, we were a constituent of Revolutionary International Movement (RIM) along with other revolutionary Communist parties like Revolutionary Communist Party of USA and Partido Comunista Revolucionario of Chile. The collapse of Soviet Union and the student upsurge and massacre at Tiananmen Square, China raised big question in the minds of many who had been committed to revolutionary change and socialism. Genuine doubts came up on the leading role of Communist party and the concept of dictatorship of the proletariat.

I was convinced that in a soc list system, the entire means of production are governed by a few individuals at the top of the hierarchy. So socialization in the absence of a concrete programme for decentralization of political power will prove to be counter-productive, as happened in Soviet Union and many other East European countries. Enlightened by such thoughts, I published a book captioned *The Democratic Perspective of a Communist* in 1991 which thoroughly analysed the Marxism in the backdrop of various socio-economic theories. I felt that parliamentary democracy is comparatively better than the Communist dictatorship which was a retrogressive historical process. With such conviction, I left the movement in 1991.

How far the Maoists could contribute to the resurgence of Adivasis and Dalits by bringing them under the influence of their ideology?

In fact, the Maoist strategy is to hijack the movements/ struggles of Adivasis and Dalits and effectively use them as protective shields in their confrontation with the State and its superstructures. In that process, they vigorously take up their issues such as denial of land/tenancy rights, minimum wages and various shades of oppression and exploitation. What is now happening in States like Odisha, Chhattisgarh, and Jharkhand and so on is the repetition of the same strategy in which Maoists are claimed to have leading heroic struggles to protect '*Jal*, *Jameen* and *Jungle*' (Water, Land and Forests), closely intertwined with the very existence of Tribals. In many areas, the Maoist-extension outfits or cultural forums consciously project their indigenous culture and customs using specific cultural themes and symbols giving an impetus to the Maoist movement. Jana Natya Mandali of Andhra Pradesh and Janakeeya Samskarika Vedi (JSV) of Kerala were two clear examples.

The Maoists, in many respects, have inherited the ideological legacy of Communists while dealing with Tribals and Dalits. Dominated by the Marxist-Leninist ideologies of class-struggles, the Communist parties in India had never accepted the reality of caste in their policies and programmes. They failed to understand that the synthesis of Marxism and Ambedkarism is the only hope of the tearing millions of Indians. The intricate caste-class dynamics of the Indian society and the social inequalities and exploitation of the low castes as brought out by many social reformers like Jyoti Rao Phule (Maharashtra) as early as the 19th century found that such a synergy might have helped to smash the oppressive structure of caste system. For many decades, mainstream Communist parties treated Dalits and Adivasis purely on class lines denigrating their caste/community identity as a result of which their genuine issues could not be properly dealt with; nor the party could permanently win their confidence.

Even Maoists are not an exception to this trend. For example, though the Maoist Communist Centre (MCC) in Bihar was built up on caste lines by rallying Dalits and the marginalized to counter the onslaught of the 'private armies' floated by the Upper castes, leadership always gave it (MCC) class-orientation. Many pioneer Maoist leaders left the movement protesting against approach. For example, KG Sathyamurthy of Andhra Pradesh who was the General Secretary of People's War Group (PWG) for many years joined Bahujan Samaj Party (BSP) on his conviction that radical Ambedkarism, just like Maoism has much relevance in the Indian polity. In short, Dalits and Tribals in many areas have lost faith over Maoists and are keen to float their own outfits.

Do you think that the socio-economic disparities, developmental aberrations and the widening gulf between the rich and the poor are the main reasons for the rise of Maoism?

Certainly, these factors contribute much to the growth of Maoism. If we analyse the spread of Maoism, we can see that Maoists could build up their influence in backward and under-developed areas. As ours is an agrarian-based economy, the land and land related activities play a decisive role in the socio-economic advancement of the large majority of people and their overall development. Wherever land resources were effectively distributed and properly harnessed for the larger interests of masses, the socio-economic disparities have drastically come down. That is why it is well argued that wherever land reforms have taken place, there are no major Maoist activities. Unfortunately, except a few States like Kerala and West Bengal, the land reforms could not be effectively implemented for many decades. The Maoists, from the very beginning could exploit such issues to their advantage. Thus, the ideologues in CPML in late 1960s identified landlordism versus masses as the main problem that the country had faced at that time. Their strategy was that the landlordism which is the main basis of imperialism/capitalism should be smashed. Thus, the party meticulously followed the strategy of the 'annihilation of landlords' which could initially create favourable response from the oppressed tenants and landless poor.

The land related issues have now attained new dimensions after emergence of market economy and the rise of corporate power. Many battle-fronts have been now opened in States like West Bengal, Chhattisgarh, Odisha, Jharkhand and Maharashtra between Corporate giants and indigenous people on the issue of land acquisition for major industries. In many instances, the Maoists are playing a proxy war instead of declaring an open war against the Corporate Mining lobby or the neo-colonial development policies of the governments. It is high time that the government should formulate judicious policies to thwart such moves by Maoists. No doubt, genuine developmental needs should not be stalled in the name of the constitutionally sanctioned special rights/privileges to those communities. At the same time, they should not be at the cost of their right to live with dignity. Basically, their traditional right over such land used for such projects should be acknowledged and compensated through special incentives or facilities, granted by the governments or the MNCs.

In your opinion what steps need to be taken to tackle the increasing Maoist threat?

The Maoist challenge should be fought with both ideologically and practically. The reality that Maoism has strong ideological foundation that upholds an egalitarian society free of exploitation and oppression should not be buried under the carpet. The sections of intellectuals and the youth who visualize such a society and empathize with the marginalized and the under privileged are easily attracted to the movement. Hence the first and foremost task is that ideology should be theoretically and ideologically smashed and those cadres have to be reorganized and rehabilitated on the strong democratic structure.

The second aspect is socio-economic development. The question is why the development process is not spreading to all the areas and different sections? Why the Tribals, Dalits and other peripheral communities are discriminated and excluded from the development paradigm? That is mainly because of the weakness of the State machinery. That weakness in the norms of administration and governance should be overcome with stringent corrective mechanisms mainly at the behest of the political executive.

Thirdly, as the Maoists are revolting against the State, there is every justification for the State to use its power against the Maoists. The only thing is that the power should be used lawfully and properly. For example, Maoist movement was almost wiped out from Andhra Pradesh through modern democratic transformation and the work of the State machinery. On the other hand, new States like Jharkhand,

Chhattisgarh, etc, have no such strong State apparatus to effectively operate in the most backward and under developed areas which are the citadels of Maoists.

The role of civil society is equally important especially when the august democratic institutions in the country are subjected to serious stress and strains due to corruption, mal-governance and political expediency. The four main pillars of democracy namely Legislature, Executive, Judiciary and the media which have the solemn duty of safeguarding the system are in the midst of serious controversies as a result of incompetence and partisan interests. The Maoists and other radical groups are engaged in conscious efforts to undermine such institutions through orchestrated campaign and propaganda. The viable solution to overcome the degeneration of those 'four estates' and counter such challenges from radical groups is the formation of 'Fifth Estate'. The Fifth Estate, as envisaged by us is an apolitical forum, a civil vigilante movement functioning as a guiding or corrective force to strengthen democratic institutions especially by ensuring transparency in the functioning of State establishments from village level, by availing the existing constitutional and legal channels. (Personal interview at his residence during July 2013.)

(ii) Ms AJITHA – FIREBRAND MAOIST CADRE OF YESTERYEARS

K Ajitha – daughter of Kunnikkal Narayanan and Mandakini Narayanan – pioneer Maoist couples of Kerala was indoctrinated to Marxism at the age of 15. Inspired by the Naxalite movement in West Bengal, at the age of 19 she participated in the attack on Pulpally Police Station in 1968, which resulted in the killing of two police personnel. After 9 years of incarceration, she came out of jail in 1977 and parted ways with the Maoist movement and started working for a feminist movement in Kerala by forming an outfit namely:

'Bodhana' (awareness) which soon became defunct. In 1993, she formed another women group 'Anweshi' (searcher) which takes up multiple issues of oppression from gender to indigenous and environment issues. Ajitha/Anweshi has been creating waves in Kerala for the past few years legally fighting many sex scandals/cases in which senior politicians are involved. (Ajitha was interviewed at her residence on the suburbs of Calicut city on July 17, 2013.)

What attracted you to Maoist movement at the prime of your life?

My main source of inspiration was the Naxalbari armed uprisings of late 1960s. Incidentally, both in Bengal and Kerala, CPM led governments were in power at that time. Many cadres in the party were against the political line of CPM towards the movement. The hard-line of Marxist government in West Bengal to crush the movement by using force frustrated many of us. Protesting against such approach, many CPM cadres including my parents joined the early Maoist movement in Kerala. As an activist of the movement, I was entrusted with the task of the translation of the works of Charu Majumdar and others from English to Malayalam and its dissemination among the cadres/supporters.

I was a pre-degree (Plus II) student at that time; more than the studies what attracted me was the new ideology of armed struggle to end the exploitation of the poor sections like Tribals and landless peasants. The condition of Adivasis and tenants was most pathetic at that time; not only that they were deprived of wages but also that they were treated as animals with brutal punishment by the landlords on flimsy grounds.

We had any number of such horrible stories; a two year Adivasi infant was thrown to death for killing a chicken and the infuriated landlord had repeatedly raped the infant's mother working as maid in his house to compensate the death of her infant! An Adivasi youth who pleaded for wages in cash was thrashed and kicked to death; his young wife was forcibly taken from his hut; raped in front of hapless Adivasis and later hanged to death. Fear gripped the Adivasi hamlets; there was none to raise their small finger against the wickedness and atrocities of some landlords.

The immediate reason for the attack on Pulpally Police Station in 1968 was the attempts by the Forest and Pulpally Devaswom authorities to evict over 7,000 farmers settled there for years. The decision of the CPM led government to go ahead with the eviction by using armed police created much tension in the area. The Maoist cadres decided to make use of the situation by resorting to armed violence on Naxalbari lines.

What was your personal experience as the only female member of the first Maoist 'action squad' in Kerala involved in the attack on Police Station?

The Police Stations were our first targets. Two separate action squads were formed – one led by my father Kunnikkal Narayanan to attack Thalassery Police Station in Kannur district and the other under the command of comrade Varghese to target Pulpally Police Station in Wayanad district. Our squad comprised Varghese, Thettamala Krishnankutty, Kurichiyan Kunjiraman, Kisan Thomman and Philip M Prasad, besides local Adivasis who supported us. As per our plan, the first squad was to attack Thalassery Police Station on November 22 and steal the weapons; whereas our squad was to target Pulpally Police Station on November 24 and after the action both the teams were to converge in the jungles of Wayanad district to chalk out future plan of action.

Our squad attacked the Police Station as per the plan; but we could not steal any arms, as police had already shifted weapons anticipating attack. The armed attack left 2 policemen, a wireless operator and a sub inspector dead. On the way, we trespassed into the houses of two notorious landlords; threatened them at gun point; forcibly seized food grains, gold ornaments and the title deeds of Adivasis and tenants and distributed among Adivasis who accompanied us. Then we withdrew to the jungles and waited for the communication from the comrades of first action squad. However, as their 'action' had fizzled out, neither they could contact us nor to reach the pre-determined rendezvous in jungles.

Thus, we decided to move to safe hideouts through jungle routes. For me the most difficult task was to waddle through the shallow waters of river Kabini full of sharp rocks and leeches. With swollen feet, I struggled and moved ahead, sometimes assisted by comrades. For the smooth journey through the jungle, I left my traditional attire of *saree* and switched over to shirt and pants given by male comrades. We slept in deep jungles and ate whatever we got on the way. We had scaled down some steep and unknown mountain-ranges bordering Kerala and Karnataka. Subsequently, I came to know that one such mountain scaled by us had been named as 'Ajitha Mountain' by the Adivasis.

Soon, we came to know that police had been trailing us. Thus we took all precautions to confront the police. Kisan Thomman, who was an expert in making country made bombs and crude detonators was moving ahead with explosives. But tragedy struck him on the way when the carry-bag containing the crude explosive devices sling from the branch of a tree fell down and exploded. From a short distance, we heard the sound of loud explosion which we initially mistook as police firing. Stealthily, we moved ahead and saw Kisan Thomman fully wounded and profusely bleeding was breathing his last. His only plea was to end his ordeal by shooting him dead. He was in such a bad shape that we were unable to move him to a safe hideout. Reluctantly, Varghese asked one of the comrades to shoot him dead. His dead body was cremated in the jungles and continued our journey.

Having failed to establish contacts with the Thalassery Squad, we decided to cross over to Mysore side through the jungle routes. Scaling down steep hillocks and crossing rivers and ravines, we ultimately landed at a small township where we waited for the sole private bus plying in that route. As the vernacular media prominently published our photographs describing us as dacoits, the local people immediately recognized us. The local church alerted the people by continuously ringing the church bell. Soon, the people rounded us; Varghese well aware of the topography of the area swiftly escaped. The police rushed to the spot and took us into their custody.

The police used brutal third-degree methods; the male comrades were the worst victims who were asked to torture me by using a cane. Some sexually perverted police personnel tried to test my 'virginity' by using most abusive language and physical advances. At their instance, I was displayed before the public with minimum clothes. Some such photographs published in the leading vernacular media are still kept in their archives as "the teen age female member of the first Naxalite action squad in Kerala"!

Despite significant strides made by Maoists as early as late 1960s, why the movement fizzled out in many States like Kerala?

In general, the major flaws in strategy and lack of unity in the movement led to its decline in many States. In the case of Kerala, a number of factors unique for the State checked its spread. In fact, the State had witnessed radical social reform movements during 19th and 20th centuries, which helped to minimize social and economic exploitation of the under-privileged. More significant were the reformist welfare policies initiated by the successive governments particularly of the Left since 1957. A number of projects and schemes such as welfare pension for the aged, widows, unemployed, agricultural workers, house or land for the landless etc, had been implemented. These schemes have considerably changed the socio-economic milieu of the State and marginally contributed to the upliftment of downtrodden and exploited sections, the traditional sources of support of the Maoists.

The second and more significant factor was the steady exodus of the youth from Kerala to the Gulf during early 1970s. Not only the educated youth, but semi-literate ones migrated in large numbers to Gulf countries as a result of which the intensity of unemployment problem had come down. The inflow of Gulf money to the State boosted up the domestic economy leading to the marginal improvement in the living conditions of under-privileged sections especially in Northern districts of Kerala where the Naxalites had their main pockets. This led to the emergence of a new class dominated by material interests, more than ideologies.

The political parties played a significant role in containing the growth of the movement. Apprehending erosion in their support base, almost all political parties notably the CPM opposed the movement tooth and nail. The above approach enabled the State to adopt most repressive measures against the movement. Not only the committed cadres but the sympathisers and supporters were hunted by the police throughout the State. Even women and children were not spared. The declaration of National Emergency helped the State to adopt draconian measures to crush the movement. The police took many of the supporters into custody and resorted to inhuman torture. The early Maoists cannot withstand such organised onslaught.

Another factor that adversely affected the movement was the ideological differences within the party. We (I, my father and others) identified imperialism as the principal contradiction which should be demolished through guerrilla warfare systematically built up by the party. On the other hand, another set of comrades, influenced by the ideologies of Charu Majumdar, felt that feudal landlordism is the principal contradiction that should be fought with by vigorously pursuing the line of the annihilation of landlords, branding them as class enemies. While opposing the killing of landlords, we justified the attack on Police Stations interpreting it as part of the guerrilla strategy of attacking the State in pursuance of armed revolution. Such polemics among the cadres demoralized section of comrades who became inactive.

Such ideological differences infested the extension outfits and cultural bodies like Janakeeya Samskareeya Vedi (JSV) which tried to build up the mass base of the movement through mass and cultural activities. For example, some of the campaigns like the 'public trial' of corrupt doctors/government officials evoked mass response in many places in the State. But, the polemics in the movement on the question of mass-based activities (mass line) or typical armed uprisings (military line) ultimately forced the party to abandon such tactics. When such polemics precipitated in the organization, the vociferous advocates of military line went for 'Kenichira action' in which a landlord Madathil Mathai of Wayanad district was eliminated in 1981. With the Kenichira action and the subsequent repressive measures by the police, the movement withered away. In such a scenario, the JSV was dissolved and the cultural activists of the movement took different path.

Though the various splinter groups such as CPML-Red Flag, CPML-Liberation, 'Porattom' etc, made regrouping efforts, they could not make much head way in building up the party. The Porattom having pro-Maoist line has the main following among the Adivasis, Dalits and landless peasants. A couple of their known leaders now operate in underground. Without any major mass base or support from any particular section, they could not create any impact in Kerala society, except the occasional regrouping efforts of Maoists in the inter-State tri-junction of Western Ghats bordering Kerala, Tamil Nadu and Karnataka.

Do you think whether land reforms and related issues are still exploited by Maoists?

As land is inextricably interrelated to the livelihood of majority of rural and backward sections, the Maoists definitely try to exploit land related issues. In Kerala, our initial strategy was to exploit such issues by actively involving in various struggles against the eviction of farmers. Though the First Communist government of 1957 introduced sweeping Land legislations, the actual implementation of those Acts gained momentum after the Maoist actions of late 1960s. Always the Leftists tried to take credit out of these reforms.

I always argued that these reforms should be viewed in two different angles. Firstly, through the abolition of tenancy leading to radical changes in landlord-tenant relations, the feudal landlord culture slowly vanished from Kerala society. That has paved the way for more revolutionary changes. Secondly, the landless Adivasis and Dalits were not much benefited out of these reforms as there was no effective restoration of alienated Tribal land or the redistribution of land among these sections. Instead of the actual tillers getting the ownership right of land, intermediary communities/castes were more benefited out of these reforms. Thus, there was no major socio-economic advancement of Adivasis/Dalits in the society. The main loophole in those Reforms was the exemption of major plantation groups and large land-holdings owned by Religious and educational bodies from the ambit of Land Ceilings. Thus, the large estates of major groups like the Tatas,

Harrison etc, remain untouched even in Tribal dominated areas where Tribals are in struggles for their land. It was in this backdrop that VS Achuthanandan; prominent CPM leader and ex-Chief Minister made an open call for the 'Second Land Reforms', which was misconstrued by his detractors as a 'Maoist inspired slogan'. Keeping apart such political rhetoric and debate, a permanent solution to the land related struggles in the State could be worked out only through radical reforms ensuring redistribution of land to Adivasis, Dalits and other landless sections.

How far the new Social and indigenous Movements act as deterrents against Maoists?

I feel that the growth of social and indigenous movements of the marginalized and under-privileged sections is a major trend throughout the country. The struggles by the Tribals and the rural peasants in States like West Bengal, Odisha, and Chhattisgarh were clear manifestations of this trend. Despite organized efforts, Maoists had only limited success to exploit these movements. Kerala is now passing through a myriad of new movements especially of the marginalized, under-privileged and unorganized sections. Many of these movements focusing on environment/ecology, health hazards/sanitation, drinking water, gender issues etc, are localized and initiated at the instance of civil society activists. After parting ways with the Maoists, I started 'Anweshi' (Searcher) with the main aim to take up women issues especially the exploitation of marginalized women and the apathy of the State/its establishments to do justice to the victims. We resort both legal and open campaigns to fight for the cause of women. However, in many instances, the political parties adopt a negative approach towards such moves by independent women bodies. Ironically even in gender issues, mainstream parties are guided by vote bank politics instead of considering the larger interests of women. We, many ex-Maoists, are engaged in other campaigns and movements highlighting the issues of Adivasis, Dalits and other weaker sections. In fact, such movements, to a great extent, could counter the moves of Maoists to make inroads into Kerala society.

(iii) GRO VASU – TRADE UNION ACTIVIST-TURNED MAOIST

Anyinoor Vasu alias Gro Vasu is one of the pioneer leaders of Naxalite/Maoist movement in Kerala, who along with A Varghese of Wayanad district participated in the first Naxalite action in the State during 1968. Despite police repression and incarceration, he continued in the movement. However, because of his serious ideological differences he left the movement and concentrated in labour unions with Maoist perspective. The agitations against Mavoor Gwalior Rayons Factory in Calicut, noted for the unique combination of labour struggle with environmentalism were ground breaking in the history of such movements in the country. Vasu popularly known as Gro Vasu (after his association with Gwalior Rayons Workers Organization) presently settled in Calicut city is actively involved in various environmental and social issues in Kerala with pro-Maoist orientation. Vasu was interviewed at his one room house, in Calicut in July 2013.

How you were attracted to early Naxalite/Maoist movement in Kerala?

The legacy of Naxalite movement in Kerala can be traced to the Communist parties. We, the pioneer leaders of the movement such as Kunnikkal Narayanan, Ajitha, KPR Gopalan, Philip M Prasad, K Venu, Thettamala Krishnankutty and A Varghese were associated with Communist Party of India (Marxist) or its Kisan, youth or student fronts. Many of us were disillusioned over the various policies and programmes of CPM especially their alliance politics with parties and groups ideologically opposed to Marxist-Leninist ideology. More importantly, the party's total subservience to parliamentary democracy negating the strategy of revolutionary struggles created serious schism in the party. By opposing the political line of CPM, we could effectively mobilize the marginalized and under-privileged especially the landless poor and the Adivasis.

We were in the forefront of various campaigns against the eviction-moves of farmers in our area. When the CPM led government was going ahead with eviction using force, we decided to resist the move by resorting to violence. The oppression and exploitation of Tribals and the landless poor and the helplessness of the political establishment to seriously deal with such issues attracted me to radical movements like Maoism. Taking inspiration from the teachings of Mao that one should gain expertise on war strategy by actually participating in the war, we organised 'Naxalite actions' in Kerala on the same lines of the early Naxalite uprisings in West Bengal. Our targets were a couple of Police Stations and landlords known for their brutality and inhuman treatment of their tenants and daily wage earners. There was no proper tactics or planning in undertaking these actions. Whatever may be the lapses in our operations, they should be interpreted as the first practical expressions of an armed struggle by Maoists in Kerala.

What according to you were the major reasons for the decline of the Maoist movement?

Many of the 'Maoist-watchers' interpret the movement as a basic law and order problem and prescribe a number of solutions to deal with it. I am against such superficial approach. Without closely examining the historical, economic, social and ideological issues closely intertwined with the movement, no realistic assessment on the Maoism could be made. Such an approach is essential while analysing the reasons for the decline of Naxalism in Kerala. Historically, the Kerala society witnessed many social reformist movements which had decisive influence over the social structure and class relations. The first one was the role of Christian churches and Missionary groups which through their pioneer educational and welfare oriented activities paved the way for a social renaissance leading to better awareness on the right and privileges of the Adivasis, Dalits and the under-privileged. Their impact was more in Central Travancore and Southern districts of the State. This resurgence among Dalits and under-privileged influenced other social developments like the Temple Entry Proclamation in 1936 by which the ban over the low castes to enter the temples in Travancore State was abolished.

On the other hand, in Northern Kerala particularly in Malabar, the overwhelming majority of Muslims who were at the lowest strata of the society could improve their social status by virtue of the patronage given to them by the Samorin (local ruler) in his confrontation with the British. Muslims constituted a major chunk of Samorin's army including the legendary fighter Kunjali Marakkar. Moreover, the Moppillah Rebellion of 1921, despite its communal overtures, contributed to the consolidation of Muslims in the region. Such trends were further augmented by the activities of Islamic religious bodies which had wide spread influence among all sections of Muslims including the poor class.

-The social reformers like Sree Narayana Guru, Ayyankali and Captain Palppu etc played a significant role in the social renaissance movement in Kerala particularly in the upliftment of the downtrodden and under-privileged. These factors greatly influenced the social fabric of Kerala society in which the plight of Adivasis, Dalits and other backward sections was not as much acute or miserable as their counterparts in many other States where Maoists could establish strong bases. It is not an exaggeration that around 40% of total poverty and malnutrition deaths in the world are reported from India which can be equated with sub-Saharan countries. Ironically, the Maoist affected States in the North account for the largest number of such maladies.

Another factor that adversely affected the radical movements like Maoism was the large scale migration of youth to Gulf countries. While 1960s was the decade of acute unemployment in Kerala with large number of youths loitering in the streets, 1970s witnessed the steady influx of educated and semi-literate youth to Gulf countries where they could find suitable jobs with better wages. The Gulf 'bonanza' not only lessened the burden of unemployment but also substantially improved the domestic economy and the living conditions of the under-privileged. Many of the frustrated and depressed youths who hoped salvation through movements like Naxalites became more realistic and developed 'petty-bourgeoisie' tendencies. Even the jargons like armed class struggles became an anathema to them. Ironically, this transition was not a temporary phenomenon. The globalization and liberalization which opened a flood gate of neo-capital opportunities for the educated youth and industrial entrepreneurs thoroughly changed the 'psyche' of these sections. Idealism and ideologies have become dead for many of them. They virtually become the robots of Information Technology (IT) and Electronic revolution.

The present Maoist leadership or other radical movements have limitations to overcome these challenges. But, it is equally illogical to think that Maoists as a major armed insurgency movement in India with a long term strategy would cease to operate in Kerala. They would learn lessons from the past mistakes and work out alternative strategies. But I am quite certain that the present Maoist leadership in Kerala is unable to formulate such strategies; or organize the masses under the banner of the party. Definitely, the Zonal Committees or senior Central leaders would be assisting them in this regard.

But, the problem with neo-Maoists is that they are experts in conceptualizing the theories or ideologies of great revolutionaries, but lack practical wisdom in applying them at ground level. This was also one of the major reasons for the decline of the movement in Kerala during 1970s and 1980s when intellectuals from reputed educational institutions or other establishments were at the leadership. Purely guided by the teachings of Mao or other revolutionaries and without analysing the ground realities of the State, they led the movement totally negating the basic canons of armed struggle. Those who opposed such authoritarian trends were unceremoniously ousted from the movement in the name of ideologies. Subsequently, the same leaders after leaving the movement admitted their mistakes for not giving correct direction for the Naxalite movement in Kerala when the party had good mass base. I firmly believe that a revolutionary movement that lost its steam during crucial phase cannot be easily revived by such confessions.

How do you look at land reforms and related issues in the spread of Maoism?

No doubt, Maoists still exploit land related issues to their advantage. Earlier it was on the question of landlordism versus tenancy; now it is between the Tribals/landless poor and the State which acquires their traditional land for the Multinationals. Though the initial struggles of Maoists were against landlordism, they could not do much in exposing the opportunist stand of mainstream parties on the issue. In fact, the land reforms in many States did not help in the process of the distribution of land to the actual cultivators such as Adivasis, Dalits and landless peasants. Because of this drawback, the actual purchasing power of these sections did not improve. This had more devastating effect over Adivasis who lost their ownership over their traditional land-holdings due to the steady influx of settlers; had left with no source of livelihood. The malnutrition and starvation deaths of Adivasis in Tribal-dominated areas of the State were the result of such land deprivation among Tribals. Even now, large areas of Tribal and forest land are illegally occupied by large plantation groups which enjoy the support of political parties. So long as this situation continues, the land related issues in Kerala cannot be resolved. However, the Maoists with weak organizational set up in the State are unable to exploit these issues to their advantage.

Do you think whether the indigenous movements of Adivasis and other groups have the potential to check the spread of Maoism?

Just like the new movements of various sections in the civil society, emergence of indigenous movements of Tribals and Dalits, to a great extent, checked the growth of Maoist movement. But the irony is that many such outfits come under the shadow of the Maoists when their genuine issues were repeatedly ignored or neglected by the State and its agencies. I feel that apathetic attitude of bureaucracy towards those groups is the main reason for such policies.

In the context of Kerala, indigenous Adivasi movements could occupy considerable space in the Tribal community, much to the chagrin of mainstream political parties. The Adivasi Gothra Maha Sabha (AGMS), as the first autonomous body of Adivasis could create considerable awareness among Adivasis through their various campaigns and struggles mainly on the issue of restoration and redistribution of alienated Tribal land among landless Adivasis. However, the ethnic diversity, inter-clan rivalries and differences in socio-economic settings, create major impediments for AGMS to emerge as the sole representative body of the entire community. Despite the active association of many ex-Maoist activists with AGMS, the outfit could successfully resist the attempts of Maoist groups to hijack it during the crucial phase of their land related struggles at 'Muthanga' in Wayanad district. The autonomous line of AGMS in many respects influenced the historic land struggles at Chengara (Pathanamthitta) when the organizers (Sadhu Jana Vimochana Samithi) outrightly rejected the offer by various Maoist groups to participate in the struggle. The urge of indigenous groups to stand on their own feet counterpoises Maoist strategy to make inroads into the community.

(iv) CIVIC CHANDRAN – MAOIST CULTURAL ACTIVIST

Civic Chandran, a noted Malayalam poet of post-modernism and a political activist was actively associated with Maoist movement especially its cultural front since the early 1970s. He was the main organizer of Janakeeya Samskareeya Vedi (JSV) which played a leading role in popularizing the Maoist ideologies through the media of art, culture and literature. Because of ideological differences with Maoist party (Central Reorganizing Committee -- CPML), the outfit was dissolved in late 1980s. He is now in the forefront of various neo-renaissance movements espousing the cause of the neglected and the marginalized sections of the Kerala society. (He was interviewed at his home in July 2013.)

In your opinion, how far the pro-Maoist cultural activities contributed to the growth of Maoist movement?

In many States, Maoists used the cultural front as an effective forum to disseminate the ideology among more and more sections especially the Tribals and Dalits by using their cultural symbols. It was quite successful in Andhra Pradesh where the literary-cultural front functioned as the open face of the movement by ideologically defending the Maoist groups and their activities. Similarly, one of the major post-Emergency trends of the Maoist movement in Kerala was the cultural and literary activities under the banner of Janakeeya Samskareeya Vedi (JSV). Through literary pursuits and street plays, JSV could popularize many of the themes and ideas of the Maoist party especially the landlord-tenant relations and the exploitation by feudalism. Attempts were made to immortalize Comrades like Varghese (killed in police encounter) through street plays and skits in which Adivasis played the key characters.

The elite middle class in Kerala who were usually averse to peoples' art forms have favourably responded to such activities. Thus, the slogans of Maoists could be effectively spread in the Kerala society. JSV's role in many respects was similar to that of Jana Natya Mandali and Gaddar's cultural agenda in Andhra Pradesh. The Vedi effectively played its social reformist role by extending support to party's 'public trial' of corrupt doctors and government officials. But, a conflict always existed on the status of a cultural activist and armed cadre in any revolutionary struggle. Very often, the party ideologically wedded to the concept of armed revolution favoured the latter on the ground that mass or cultural activities are not conducive for armed struggle by Maoist party. Such conflicts forced the organizers to dissolve the JSV.

How far the Adivasis and other weaker sections could be attracted to Maoism?

In fact, the main targets of Maoists were Adivasis and other vulnerable sections who were wooed to the movement by actively taking up their issues. But, the party had limited success in ideologically indoctrinating them as manifest by the experiences in Andhra Pradesh where Tribals deserted them en masse during the late 1990s when the police stepped up operations against Maoists. The situation was not much different in other States where Tribals or Dalits were herded together under the movement through force, coercion or intimidation.

For example, though Adivasis participated in early 'Maoist actions' in Kerala, Maoists failed to organize them on Marxist-Leninist lines. Illiterate and ignorant of the class or social realities, they were attracted to the movement at the instance of pioneer Maoists like Varghese who worked among Adivasis and the poor landless taking up their issues of exploitation by the landlords. With killing of Varghese during police encounter in Thirunelly area of Wayanad district in February 1970, Adivasis of the area were once again left to the mercy of mainstream political parties.

In the neighbouring Kannur district, dissident leaders of Communist Party of India (Marxist) played a leading role in organizing Adivasis, peasants and landless under the movement. Kunnikkal Narayanan and others started the first armed uprising in the area in which Adivasis/Dalits participated. In the subsequent police repression, the movement withered away and the terrorized Adivasis kept away from the movement. The attempts of various Maoist groups to reorganize the Adivasis could not meet with any tangible success mainly due to the emergence of indigenous Adivasi outfits, the mobilization of Adivasis on political lines and the lack of dynamic leaders among the new Maoist outfits.

How do you assess the present Adivasi scenario in Kerala?

Despite a plethora of developmental and welfare programmes exclusively meant for Adivasis, they continue to be the most deprived and neglected social group in Kerala. Numerically as a small group of less than 2% of total population in Kerala, they could not emerge as a significant vote bank in the State politics.

Basically, Adivasi dilemma in Kerala is closely intertwined with land issues. The traditional land-holdings of Adivasis have steadily declined with the influx of settlers from plains that began in late 1970s. The Adivasis were outnumbered by these settlers who enjoyed the political clout. Slowly and steadily, the settlers by using dubious means managed to occupy large bulk of Adivasi land depriving them their basic source of livelihood.

Added to this was the entry of major plantation groups in Tribal belt where Adivasis turned into the cheapest labour. Thus, the traditional way of cultivation of a variety of pulses and grains that were their main sources of food became alien to them. This has opened a vicious circle of maladies such as malnutrition, addiction to liquor, health hazards, and indebtedness and different forms of exploitation. For example, in Wayanad district alone there are around 200 identified unwed mothers whose cases are totally neglected by the law enforcement agencies and the administration.

The successive governments in the State have enacted various legislations for the restoration of Adivasi land; but these acts could not be enforced due to the resistance by the settlers lobby backed by political parties. The protracted struggles by Adivasi Gothra Maha Sabha (AGMS) particularly the 'Muthanga episode' have gradually changed the scenario. The major challenge before the governments is the identification of Tribal land, its restoration and redistribution to the Adivasis.

However, the distribution of small tracts of land to Tribals in areas alien to them would not help to solve the issue. Their sustainability through cultivation in their own land is the main question. At typical example is the Tribal belt of Attapaddi in Palakkad district which has come to lime light due to series of malnutrition deaths of new born Adivasi children. Attapaddi is the only Tribal block in Kerala with a number of government establishments exclusively for the development of Tribals. The

Centre and State Governments have pumped substantial funds for different schemes such as housing, sanitation, drinking water, elementary education, health, self-employment, traditional agriculture etc. The unholy nexus between political intermediaries/contractors and government officials is the biggest impediment that adversely affects the socio-economic upliftment of these sections. The more such government intervention, the greater would be the adversities in Adivasi hamlets.

A unique example is the Attappadi Hill Area Development Society (AHADS) in the Tribal block of Palakkad district. The society was designed by Professor Unnikrishnan in 1996 and made operational in 2000. This 45 US million dollar project with around 85% support from Japan Bank for International Cooperation was aimed at restoring the ecology of the degraded forest and Tribal belt of Attapaddi area and build livelihood security through massive ecology restoration project. The execution of the project was entrusted to Watershed based users' Association; Adivasi hamlet based Developmental Committees and Joint Forest Management Committees with the help of more than 3000 elected representatives, most of them belonging to Adivasi community. The Society could make some contributions in developing the basic infrastructure especially in the areas of housing and drinking water facilities. But its abrupt suspension of operations from the scene has caused more problems for the Adivasis. Moreover, the project failed to provide sustainable resources for the livelihood of Tribals. Thus, by merely providing some basic infrastructure to Tribals will not help to improve their overall development.

One disgusting trend is that Adivasis were never allowed to voice their independent views. Their elected representatives in local self-government bodies are forced to function either as silent spectators or as mere dummies of powerful lobbies. Thus, practically, the much hailed decentralization of democratic institutions for the active participation of Tribals and the under-privileged sections in decision making process is nothing but a myth. If that being the case of elected Adivasi representatives in an enlightened society like Kerala, one can very well imagine their plight in Local self-governing bodies in many other States where Tribals are treated as untouchables and slaves!

Definitely, the emergence of new Adivasi organizations has helped to improve their awareness. In this connection the role played by CK Janu of Wayanad is most significant. Perhaps, Janu is the first popular Adivasi leader from Kerala who tried to give an autonomous character to the Adivasi movement in the State. The earlier efforts by various political parties were to retain them as traditional vote banks by exploiting their backwardness and ignorance. In organizing the Adivasi Gothra Maha Sabha (AGMS) led by Janu, the erstwhile Maoist leaders like Geethanandan had a decisive role. In fact, AGMS and Janu came to lime light through their struggles for the restoration and redistribution of Adivasi land for the Tribals. Their historic struggle in the capital city of Kerala in 2001 by erecting temporary huts by the agitators was the real demonstration of the mobilization capacity of Janu and other AGMS leaders. The outcome of this struggle was the signing of an agreement with the government for the redistribution of land to the Tribals; which subsequently led to other notable land related struggles in Kerala at Muthanga (Wayanad), Chengara (Pathamanthitta).

(v) Ms CK JANU – VOICE OF ADIVASI MOVEMENT

CK Janu, belonging to Adiya community of Wayanad district has emerged as the undisputed leader of Adivasis in Kerala. Her emergence as a Tribal leader articulating Tribal questions especially the sources of power, land, property rights and self-rule revolutionized the process of Tribal politicization and empowerment. Through various struggles demanding restoration of alienated Tribal land and its redistribution among the Adivasis, Janu attracted international attention. Janu earlier associated with the agricultural workers' front of Communist Party Marxist (CPM) and Geethanandan, who led a Marxist-Leninist faction, are the architects of Adivasi Gothra Maha Sabha (AGMS), the sole mass-based Adivasi movement in Kerala. (Janu was interviewed in her house during June 2013.)

As an Adivasi leader, how do you look at the participation of Adivasis in Maoist movement?

I never think that Adivasis or Tribals *suo motu* join movements like Maoism; on the other hand compelled by circumstances they support such movements. For example, during the early phase of Naxalite movement in Kerala, sections of illiterate and exploited Adivasis especially of Wayanad district participated in Naxalite-inspired activities. But these sections were totally ignorant of the Maoist ideology or strategy. Varghese, the Naxalite leader with Communist background, who participated in the attack on Pulpally Police Station in 1968 tried to organize them on class lines. He won over their support by taking up their issues such as low wages and continued exploitation by landlords. The elder generation still remembers him not as 'Maoist' but as their own 'man'. The growing awareness among Adivasis was mainly due to their political mobilization and the formation of autonomous bodies like AGMS. This has greatly helped to contain the spread of Maoist and radical ideologies among the Adivasis. We, under the banner AGMS intervened on a number of Adivasi issues and tried to create social awakening in the community.

Do you think whether the vexed land related issues of Adivasis have been exploited by Maoists?

The Naxalite/Maoist groups from the very beginning tried to exploit land related issues to build up their pockets of influence. In fact, the early Naxalite actions in the State were engineered focusing on the issue of eviction of farmers in Wayanad district. Later, some groups like Porattom resorted to extensive campaign and propaganda on the issue of Tribal land alienation and apathetic attitude of successive governments in doing justice to Tribals through the restoration and redistribution of alienated Tribal lands among landless Tribals. But the successful struggles launched by AGMS on such issues helped to counter the Maoist strategy. We could also resist the gestures of various Maoist groups extending support to our protracted struggles demanding restoration of alienated Tribal land.

But, the ground reality is that land related issues are still volatile among Adivasis. Though land reforms had made major changes in Kerala society, the benefits for Adivasis were limited. This was due to the exemption of plantations from the provisions of the Land Ceiling Act, which facilitated the landlords and major groups to retain their land-holdings. Further, many plantation groups illegally occupied Tribal and forest land with the connivance of the revenue authorities leading to sharp decline of forest and Tribal lands in many places. Typical examples are the case of Tatas and Harrison Plantations. The Adivasis are now deprived of their traditional land, viable employment, and food or health facilities. Thus, in places like Attapaddi in Palakkad district, there are a number of malnutrition deaths of new born Tribal babies, which is a national shame. The government officials and elected representatives who are constitutionally bound to safeguard the life and safety of all citizens should be charged for the offence of murder for such utter callousness and negligence.

Basically, all these problems are related to Tribal land alienation. The Dalits and other under privileged sections are also victims of such exploitation. A permanent solution to the land related issues in Kerala can be worked out by capturing the illegally occupied land by these groups and redistribute them to the Tribals and the landless people. But, the mainstream political parties are not sincere in taking such drastic measures.

The AGMS is building up campaigns/agitations on the above lines. The 2001 agitation by AGMS in front of Kerala Secretariat by erecting huts occupied by Adivasi agitators was a landmark event in the history of land struggles in Kerala. The subsequent 'Muthanga agitation' (forcible occupation of forest land near Muthanga Wildlife Sanctuary, Wayanad) attracted national attention. Over the years around 25,000 people could be benefited out of AGMS-led land struggles by way of allotment of land or house sites. As the successive governments have not implemented their commitment in respect of the redistribution of land to Adivasis, AGMS continue their struggles and campaigns highlighting these demands.

Do you think that 'Adivasi' or 'indigenous' identity projected by Adivasi movements is a promising means for their liberation?

I strongly feel that the Adivasi issues have started getting some attention from the governments especially after the organized moves by AGMS to project their indigenous identity. From the very beginning, we have distanced from all political parties, as we are convinced that these parties would not work for the larger interests of Adivasis. Moreover, AGMS during initial stages had to face stiff resistance from parties like CPM, as they feared that autonomous Tribal bodies would erode their vote banks among Tribals. These parties adopted different strategies to discredit our movement through slandering campaign attributing our links with Maoists and extremists or foreign agencies. Attempts were made to woo prominent leaders by offering positions in their parties. I was offered a safe Assembly seat from Wayanad district during the 2011 Assembly polls. The NGOs and civil society representatives were motivated to resort to orchestrated campaign that our land related struggles posed serious threat to nature and environment in ecologically fragile areas. Many NGOs, just like political parties adopted a hostile approach towards us giving us clear indication that the civil society is not favourably disposed towards the issues and demands of the under-privileged and marginalized sections.

Though we could overcome these challenges, leadership crisis in Adivasi community is one of the major issues. Unlike other social groups, Adivasis are the most backward and are forced to depend on their daily labour for livelihood. Thus, majority of Adivasis including the educated younger generation are reluctant to engage in community related activities. Our movement also faces this dilemma, as obviously we have no second line leaders. I have fully dedicated to the movement; remained unmarried and worked as a full timer which others are not accustomed to.

Another disgusting aspect is the organized moves of mainstream parties to net in upcoming Adivasi leaders by extending fall promises and offers. Many of them fall in their trap and emerge as strong votaries of those parties and fully ignore the issues/problems of the community. Added to this is the dearth of funds as we do not encourage fund collection from outside sources. Bulk of our funds is mobilized from our own cadres and Adivasi community in general. Thus, our indigenous identity in many respects is both a promise as well as challenge.

(vi) LATE JUSTICE VR KRISHNA IYER (RETIRED) – LEGENDARY PERSONALITY OF JUDICIARY

He spoke out his free and candid views on issues of Tribals and the under-privileged. A humanist, active crusader and ceaseless champion of social justice and Human Rights, he highlighted the loopholes in the implementation of land reforms as major causative factor for increasing Tribal unrest and inter-related issues like growth of Maoism. (This interview was conducted during May 2013.)

In your opinion what attracts Tribals to movements like Maoism?

Tribals from ancient times had certain community rights commonly enjoyed even in forests and jungles. But alas, today, the Tribals are deluded of these jungle rights. They have no homes or places of shelter. They have no means of livelihood because their free spaces are given away on commercial terms to foreign interest. De facto discarded as flotsam and jetsam by the State and de jure proffered jungle slices which do not exist, these Tribal communities have not been a trace of what belonged to them. No wonder that Maoists are expanding their invasionary jurisdiction far from being eliminated. They grow in strength since Tribals do not make corruption as their way of life. The transformation of society into one of classless humanity is a proposal of despair.

How far the land related issues precipitate Tribal unrest that is exploited by Maoists?

The social disease of alienation of Tribal land-holding for years is yet to be cured in many States. In fact, we had seriously initiated various land reforms in Kerala as early as in 1957; yet Tribal land alienation continues to be major issue of concern. In 1975, the Kerala Legislature unanimously enacted the Kerala Scheduled Tribe (Restriction of Transfer of Lands and Restoration of Alienated Land) Act which imposed a complete ban on the transfer of Tribal land to non-Tribals. Had this Act been implemented with social passion, the Tribal land alienation problem should have been resolved. Unfortunately due to political compulsions and obviously to safeguard the interests of non-Tribal settlers in the Tribal land, the Act could not be effectively implemented by the successive governments. Thus Tribal protest against unjust privation appears in one form or other. The Maoist groups trying to hijack such protest declared solidarity with the Tribals and resorted to some sporadic actions such as the detaining of Collector in Palakkad some years ago. The militant mood may explode justly any day, needless of the *lathi*-wielding men in khaki unless the Tribal land question is settled with justice, equity and good conscience weaving a jurisprudence which treats Tribals as humans with title to survival. To recover the lost land from the encroachers, the Government had to implement the law with conviction for the cause, compassion for the powerless.

Apart from Tribal unrest and land related issues, what are the other major issues exploited by Maoists?

No doubt, it is corruption. If there is one word which universally vitiates the three State instrumentalities namely, the Executive, the Legislative and the Judicative, it is corruption. Everywhere there is corruption. Corporations which are new instruments of administration suffer from this vice. It is so omnipresent that even the judiciary which commands high esteem from the people no longer resists corruption. Even the judges of the Supreme Court these days are suspect. I have been told by several friends there is no hope for corruption free administration. That is why movements like Maoism or Naxalite instrument gaining ground in many areas.

As a man of Judiciary with great innings, how you look at these issues?

Fundamental Rights no longer inspire many people because the judicial remedy namely litigation is itself expensive and takes more than a life time to get justice in its finality. Violence makes peaceful life under the law or a stable society without criminality a difficult proposition. But disillusionment about corruption in the present system of Government is diehard. Even elections and universal votes have become expensive and beyond the reach of the common man. But the administrative machinery is beyond political parties. They are organized through corrupt means to control the governance of the country. What Anatole France in a cynical poem once quoted holds good in our current system:

> The law locks up the man or woman
> Who steals the goose from off the common?
> But leave the greater villain loose
> Who steals the common from off the goose?

What are your suggestions to overcome the present challenges in the polity and system?

Change this system we must if truth and peace are to be an asset of governance and the poor are to claim the fundamental right to live in dignity as a constitutional demand. Who governs this country politically and economically? – the Cabinet. Parties which command a majority in the House of the Legislature form the Cabinets. How are Cabinets composed? By political parties which have a majority of legislators to vote with them. How do legislators secure a seat in the House? Through elections often manipulated by huge expenditure. In short, the poor who are in a majority in the nation are voiceless in practice since franchise of the little man is purchased by the purse of the rich. That is how the rich Houses make the law and Law India becomes Swaraj of the haves and the have-nots are alien to the Establishment. We won Swaraj from the British Empire with great expectations but expectations darkened into anxiety, anxiety into dread and dread into despair. Sincere reforms at various levels – Executive, Legislature and Judiciary – are the only solution to overcome these challenges.

(vii) JACOB LAZER – PUCL, KERALA

Jacob Lazer, a pro-Left activist, is actively associated with various labour, environment, Adivasi and civil liberties movements in Kerala. He is active in the State unit of People's Union for Civil Liberties. As a member of Kerala PUCL team, he visited Nandigram and Singur and conducted first hand study on the mass movement there, particularly the land-related issues of Tribals and rural poor and the involvement of Maoist groups.

As a civil rights activist with pro-left proclivities, how do you assess the present status of Maoist movement?

I firmly believe that inequalities in the society do contribute to the emergence of extremist or violent movements like Maoism. In a country like India where more than 85% of the total population depends on agriculture for their livelihood, the land related issues contribute to such inequalities. In States where the landlords and landed gentry dominated the socio-economic and political set up, the implementation of land reforms was tardy. These forces have considerable sway over all political parties including the Left parties. We have personally experienced this trend during our fact finding mission to Singur in West Bengal in the wake of the protracted struggle by peasants and rural poor against Tata's venture there. The rural poor revealed to us that they had no title deed of the land which they occupied for many decades.

The situation is worse in many States like Jharkhand, Chhattisgarh, and Odisha where the issues like restoration of alienated Tribal land are alive. Added to this, there is large scale displacement of Tribals from their traditional land due to the entry of a number of Multi nationals engaged in mining and industrial ventures in the Tribal belt. Viewed in this backdrop, the land related issues are not as much acute in Kerala as compared with the Central Indian States.

Issues like the restoration of alienated Tribal land continue to exist in some districts of Kerala; the powerful non-Tribal lobby backed by political parties tries to defeat the efforts of successive governments to restore and redistribute the land among Tribals. The indigenous Tribal organizations like Adivasi Gothra Maha Sabha (AGMS) could effectively build up their support base among Tribals by taking up land related issues. Though ex-Maoists like Geethanandan tried to give Maoist orientation to the movement; they maintained their independent identity. Further, the political mobilization of Adivasis, to a great extent has checkmated the moves of Maoists to woo Tribals to their camp.

The Maoists cannot make any significant headway in Kerala society due to a variety of factors. The first and foremost reason is the new 'psyche of Keralites'. An average Keralite has a strong desire to remain happy and contented irrespective of what is happening around him or her. With growing neo-liberal influences and steady growth of market economy, this has become a mass psyche, which is perhaps the major stumbling block for Maoists or other radical groups to organize the youth and middle class on militant or revolutionary lines.

The second and more important factor is the vacuum of leadership. The situation was much different during late 1960s and early 1970s when the initial movement was built up by a set of middle class intellectuals moulded in the organizational furnace of Communist parties and well exposed to the Tribals and the marginalized. The new generation leaders have neither such political exposure nor any rapport with the traditional sections like the marginalized and the under privileged. Their diehard ideologies or mere rhetoric on the neo-colonial policies of the State that work against the interests of the common masses will seldom evoke much response among Tribals or other marginalized sections.

But the hard reality is that the developmental and welfare schemes of the successive governments for the upliftment of these sections failed to achieve the desired results in commensurate with the quantum of funds allocated under various schemes or sub-plans. Why this happened in a State whose model of development has been hailed by eminent economists like Nobel laureate Dr Amartya Sen? The answer is simple. An unholy nexus of petty bureaucrats, political intermediaries and contractors through large-scale irregularities and malpractices have virtually sabotaged these programmes. The mainstream political parties irrespective of their ideologies could not do much in containing the menace. Thus, instances like malnutrition and starvation deaths do occur in Tribal hamlets; steady alienation of Tribal land continue; the number of unwed mothers increases and the exodus of non-Tribals to Tribal areas continue unabated. The Maoists try to exploit such issues interpreting them as the fall out of the neo-colonial policies pursued by the State and its various agencies.

Bibliography

Books

Aiyappan, A, *The Paniyas: An Ex-Slave Tribe of South India*, 1992, Institute of Social Research and Applied Anthropology, Calcutta.

Ball Colin and Dun Leith, *Non-Governmental Organisations – Guidelines for Good Policy and Practice*, 1996, The Commonwealth Foundation, London.

Edward Duyker, *Tribal Guerrillas: The Santals of West Bengal and the Naxalite Movement*, 1987, Oxford University Press, Delhi.

Govinda Chandra Rath (Ed), *Tribal Development in India: The Contemporary Debate*, 2011, Sage Publications, New Delhi.

Jerkins and Klandermans, *The Politics of Social Protest: Comparative Perspective on State and Social Movement*, 1985, Minnesota Press, Minneapolis, USA.

KV Thomas, *Left-Wing Extremism and Human Rights: The Role of Civil Liberties Groups in Andhra Pradesh*, 2014, Sage Publications, New Delhi.

O'Neill Bard, *Insurgency and Terrorism: Inside the Modern Revolutionary Warfare*, 2001, Potomac Books, New York.

Prakash Singh, *The Naxalite Movement in India*, 1995, Rupa Publications, New Delhi.

PK Mohanty, *Encyclopaedia of Scheduled Tribes in India* (5 Volumes), 1977, Gyan Publishing House, Delhi.

PRG Mathur, *Tribal Situation in Kerala*, 2007, Kerala Historical Society, Trivandrum, Kerala.

R Rajeevan, Dr, *Towards Political Empowerment: Political Socialization and Political Participation of Tribal Community in Kerala*, 2010, Kalpaz Publications, New Delhi.

Sumanta Banerjee, *India's Simmering Revolution: The Naxalite Uprising*, 1984, Zed Books Ltd, London.

Tharamangalam, J, *In Kerala: Paradoxes of Public Action and Development*, 2006, Orient Longman, Hyderabad.

Uday Kumar, *Defeating Naxalite: Ways and Means to Defeat Naxalism*, 2012, Lucky International, New Delhi.

VR Raghavan, *The Naxal Threat: Causes, State Responses and Consequence*, 1977, Vij Books India Pvt Ltd, New Delhi.

Articles in Books/Journals/Newspapers

Ahuja, P, "The Fire Within: Naxalite Insurgency Violence in India", 2007.
(www.tandfonline.com/doi/pdf/10.1080/09592310701400861 last accessed on December 15, 2016.)

Anand S, "Understanding the Khairlangi Verdict", *The Hindu*, October 5, 2008.

Anil Boiyini, "Explaining Success and Failure: Counter-Insurgency in Malaya and India", 2010.
(https://calhoun.nps.edu/handle/10945/5038 last accessed August 16, 2015.)

AG Noorani, "Of Stalin, Telangana and Indian Revolution" *Frontline*, Volume 28, Issue 26, December 17-30, 2011.
(www.scribd.com.doc/89059088/communist-memories/A-G.Noorani accessed on January 31, 2016.)

Arunava Narayan Mukherjee, "The Naxalite Movement", in

Samarak Swain (Ed), *Social Issues of India*, 2011, New Vishal Publications, New Delhi, pp 188-92.

Bela Bhatia, "The Naxalite Movement in Central Bihar", *Economic and Political Weekly* (*EPW*), 40(15), April 9-15, 2005.

Binoj Jose, "Peace and Eco-Social Justice: Failed Distributive Justice, Violence and Militancy in India", Public Policy and Administration Research, ISSN 2224-5731 (Paper) ISSN 2225-0972 (Online), Vol 1, No 3, 2011. *Peace and Eco-Social Justice* (www.iiste.org).

Biplab Dasgupta, "The Naxalite: An Epilogue" *Social Scientist*, Volume 6, No 12, July 1978, pp 3-24. (www.istor.org/stable/3516672 accessed on February 12, 2017.)

Cedric Gouverneur, "India's Undeclared War", *Le Monde diplomatique* (December 2007).

Chandran, Deepa, "The Paradox within Paradoxes: Emerging Signs of Change in the Unappealing Tribal Scenario in Kerala", 2012, Centre for the Study of Regional Development, JNU, New Developing Country Studies, ISSN 2224-607X, Vol 2, No 6/2012.

Charu Majumdar, "A Few Words about Guerrilia Actions", *Liberation*, February 1970.

Chattukulam, J and MS John, "Tribal Development: The Recent Experience of Kerala". (shodhganga.inflibnet.ac.in/bitstream/10603/2732/11/11_ introducation.pdf accessed on December 12, 2017.)

Dilip Simeon, "Permanent Spring", *Seminar*, No 607 (March 2010), (www.india.seminar.com).

Edward N Muller and Mitchell A Seligson, "Inequality and Insurgency", *American Political Science Review*, Vol 81, No 2 (June 1987), pp 425-452.

Fearon, JD and Laitin, David "Ethnicity, Insurgency and Civil War", *American Political Science Review*, Vol 97, 2001, pp 91-101.

Gautam Navlakha, "Day and Night in Maoist Heartland", *Economic and Political Weekly* (*EPW*), Vol XIV, No 16, April 2010.

George Mathew, "Dr Amartya Sen and the Kerala Model", *The Hindu*, January 9, 2001. (www.thehindu.com/2001/01/09/stories/05092523.htm last accessed on October 15, 2016.)

George J Kunnath, "Becoming a Naxalite in Rural Bihar: Class Struggle and its Contradictions", *The Journal of Peasant Studies*, 33(1): 89-123, 2004.

John Harris, "What is Going on India's 'Red Corridor'? – Questions about India's Maoist Insurgency", *Pacific Affairs*, Vol 84, No 2 (June 2011), pp 309-327.

Joseph Flavian Gomes, "The Political Economy of Maoist Conflict in India – An Empirical Analysis", Working Paper 12-18, Economic Series, June 2012, Universidad, Carlos III, Madrid, Spain.

Joseph Tharamangalam, "The Perils of Social Development without Economic Growth: The Development Debacle of Kerala, India", *Bulletin of Concerned Asian Scholars*, Vol 30, No 1, 1998, pp 23-34.

Kjosavik Darley and Shanmugharatnam, "Integration or Exclusion? Locating Indigenous Peoples in the Development Process of Kerala, South India", 2004, *Forum for Development Studies*, 31(2), pp 231-274.

Kristian Hoelscher, Jason Miklian and Krishna Chaitanya Vadlamannati, "Hearts and Mines: A District-Level Analysis of the Maoist Conflict in India", *International Area Studies Review*, June 22, 2012, pp 435-449.

Mariamma J Kalathil, "Withering Valli: Alienation, Degradation and Enslavement of Tribal Women in Attapaddy", CDS, Trivandrum, 2004, pp 82-202.

PV Ramana, "The Maoist Movement in India", *Defense and Security Analysis*, 22, No 4, December 2006.

Praveen Swami, "For a Review of Counter-Insurgency Doctrine", *The Hindu*, Opinion page dated April 13, 2010. (http://www.thehindu.com/opinion/lead/For-a-review-of-counter-insurgency doctrine/article16366244.ece last accessed on November 15, 2016.)

Priyanka Vora and Siddhant Buxy, "Marginalization and Violence: The Story of Naxalism in India", *International Journal of Criminal Justice Sciences*, 2011, 6(1-2) pp 358-371.
(www.oalib.com/references/10339654 last accessed on November 23, 2016.)

Ramachandra Guha, "Adivasis, Naxalites and Indian Democracy", *Economic and Political Weekly*, Vol 42, No 32 (August 11-17, 2007), pp 3305-3312.

Sreekumar, TT and Parayil G (2006), "Interrogating Development: New Social Movements, Democracy and Indigenous People's Struggles in Kerala", in J Tharamangalam (Ed), *Kerala: The Paradoxes of Public Action and Development*, Orient Black Swan, New Delhi, pp 56-80.

Sreekumar, TT and Parayil, G (2010), "Social Space, Civil Society and Transformative Politics of New Social Movements in Kerala", in K Ravi Raman (Ed), *Development, Democracy and the State: Critiquing the Kerala Model of Development*, Routledge, New York and London, pp 237-253.

Sreerekha, MS, "The Story behind Kerala's Landless: The Story of Aralam Farm", 2010, *Economic and Political Weekly* (Special Article), 45(21), pp 52-62.

Steur, Luisa, Ms, "Adivasi Mobilisation: 'Identity' versus 'Class' after the Kerala Model of Development", *Journal of South Asian Development*, 4:1(2009), 25-44, Sage Publications, London.

Venkitesh Ramakrishna, "Maoist Connection", *Frontline*, Vol 24, Issue 25, December 22, 2007–January 4, 2008.

VR Krishna Iyer, "Atrocities on Adivasis", *The Hindu* (http://hinduonnet.com dated 16/08/2003).

Walter Fernandez, "Internally Displaced Persons: Challenge to Human Dignity", *Vidyajyoti Journal of Theological Reflection*, 71(1), January 2007, pp 43-51.

Documents/Seminar Papers

Census of India Report, 2011.

"Document on the Programme of the Communist Party of India (Marxist-Leninist)", May 1970.

Government of India, "Development Challenges in Extremist-affected Areas", Report of the Expert Panel to the Planning Commission, 2008.

Government of India, Ministry of Home Affairs, Annual Report 2004-2005 and 2010.

Government of India, Report of the Ministry of Tribal Affairs, 2006.

Government of India, Ministry of Rural Development (MRD), 2006, Report of the Expert Group on the Alienation of Tribal Land and its Restoration, New Delhi.

Government of India, Ministry of Forests and Environment, Forest Survey Report, 2011.

Human Poverty and Socially Disadvantaged Groups in India. (www.undp.org/....intent/dam/India/docs/human_poverty accessed on February 12, 2016.)

"India Human Development Report 2011".

(http://www.im4change.org/docs/340IHDR_Summary.pdf accessed on March 26, 2016.)

Institute of Peace and Conflict Studies Special Report, 25 June 2006, "Left Extremism in India: Naxal Movement in Chhattisgarh and Orissa" by Rajat Kumar Kujur. (http://ipcs.org/pdf_file/issue/576885354IPCS-Special-Report-25.pdf accessed on March 25, 2016.)

Institute for Defence Studies and Analyses, "The Maoist Movement in India" by PV Ramana. https://idsa.in/profile/pvramana last accessed on September 19, 2017.)

IPCS Conference Report, March 2012, "The Naxal Problem: Understanding the Issues, Challenges and Alternative Approaches".

Kerala State Economic Review, 2010-11.

Maoist Documents: Party Programme – South Asia Terrorism Portal. (www.satp.org/satporgtp/countries/india/maoist/documents/papers/partyprogram.html last accessed on October 15, 2016.)

"Maoist Document Strategy and Tactics", Central Committee (P) CPI (Maoist). (www.satp.org.saportop/communist/countries/maoist/documents/papers/strategy.htm accessed on February 20, 2016.)

"Naxalism – The Malady and the Remedy". (www.Dsaert.org/October-2010/141/naxalism-the-malady-and-the remedy-by-en-ram-mohan accessed on February 17, 2016.)

NHRC Annual Report, 2001-02

The Communist Party of India (Marxist): New Programmes", New Delhi, March 2001.

The Imperial Gazetteer of India, 1911.

"The Economic Costs of Naxalite Violence and the Economic Benefits of a Unique Robust Security Response", 2012. (https://aae.wisc.edu/mwiedc/papers/2011/singhal_saurabh.pdf last accessed March 15, 2016.)

World Bank Report, 2015.

Index

Abdul Nasser Madani, 195, 196
Action Groups, 96
'Activist bodies', 68
Activist groups, 67, 68, 143, 149, 151
Activities of
  Central Reorganizing Committee (CRC)-CPML, 157
  Islamic religious bodies, 255
  Maoists, 62
Adibhatla Kailasam, 36
Adijana Sabha (Adivasi Sabha), 132
Adivasi Aikkya Samiti, 155
Adivasi Federation, 155
Adivasi Gothra Maha Sabha (AGMS), 10, 122, 130, 131, 141, 153, 156, 158, 160, 161, 162, 163, 182, 183, 184, 185, 217, 230, 258, 259, 262, 264, 265, 267, 273
  achievements of, 162
  autonomous line of, 182, 259
  death knell of, 164
  detractors of, 164
  formation of, 185
  foundation stone of, 155
  impediments for, 259
  indigenous identity of, 164
  led land struggles, 267
  successful struggles launched by, 266
Adivasi land alienation, 9, 137, 141, 161, 162, 179, 181, 217, 218
Adivasi Land Reforms Committee, 133
Adivasi movement(s), 156, 157, 182, 258, 264
  in Kerala, 265
Adivasi Organizations, 124
Adivasi Sangham, 150, 151
Adivasi support to
  Maoist insurgency, 40, 176, 193
  Maoists, 9
Adivasi Vikasana Pravarthaka Samiti, 155
Adivasi Vimochana Munnani (Adivasi Liberation Front), 94, 155
Adivasi-Dalit land struggles, 96
Adivasis or Tribes, 123-24
'Adjustment politics' between CPI(M) and their political opponents, 192
Ajitha, K, Ms, Advocate, 15, 79, 92,

97, 179, 185, 221, 222, 245, 253
daughter of Kunnikkal Narayanan and Mandakini Narayanan, 244
Firebrand Maoist Cadre of Yesteryears, 244-53
'Ajitha Mountain', 247
Ajit Kumar Singh, 115
AK Saseendran, 190
episode, 190
in the sex scandal, 200
Alienation of Adivasi land, 179, 180, 181, 218
Alienation of land, 109
Alienation of Tribal land, 41, 107, 131, 139, 269, 274
by force, fraud or manipulation, 51
by powerful non-Tribal lobby, 57
All India Babri Masjid Action Committee (AIBAC), 195
All India Coordination Committee of Communist Revolutionaries (AICCCR), 29, 30, 36, 81
All India Coordination Committee of Revolutionaries (AICCR), 29
All India Milli Council, 195
All India Muslim League (AIML), 195
All India Muslim Personal Law Board (AIMPLB), 195
All India Youth Federation (AIYF), 85
All Kerala Tribal Workers' Union (Pathanamthitta), 155
'Alliance politics', 194
Alphons Kannamthanam, ex-IAS officer as Union Minister, 213
Amartya Deb, 122
Amartya Sen, Dr, Nobel Laureate 103, 274
Ambedkarism, 241
Amendment in Indian Forest Act, 57
Amit Shah (National President, BJP), 207
Amulya Sen, 32
Andhra Pradesh Revolutionary Communist Committee (APRCC), 31
Anikkad Varghese, Naxalite/Maoist leader, popularly known as 'Naxal Varghese', 79, 85, 119, 127, 129, 233, 246, 247, 248, 253, 260, 261, 265
killing of, 79, 233, 261
Annihilation of class enemies, 8, 216, 219
strategy of, 30, 80, 161
Annihilation theory, 31, 85, 234
Anti-Lin Biao camp, 32
Anti-Majumdar camp, 32
Anti-Maoist operations, 11, 82, 132, 224, 225
by security forces, 90
Anti-Maoist strategy, 223
Anti-PWG operations, 63, 64
'Anweshi' (Searcher), 252
Anyinoor Vasu alias Gro Vasu, 253
Apolitical movement, 155
Application of Marxism on Chinese conditions, 25
Areas of Maoist conflict, 36
Armed insurgency movement in India, 256
Armed revolution, 220, 231, 250
concept of, 260
for overthrowing the government, 58
Armed revolutionaries, 70
Armed revolutionary movement, 127
'Armed Senas', 44

Armed struggle(s), 24, 25, 26, 27, 34, 77, 78, 83, 86, 92, 128, 186, 193, 220, 236, 237, 238, 239, 257, 260
against national oppressors, 86
by Maoists in Kerala, 254
for political power, 237
new ideology of, 245
of pre-Independence period, 25, 54
opposing the strategy of, 87
strategy of revolutionary, 206
Armed uprising(s), 250, 261
in Naxalbari, 216
Armed violence on Naxalbari lines, 246
Armed warfare, 25
Artificially depressed wages, 46
Arundhati Roy, Ms, Booker Prize winner, 82
Arun Jaitley (Union Finance Minister), 207
Ashit Chatterjee, 30
Atrocities Act, 43
Attappadi, 142, 155, 169, 172
Adivasi related issues in, 134
as the first Tribal Block, 171
ban on cattle rearing in, 173
case of, 10, 173
Tribal regions of, 133
Attappadi Adivasi Sanghatana (Attapadi Adivasi Forum), 132
Attappadi Hill Area Development Society (AHADS), 143, 173, 263
Attappadi Wasteland Comprehensive Environmental Conservation Project, 173
Ayyankali, 104, 255
Ayyankali Pada (Maoist group), 89, 90, 161
Backbone of Maoist uprisings, 36
Backward and under-developed areas, 180, 241
of the country, 35
Balachandran Chullikkad, 129
Bar Licences Bribery case, 187, 197
Bard, 122, 123
Basheer Madala, 153
Below Poverty Line (BPL), 47
Better governance, 6, 11, 222, 223
Bhoodan movement, 56
Bhooparishkarana Samithi (Land Reforms Committee), 131
BJP, 98, 99, 100, 155, 188, 191, 204, 205, 206, 207, 210, 212, 213
BT Ranadive, 26
Building up revolutionary mass bodies of the Adivasis, rural peasants and the under-privileged, 33
Bureau of Police Research and Development (BPR&D), 98, 117

'Carrot and stick policy', 6
'Caste Senas' (private armies), 34
creation of, 40
Census, 2011, 38, 39, 103, 107, 208
Central Bureau of Investigation (CBI), 198
Central Organizing Committee (COC), 32
Central Reorganizing Committee (CRC), 33, 83, 84, 85, 86, 87, 88, 89, 157, 158, 237, 238
dissolution of, 89
of CPML (CRC-CPML), 237
position on 'public trial', 237
Central Reorganizing Committee Communist Party of India Marxist-Leninist (CRC-CPML), 83, 85, 101, 135

Chaitanya Saravanti, 68
Chandra Pulla Reddy, 31
Changing socio-economic scenario, 173
Charu Majumdar, 8, 28, 29, 31, 32, 33, 79, 80, 81, 194, 233, 234, 237, 238
  annihilation theory, 33
  arrest and subsequent death of, 31
  counterpoising of mass struggles and mass organisations to guerrilla struggle, 83
  father of the Maoist movement, 58
  ideologies of, 250
  legacy of, 32
  line of annihilation of class enemies, 78
  proletarian revolutionary line of, 83, 237
  revolutionary line of, 32
    annihilation of class enemies, 216
  slogan of annihilation of class enemies, 79
  strategy for Indian revolution, 31
  strategy of annihilation of class enemies, 29
  tactics of, 32
  translation of the works of, 245
  well-known opposition, 83
  unfurled the flag of revolt, 78
Chattukulam John, 121
Checkmated efforts of Maoists and radicals, 122
Checkmated moves of Maoists to woo the Adivasis, 182
Checkmated moves of Maoists to woo Tribals, 273
Chengara land struggle, 141, 160
Chenna Reddy, Dr, 63
Chinese Communist Party (CCP), 32, 193
Civic Chandran – Maoist Cultural Activist, 15, 129, 182, 185, 259-64
Civil liberties movements in Kerala, 272
Civil society, 7, 11, 24, 46, 67, 69, 129, 163, 225, 258, 268
  activists, 252
  broader form of, 232
  cynical approach of, 227
  movements, 144
  representatives, 267
  role of, 244
Civil supplies corruption, 187
Civil vigilante movement, 244
CK Janu, Ms – Voice of Adivasi Movement, 15, 137, 155, 156, 157, 164, 176, 183, 184, 185, 230, 264-68
Collapse of Soviet Union, 239
Commissioner of Scheduled Castes and Scheduled Tribes, 138
Communist movement, 7, 77, 206
  developments in international, 27, 239
Communist Party Marxist (CPM), 80, 150, 155, 156, 157, 193, 194, 195, 196, 197, 198, 204, 205, 206, 232, 245, 249, 254, 265, 267
  backed independents, 200
  cadres, 245
  conflict with declared economic policies of, 201
  disillusioned over the various policies and programmes of, 253
  dissident leaders of, 261

deviation from its strategy, 194
leaders off the hook, 192
leadership, 207
in Kerala, 199
led government(s), 245, 246, 254
on Shah Bano case, 195
workers killed, 204
Communist Party of China (CPC), 29
Communist Party of India (CPI), 24, 25, 26, 27, 87, 150, 194, 195, 196, 212, 222
formation of pro-Soviet, 27, 77
formation of Soviet-backed, 193
leadership, 222
Communist Party of India (CPI) (Maoist), 35, 41, 59, 63, 66, 94, 97, 101, 123, 186
network of, 63
strategy of, 106
Communist Party of India (Marxist-Leninist), 29, 31, 32, 33, 58, 87, 90, 97, 101, 157, 160, 232, 235, 89, 94, 231, 250
Central Reorganizing Committee, 259
groups, 58
ideologues in, 181, 242
led governments, 54
Maoist Unity Centre, 89
movement, 236
strategy and tactics, 238
Communist Party of India/Marxist (CPI-M), 7, 28, 30, 54, 62, 78, 80, 87, 98, 99, 100, 120, 127, 150, 154, 175, 188, 192, 194, 204, 205, 206, 207, 209, 211, 212, 222, 253
China-supported, 193
conflict, 28
formation of, 27
fortresses of, 206
ideological differences in, 215
leadership, 203
leaders of, 192, 206
led government, 79, 196
led LDF, 210
radical cadres of, 28
rule, 193
to join hands with Congress, 211
violence and jihadi terror, 207
workers, 100
Communist Party of Soviet Union (CPSU), 193
Communist Revolutionary Party, 81
Concept of Mao's people's war, 238
Concept of Democracy by a Communist, The, 232
Conceptual definition of an insurgency, 122
Conducive climate for Maoists and other insurgents, 13
Contain the influence of Maoists among Tribals, 118
Contain the spread of Maoist and radical ideologies, 265
Cottage industries based on natural resources, 152
Counter-Maoist operations by security forces, 36
Counter-Maoist strategy and tactics, 214
Counter-Maoist strategy, 214
CPML (Liberation), 32, 33, 40, 160, 250
CPML-Naxalbari, 89, 101
CPML (Party Unity), 33, 40, 58, 59
formation of, 32
CPML (Rauf), 87
CPML (Red Flag), 160, 239

CPML (Unity Committee), 32
CPML-RF, 88
Cross-border terrorism, 5
Cultural movement, 128
Cultural Revolution, 30, 32, 231

Dakshin Desh, 32
Dalits (Scheduled Castes), 35
Dalits and Adivasis: Traditional Sources of Support of Maoist Movement, 35-45
David D Laitin, 116
DD Nag, 116
Dean Joros, 118
Deepa Chandran, 121, 146
Deepak Aneel Boyini, 118
Democratic revolution, 25, 26, 84, 86, 128, 237
Democratic Youth Federation of India (DYFI), 85, 99
Demolishing Maoists Training camp, 97
Depressed Classes Renaissance Front, 129, 157
Describing the Maoists as true patriots, 64
District Gothra Sabha, 158

E Ahmed, 211
Edward Duyker, 116
Edward N Muller, 116
EK Nayanar, former CPM Chief Minister, 198
Elamaram Kareem, former State Industries Minister, 199
Electronic revolution, 256
Emergence of CPML (People's War), 35
Employment opportunities, 46, 51
Enactment of The Kerala Private Forests (Vesting and assignment) Act, 1967, 169
Environment stabilization, 68
EP Jayarajan, 197, 198, 201, 203
  episode, 198
  self-glorifying music album of, 199
  State Industries and Sports Minister, 197
Errors in the CPML movement, 236
Establish power through armed struggle, 11, 224
ET Mohammed Basheer, 196
Ethnic conflicts and insurgency in the North-East, 5
Ex-Maoist activists, 182, 259
Ex-Maoists or pro-Left intellectuals and activists, 68
Expert Group on Prevention of Alienation of Tribal Land and its Restoration, 43
Exploitation of
  Adivasis, 9, 137, 234
  marginalized women, 252
  low castes, 241
  poor sections, 245
  under-privileged, 248
  Tribals, 108
Exploited by Maoist(s), 116, 121, 138, 168, 174, 179, 180, 218, 219, 224, 227
Extra-judicial killings, 11, 224

Faction-ridden Congress in Kerala, 212
Fall of Lin Biao, 32
Fedayeen-e-Khalq, Marxist-Leninist group, 95
Feminist movement in Kerala, 244
Feudal and semi-feudal forces, 44
Feudalism, 55, 105

Feudal landlordism, 56, 58, 216, 234, 250
  exploitation by, 260
Feudal landlord(s), 7, 42, 217
  culture, 251
  tendencies, 139
Fifth Estate, 244
  formation of, 244
'Filmy dialogues', 200
First ever corruption-related prosecution of a Politburo member of CPM, 198
Forest Conservation Act, 1980, 57
Formation of
  united all India revolutionary Communist movement, 239
  Wayanad Adivasi Swayam Sevak Sangham (WASSS), 150
'Four estates', 244

Gender justice, 68
Genesis and spread of Naxalite/ Maoist movement in Kerala, 78
Geographic isolation, 46
George Kunnath, 116
Girijan Sangham, 36
Girijan Sevak Samiti (Attappadi/ Palakkad), 155
Gopala Rao N, 117
'Greyhounds' – Special Task Force of Andhra Police, 64, 225
Gro Vasu – Trade Union Activist-Turned Maoist, 15, 79, 185, 253-59
Growth of Maoists in States, 62
G Sivarajan, Justice, 191
  Commission's Report, 189
Guerrilla warfare, 25, 33, 37, 40, 80, 90, 123, 186, 234, 250
Gulf bonanza, 219

Hadiya case, 208
Harassment by forest and revenue officials, 59
High Court of Kerala, 82
High intensity of Maoist activities and violence, 38, 40
High Land Development Agency (HILDA), 152
Historical Evolution of Maoist Movement, 24
History of India's Maoist organizations, 114
Human Development Index (HDI), 6, 49, 50
  for non-SC/ST, 50
  wide variation in, 50
Human Poverty Index (HPI), 6, 47, 48
  for Scheduled Castes (SCs) and Scheduled Tribes (STs), 48
Human Rights, 269
  activists, 11, 224
Hussein Randathani, 196

Ice cream parlour
  sex scandal, 192
  sex racket case, 190
Identifying Maoist-affected areas, 23
Ideological foundation of CPM in Kerala, 195
Ideology of the Islamic State, 207
Ignorant of Maoist ideology or strategy, 177, 216, 265
Illegal gratification, 191
Impact of Maoist insurgency on country's economy, 150
Imperial Gazetteer of India (1911), 123
Implementation of
  Kerala Scheduled Tribes (Restriction of Transfer and

Restoration of Alienated Land) Act, 1975, 155
Minimum Wages Act for Beedi workers, 80
Transfer and Restoration of Alienated Land Act, 121, 140
Tribal Rights Act, 161
Improvised Explosive Devices (IEDs), 115
Inder Singh Namdhari, leader of Janata Dal (United) and ex-Speaker of Jharkhand, 66
Indian National Congress (INC), 54, 63, 65, 81, 88, 98, 150, 154, 168, 186, 187, 188, 189, 191, 192, 195, 205, 210, 211, 212
image of, 187
leader(s), 190, 191, 192, 200
AK Antony, 211
K Babu, Minister, 187
K Karunakaran, 82
strategy, 212
Indian National League (INL), 195
Indian Penal Code (IPC), 191
Indian People's Front (IPF), 34
Indian revolution, 234
Indian Union Muslim League (IUML), 98, 99, 187, 190, 192, 190, 192, 194, 196, 205, 211
impregnable fortresses of, 195, 211
vote bank of, 211
Infant Mortality Rate (IMR), 49, 103, 109, 142
Influence of Maoist groups, 37
Information Technology (IT), 256
Inspired by the Russian and Chinese Revolutions, 25
Institute of Conflict Management, 23
Institute of Peace and Conflict Studies (IPCS), 115
Integrated Action Plan (IAP), 24, 69
Inter-State tri-junction, 90, 251
Iran, 95
Iranian students in India, 95
Iron control over villages, 206
IS, 207, 208
controlled areas in Afghanistan, Syria and Iraq, 207
fighting for, 207
links with, 208
strongholds, 208
Islam, 208
converts to, 208
Islamic
fighters, 207
jihadist movements, 95
revolution, 95
terror, 207
terrorism, 95
Islamic State of Iraq and Syria (ISIS), 207
Islamised Communism, 95

J Tharamangalam, 120, 175
Jacob Lazer – PUCL, Kerala, 272-74
Jacob Thomas, IPS, 201, 202
allegations of malpractices/irregularities against, 202
elevation of, 202
James D Fearon, 40, 116
Jan Sangh, 150, 206
Jana Natya Mandali, 129, 240, 260
Jana Raksha Yatra (people's protection march), 207
Janadhipathiya Kerala Congress (Democratic Kerala Congress), 187

Janadhipathya Rashtriya Sabha (JRS), 184
Janakeeya Manushyavakasha Samiti (People's Human Rights Movement), 94
Janakeeya Samskarika Vedi (JSV), 84, 128, 237, 240
  dissolution of, 158
Janandhipathiya Rashtriya Sabha (JRS), 164
Janata Dal, 196
Japan Bank for International Co-operation, 173
Jason Miklian, 119
John Zwaanstra, 201
Jose Binoj, 116
Jose K Mani, MP, 189
Joseph Flavian Gomes, 119
JSV, 86, 238, 250, 260
  activists, 128
Jungle warfare, 91, 214
Jyoti Rao Phule, 241

Kanhai Chatterjee, 32
Kannan Devan Hills (Resumption of Lands) Act, 209
Kanu Sanyal, 28, 29, 80, 87, 194
Kenichira action, 86, 250
  aftermath of, 130
Kerala Communist Party (KCP), 89
Kerala Congress (KC), 187, 189, 195, 200, 213
  led by KM Mani, 211
Kerala Conservation of Paddy Field and Wetland Act, 187
Kerala Institute of Local Administration (KILA), 109, 112, 113, 142, 146
Kerala Janata Dal (United), 211
Kerala Karshaka Sangham, 157
Kerala Land Reforms Act, 187
Kerala Model Development, 109, 146, 210, 221
Kerala Restriction on Transfer and Restoration of Lands to Scheduled Tribes Bill of 1999, 156
Kerala Scheduled Tribe (Restriction of Transfer of Lands and Restoration of Alienated Land) Act, 181, 269
Kerala Scheduled Tribe Amendment Bill, 156
Kerala State Industries Enterprises Ltd (KSIE), 197
Kerala State Karshaka Thozilali Union (KSKTU), 150
Kerala State Wetland Conservation Act, 200, 209
Khalistan, 239
  movement, 86
Kim Jong-un, North Korean leader, 193
Kiran Kumar Reddy, 64
Kisan Thomman, 79, 246, 247
KM Mani, 187, 213
  Finance Minister, 187, 189
KN Ramachandran, 87, 239
Kol uprising, 42
Koratala Suryanarayana, 62
KPR Gopalan, 81, 253
KR Gouri, Ms, 232
Krishna Chaitanya Vadlamannati, 119
Kristian Hoelscher, 119
Kujur Rajat, 114
Kunnikkal Narayanan, 78, 79, 80, 233, 246, 253, 261
Kuppu Devaraj, senior Maoist leader, 91, 97
  killing of, 221, 222
Kurichiyan Kunjiraman, 79, 246
K Venu – Ideologue of Maoist

Movement, 15, 81, 88, 177, 180, 184, 231-43, 253
exit of, 97

Lack of
access to resources, 46
adequate medical facilities, 142
agrarian programme, 238
basic amenities, 48, 140
communication, 80
development, 46
development/infrastructure, 109
economic gain, 116
governance, 168
in the rural and Tribal regions, 116
indoctrination and training of cadres on Maoist strategy, 216
irrigation facilities, 53
judicial reforms, 116
representation, 116
security, 115
social and economic development, 116
vision, 65
Laitin, 40
Land Acquisition, Rehabilitation and Resettlement Act, 2011, 53
Land alienation, 59, 108, 111, 121, 164
Tribal, 42, 92, 108, 155, 156, 181, 266, 269
Land Ceiling Act, 180, 266
Landless peasants and Tribals of Naxalbari, 78
Landlordism, 55, 105, 126, 181, 242, 257
abolishing, 54
caste-based, 215
versus masses, 242
versus tenancy, 257
Landlord-tenant relations, 251, 260
Landmark judgment in Samatha case, 51
Land reforms, 6, 28, 54, 55, 56, 104, 160, 180, 242, 251, 257, 266
fall out of, 56
half-baked, 54
helped to check Maoist influence, 229
impact of, 137, 179
implementation of, 55, 272
implementing radical, 54
in Kerala, 137, 218, 269
lack of, 46, 116
loopholes in the implementation of, 269
mainstream parties failed to implement, 54
of a radical nature, 209
oral orders to defeat, 55
successful implementation of, 180
vis-a-vis Maoist strategy, 55
Land Rights of Dalits and Tribals – Fertile Ground for Maoist Exploitation, 54-59
Land rights, 224
fighting for, 57
of Tribals and Dalits, 7
protection of, 59
restoration of alienated Tribal land and, 7
struggles by Tribals, Dalits and landless for, 54
Land rights or rights over forest resources, 177
Land struggles, 122, 131, 163, 182, 210, 217, 259, 267
Law enforcement set up in Maoist infested areas, 134

Laya, 68
Leaders immersed in shameless scandals, 212
Leaders of Maoist movement in Kerala, 15
Left Democratic Front (LDF), 99, 100, 154, 188, 191, 195, 196, 203, 204, 205, 209, 210, 212, 222
  government, 80, 190, 192, 197, 202, 203, 209
    greatest harm to the image of, 203
    style of functioning of, 201
  on solar scam, 191
  partners, 200
  shattering the coalition spirit of, 212
Left Extremist movement, 15
Left Front (LF) government, 28
Left radicals, 25
Left Wing Extremism/Extremists (LWE), 23, 46, 109, 123, 186, 214
  groups, 162, 194
  hunting grounds of, 46
  Planning Commission Report on, 23
  violence, 24, 78
Left Wing Extremists (Naxalites), 206
Legacy of Naxalite movement in Kerala, 253
Leninism, 222, 235
Liberation Tigers for Tamil Elam (LTTE) in Sri Lanka, 115
Likert model, 9, 113, 137
Lok Sabha, 163, 164, 184, 190, 195, 199, 211
Loknath Behera, 204
Love Jihad, 208
Luisa Steur, Ms, 119, 122, 128, 146

Madathil Mathai, 85, 238, 250
Maharashtra Communist Party (MCP), 89
Mala Araya Maha Sabha, 155
Malla Raji Reddy, 91, 96
Mandakini, 79
Manmohan Singh, Dr, Prime Minister, 5, 46
Maoism, 11, 25, 33, 60, 89, 97, 120, 123, 225, 231, 235, 241, 243, 254, 256, 260, 265, 269, 270, 272
  and Maoist thought, 27
  as a complex socio-politico-economic phenomenon, 116
  growth of, 241, 269
  opportunistic approach towards, 67
  reasons for rise of, 241
  spread of, 180, 241, 257, 258
Maoist, 231, 233
Maoist, 24, 28, 42, 50, 98, 105, 251
  action in Kerala, 179, 185
  activists, 157
  activities, 90, 180, 242
    and violence, 29
  agenda of redistribution of land among the landless poor, 59
  affected areas, 49
    areas of Jharkhand, 41
  affected districts, 6, 38
    from Uttar Pradesh and West Bengal, 40
  affected States, 48, 49, 256
    systematic development of, 66
  and other publications, 233
  armed guerrilla struggles, 177
  armed struggles, 80

armed uprisings, 109, 127
cadres, 246
challenge, 5, 63, 136, 243
conflict(s), 50, 119
countering the expansion, 111
extremists from Nepal, 115
groups, 40, 58, 67, 68, 81, 90, 91, 95, 121, 149, 160, 161, 182, 217, 234, 259, 260, 261, 265, 266, 270, 272
check the growth of, 112
good-will among sections of Adivasis towards, 161
inspiration to, 161
support base of, 40
ideology, 89, 127, 223, 235
and propaganda, 226
counter spread of, 150
strategy of disseminating, 129
infested areas of Andhra, Chhattisgarh, Jharkhand and Odisha, 45
infested districts in Bihar, 40
infested regions, 115
influence, 23
checking, 150
districts prone to, 222
inspired activities, 177
inspired struggles, 177
inspired violent overthrow of Indian government, 29
insurgency, 5, 7, 9, 23, 29, 119, 122-23, 128, 129, 130, 136, 138, 146, 149, 150, 195, 234, 241
as socio-political movement, 242
background of, 147
battle ground of, 36
causative factors for, 151
checkmating spread of, 146
containing, 154
different shades of, 30
factors influencing, 234
frustration and helplessness influenced, 136-37
genesis and growth of, 104, 139, 140, 148
genesis, growth and consolidation of, 215
growth and expansion of, 149
growth of, 146, 196
history of, 8, 149
in Kerala, 99, 129, 130, 149, 236
legacy of, 24
literature on, 5
in Kerala, 119
political parties supported early, 128
recommendations on, 10
root cause of, 151
spread of, 9, 138, 140, 147, 176
States affected by, 47
strategy, 123, 126, 128
strategy to face a major challenge like, 63
success in countering, 118
support by Adivasis to, 8
support of Adivasis to, 111, 146
universalizing of, 235
Kattula Sammaiah, 65
killings and violence, 104
leader(s), 63, 95, 177, 233, 241
arrest of, 81
Geethanandan, 264
Murali Kannamballi alias Ajith, 97
leadership, 95, 256
in Kerala, 219, 256

line of Marxism-Leninism, 26
movement, 6, 7, 10, 26, 32, 35, 37, 45, 46, 58, 66, 81, 82, 84, 89, 101, 117, 126, 129, 168, 184, 194, 231, 232, 240, 243, 244, 259
growth of, 45, 46, 176, 258
historical transition of, 35
in Kerala, 7, 79, 90, 136, 177, 181, 215, 245, 253, 260
spread of, 35
supporters of, 29
outfit(s), 220, 261
in Bihar, 32
perspective, 236, 253
strategy, 8, 9, 94, 95, 160, 182, 218, 240, 259
counter, 266
of dispensation of instant justi, 45
to demolish the institutions, 174
strongholds, 62
struggles, 115
thought, 27, 123
threat, 5, 65, 134, 243
as a serious law and order or internal security issue, 222
combating, 24
geographical spread of, 23
policies to combat, 11
policy to tackle, 64
solution to, 6
strategies and policies to combat, 222
violence, 115, 215
degree of, 23
'Maoist actions', 261
Maoist Communist Centre (MCC), 24, 32, 33, 34, 35, 37, 40, 58, 59, 241
of Bihar, 123
Maoist Communist Centre of India (MCCI), 35, 90
'Maoist-free', 11, 223
'Maoist inspired slogan', 252
Maoist Insurgency and the Civil Society, 67
'Maoist issue', 225
Maoist/Naxal activity, 220
Maoist Unity Centre (MUC), 33, 89
Maoists, 7, 9, 10, 11, 12, 13, 23, 36, 41, 42, 45, 46, 50, 51, 53, 55, 57, 59, 65, 66, 67, 68, 69, 79, 80, 81, 82, 83, 90, 91, 92, 94, 95, 96, 97, 98, 113, 118, 120, 121, 122, 126, 127, 128, 130, 133, 138, 139, 141, 143, 144, 145, 146, 153, 162, 165, 174, 175, 176, 177, 178, 179, 180, 181, 182, 183, 186, 214, 216, 217, 219, 220, 221, 224, 225, 234, 240, 241, 242, 243, 244, 249, 251, 252, 255, 256, 257, 258, 259, 267, 269, 273, 274
advantage of, 11
approach of parties towards, 62
assessment of, 93
attract intellectuals and youth to the fold of, 98
bid to get a foothold in the Tribal areas, 134
blunted the moves of, 217
blunted the strategy of, 130
campaigns of, 129
checkmated strategy of, 111
checkmate re-grouping efforts of, 64
checkmating strategies of, 163
citadel(s) of, 50, 63, 117, 244
collusion between mainstream parties and, 65

combating, 115
compromise with, 66
confrontation with, 214
counter moves of, 253
designs of, 161
do not uphold constitution, 224
encounter killing or police excesses against, 222
erosion in the support base of, 130
fertile ground for, 7, 127, 131, 215
fight against, 118, 214
threat of, 66
fortresses of, 221
growth and expansion of, 111
growth of, 112, 114
guerrilla type activities of, 132
in Chhattisgarh, 41
in Dandakaranya, 177, 234
influence of, 140, 223
in Kerala, 128, 233
defending the cases/issues of, 94
launching pad for, 184
links with, 82
main citadels of, 62
main focus area of, 59
main targets of, 260
military strength to fight, 6
operations against, 261
playing a proxy war, 177
political activity in constant consultation with, 66
propaganda/activities of, 153
propaganda of, 109
regrouping efforts of, 96, 251
saga of excesses and brutalities against, 82
security operations against, 64
setback faced by, 90
slogans of, 146, 260
slogans of violence and bloodshed by, 130
strategy of, 111, 132, 177
struggles of, 257
stumbling block for, 273
support of Adivasis to, 215
traditional sources of support of, 249
training camps, 115
trap of, 133
violence on the behest of, 221
violence perpetrated by, 11
wrath of, 68
'Maoist-watchers', 254
Mao's theory of partisan warfare, 25
Mao's thesis on democracy, 25
Marxism, 222, 232, 235, 240, 241, 244
philosophical foundations of, 231
Marxism-Leninism, 28, 33
concept of, 194
conceptual elements of, 236
Marxism-Leninism-Maoism, 88
inalienable elements of, 88
Marxist concept of society, 232
Marxist-Leninist, 34, 54, 261, 265
ideologies of class-struggles, 240
ideology, 234, 254
movement, 236
Marxist-Leninist-Maoist ideologies, 220, 236
Mary Tyler, Ms, 44
Merger of CPI (Maoist) and CPI(ML) Naxalbari, 8, 94
M Geethanandan, 15, 133, 157, 185, 264, 265, 273
Minerals and natural resources, 51
Minimum wages, 240
denial of, 59

denying, 170, 217
implementation of, 154
Mitchell A Seligson, 116
MK Damodaran, former Advocate General, 192
MM Hassan, 188
Mobile conventional warfare, 123
Mohammed Najibullah, 95
Moral policing activists of Shiv Sena, 204
MP Veerendra Kumar, 211
Muppalla Lakshmana Rao alias Ganapathy, 34, 35
elevation of, 34
General Secretary, 95
Murali Kannamballi alias Ajit of Kerala, 82, 89, 90, 97, 101
Muslim radical groups, 208
Muthanga, 96, 147, 210, 264
land related struggles at, 259
agitation, 160, 267
episode, 163, 262
Forest Area, 159
land struggle, 137
struggle(s), 140, 141, 147, 163, 165, 182, 217
Muthanga Wildlife Sanctuary, 159, 163, 210, 267
MV Raghavan, 195

N Janardhanan Reddy, 63
Nagi Reddy, 32
Narendra Modi, Prime Minister, 142
National bourgeoisie, 26, 193
National Democratic Alliance (NDA), 164, 184
National Development Front (NDF), 99, 208
National Emergency, 33, 81, 89, 231
challenging, 8, 78
declaration of, 235, 249
National Human Rights Commission (NHRC), 162
National Institute of Nutrition, 142
National Platform of Mass Organizations (NPMO), 87
National Rehabilitation and Resettlement Policy, 226
Nationalist Congress Party (NCP), 190, 200
'Nationality question', 238
Natural resources, 220
extraction, 119
traditional rights over Forest and other, 51
Natural resource management, 68
Naveen Prasad, 32
Naxalbari, 29, 36, 77, 101, 123, 234
armed peasant uprisings in, 92
armed struggles, 104
armed uprisings, 245
model movement, 30
movement in Kerala, 257, 265
uprisings, 30, 58, 79
Naxalite movement, 37, 45, 116, 120, 185, 233, 244
emergence and growth of, 116
growth of, 46
main support of, 35
Naxalite uprisings, 46, 254
Nayeemuddin alias Nayeem, 65
killing of, 64
State support for, 65
NDA, 188, 210, 211, 212, 213
Neo-renaissance movements, 259
Nepal, 23, 40, 97, 115, 214
Nepalese Communist Party (Marxist-Leninist), 90
'New Samara Bhoomis' (agitation fronts), 160

Nilambur episode, 92
Njattuvela Samskarika Samithi (Cultural Body), 94
Non-Governmental Organizations (NGOs), 24, 67, 68, 75, 96, 113, 149, 151, 152, 153, 165, 172, 267, 268
  agents of, 161
  bashing, 153
  conventional, 67
  progressive, 67
  proliferation of, 150
  role of civil society and, 35
  Tribal, 230
  working among Adivasis, 150
Non-implementation of Forest (Rights) Act, 2006, 146
NT Rama Rao (NTR), 64
  of TDP, 63

Oommen Chandy, Congress Chief Minister, 188, 189, 190, 191, 200
  tainted Chief Minister, 188
Ooru Sabhas, (Adivasi representative council), 158, 159
Oppression and exploitation, 84, 240
  by non-Tribal settlers, 92
  of Adivasis and Dalits and denial of justice, 215
  of Adivasis and Dalits by the landed gentry, 7
  of Adivasis and other weaker sections, 129
  of Adivasis by landlords, 217
  of Tribals and the landless poor and the helplessness of the political establishment, 254
Organization of Islamic Conference (OIC), 195

Pahlavi regime, 95
  anti-Shah movement in Iran, 95
Palppu, Dr, 104, 255
Panchayat (Extension of Scheduled Areas) Act, 1996 (PESA), 61
Panchayat Gothra Sabha Council, 158
Panchayats (Extension of Scheduled Areas) Act, 1996 (PESA), 12, 53, 226
Parayil, 121, 146
Partido Comunista Revolucionario of Chile, 239
Party Unity (PU), 34, 35
'Patriotic image', 63
Pattoor land case, 187, 197
Paul Antony, Industries Secretary, 202
PC Unnichekkan, 87
'Peaceful transition', 193
Peasant warfare, 25
'Pennant episode', 196
'People-centric approach', 6
People-centric projects and programmes, 11
People-centric strategies/strategy, 11, 24
'Peoples Court', 45
Peoples Democratic Party (PDP), 195
People's Democratic Revolution, 25, 27, 29, 78
'People's trial', 84, 85, 237
People's war, 8, 86, 94
People's War Group (PWG), 24, 32, 33, 34, 35, 37, 58, 59, 62, 63, 64, 68, 90, 123, 134, 241
  ban on, 63, 64
P Govinda Pillai, 232
Philip M Prasad, 78, 79, 246, 253

Philosophical Problems of Revolution, The, 236
Phone sex with a woman, 190
Pinarayi Vijayan
  Chief Minister, 193, 196, 197, 198, 201, 206, 207
  government, 201
  State Power Minister, 198
Pinarayi-Madani sponsored candidate, 196
Pioneer Maoists in Kerala, 216
PK Kunhalikutty (former State Industries Minister), 190, 192, 211
PK Sreemathy, Ms, MP, 197
Plachimada struggle, 143
Plachimada Struggle Committee, 143
Plachimada Struggle Solidarity Committee, 144
Planned development, 11, 221, 223
Planning Commission, 50, 112
  Expert Panel of, 46, 117
Polemics between CPM and CPI, 200
Policies and strategies of the governments in dealing with the Maoist challenge, 6
Political mobilization, 7, 8, 10, 167, 176, 265
  of Adivasis, 167, 182, 215, 219, 273
  of Dalits, Tribals and under-privileged, 62
  of Tribal communities, 121
  of Tribals and Dalits – Strategies to Counter Maoism, 60-69
  of Tribals and other marginalized sections, 122
Political movement, 105
Political response to Maoist uprisings, 140
Political socialization of Tribals, 146
Popular Front of India (PFI), 99, 208
Popularizing the Maoist ideologies, 259
Porattom, 89, 90, 94, 181, 250, 266
'Post-Maoist', 220
'Post-Naxalite', 220
Poverty eradication, 222
Poverty line in Maoist infested States, 47
Poverty reduction, 6
P Rajan, 82, 83
  episode, 82, 83
Prakash Singh, 115
Prakriti Samrakshana Samithi, 153
Pratul Ahuja, 114
Praveen Swami, 118
'Pressure politics', 187
Prevention of Corruption (PC) Act, 191
PRG Mathur, 118
Priyanka Vora, 117
Problem with neo-Maoists, 257
Pro-Chinese Communist Party of India – Marxist (CPI-M), 27
Pro-Chinese Communist Party of India (Marxist), 77-78
Pro-Left intellectuals, 113
Pro-Left Wing extremist intellectuals, 191
Pro-Lin Biao faction, 32
Pro-Maoist
  'Ayyankali Pada', 156
  groups, 181
  intellectuals, 128
  orientation, 253
  outfits, 133, 141, 142, 145, 175
  Porattom, 140, 217
  thinking, 83

Prominent CPM leader sharing platform with Madani, 196
Propagating Maoist line, 28
Proper resettlement, 12, 224
Protection of Civil Rights (PCR) Act, 1955, 12, 43, 226
Protection of rights and privileges, 11, 223
Protracted people's war, 27, 77, 123
Public perception management, 11, 223
'Public trial(s)', 45, 85, 129, 237, 250, 260
'Punnappara-Vayalar' struggles, 25, 54
PV Ramana, 118

Radical Ambedkarism, 241
Radical groups, 10, 69, 109, 111, 120, 153, 162, 183, 184, 186, 224, 244, 273
  trap of, 160
Radical movements, 254, 256
Radical social reform movements, 248
Rajas of Veda tribe, 139
Rajat Ganguly, 114
Rajya Sabha, 211
Ramachandra Guha, 46, 117
Ramesh Chennithala, former State Home Minister, 188
Rashtriya Maha Sabha (RMS), 163, 184
Rashtriya Swayamsevak Sangh (RSS), 98, 99, 100, 150, 204, 205, 206, 207
Rauf, 87
  faction, 89
Red Corridor, 23, 122, 214
Red Flag – Unnichekkan, 33, 87, 88, 89, 250
Red Star, 88
Redistribution of land, 55, 59, 251
  to Adivasis, 267
  to Adivasis, Dalits and other landless sections, 252
  to Tribals, 264
'Red-Terror', 7, 30, 62
Rehabilitation of
  Adivasis, 12, 141, 224
  Endosulfan victims, 96
  landless Adivasis, 145
Restoration of
  Adivasi land, 262
  alienated Adivasi land, 12, 162, 171, 174, 177, 182, 224
  alienated land, 171, 180, 218
  alienated Tribal land, 8, 57, 90, 111, 137, 147, 154, 160, 251, 264, 266, 272, 273
  Tribal land, 121, 150, 161
Retail Sector, 94
Revolutionary
  armed force, 237
  army, 92
  heritage, 27
  mass struggles, 194
  movement, 92, 235, 257
    growth of, 67
    in Kerala, 233, 237
  politics, 238
  resistance, 88
  struggle(s), 27, 87, 91, 260
    by the Communist parties, 54
    in Kerala, 92
Revolutionary Communist Centre (RCC), 31
Revolutionary Communist Centre of India (RCCI), 35
Revolutionary Communist parties, 90, 239

Revolutionary Communist Party of USA, 239
Revolutionary Democratic Front (RDF), 59, 94
Revolutionary International Movement (RIM), 89, 101, 239
Revolutionary Peoples' Committees (RPC), 165
Revolutionary Socialist Party (RSP), 211
Revolutionary Writers Association (RWA), 129
Rights over forest/natural resources, 53
Rise of Maoist movement and the Maoists, 46
Rivalries between the CPI(M) and the Congress and IUML, 100
Roopesh, underground Kerala Maoist leader, 96, 97, 132
RP Saxena, 116
R Rajeevan, Dr, 120, 121, 122, 128, 154, 175

Sadhu Jana Vimochana Samithi, 182, 259
Saga of anti-Pinarayi crusade, 199
Saketh Rajan, 91
Samata, 68
Sammaiah, accused in IPS officer KL Vyas's murder, 65
Sangh Parivar, 151, 207, 213
Santhosh Rana, 30
'Saritha controversy', 200
Saritha S Nair, 189
  sexually exploiting, 189
SC/ST Orders (Amendment) Act, 2002, 124
Scarcity of drinking water, 143
Scheduled Caste and Schedule Tribe (Prevention of Atrocities) Act, 1989, 12, 226
Scheduled Castes (SCs), 38, 60
Scheduled Tribes (STs), 38, 60, 119, 120, 124, 153
  areas, 159
Scheduled Tribes and Other Traditional Forest Dwellers (Recognition of Forest Rights) Act, 2006, 12
Schism between CPI(M) and CPI, 212
Secessionist-separatist movements, 239
'Second Land Reforms', 252
Security Related Expenditure (SRE), 24, 38
  scheme, 221
    anti-Maoist, 221
    anti-Naxalite, 134
Semi-feudal tendencies, 126
Senkumar, 203, 204
'Senkumar episode', 203
Separatist movements, 86
Serious sexual and corruption charges against a dozen Congress leaders, 189
Sex scams, 190, 191
Sex scandal(s), 200, 245
Sexual demeanour/misbehaviour towards women comrades or their relatives, 199
Sexual escapades, 186, 199
Sexual favours, 191
Sexually perverted police personnel, 248
Siddhant Buxy, 117
SNC-Lavalin scandal, 198
Sneha Mary Koshy, 98
Social Democratic Party of India (SDPI), 99, 205, 208, 211
Social equality, 28
Social justice, 68, 120, 269

Social movement(s), 89, 122, 130, 182, 232
Social reform movements, 158
Social reformist movements, 255
Social renaissance movement in Kerala, 104, 255
Socialist revolution, 25, 26, 67
Socio-cultural movement, 151
Socio-economic
  advancement, 136, 180, 242
    of Adivasis/Dalits, 251
  and political factors, 167, 219
  backwardness, 46, 107, 150
    of Adivasis, 174
  condition(s), 9, 136, 137
    among Adivasis, 137
    of Dalits and Tribals, 6, 50
  development, 64, 243
    indicators, 121
    of Adivasi community, 159
  developmental issues, 46
  disparities, 105, 180, 241, 242
  factors, 35, 176, 179, 214
  indicators of Adivasis, 146
  indicators of Tribals, 109
  issues, 9, 131, 137, 141, 215
    confronting Adivasi community, 179
    of Adivasis, 234
  plight of community, 161
  political factors, 40
  political movement, 222
  problems of Adivasis, 224
  situation, 28
  status of people, 146
  theories, 240
  upliftment, 263
  welfare indicators of Adivasis, 179
Socio-economic and developmental factors, 24
  indicators, 218
  issues, 6, 8, 45, 215
  promises, 46
  indicators, 146
Socio-Economic Issues Influencing Growth of Maoist Movement, 45-53
Socio-political
  circumstances, 46
  issues, 232
  movement, 222
Solar scam, 187, 191, 192, 210
'Solidarity', 151
Souvik Chatterjee, 116
Soviet occupation in Afghanistan, 95
Special Economic Zone (SEZ), 94
Special forest rights, 178
Special Infrastructure, 24
Special Investigation Team (SIT), 190, 191
Spread of Maoist ideas, 136
Spread of Maoist movement among the Tribals, 120
Sreekumar, 121, 146
Sreemathy, 197
Sree Narayana Guru, 104, 255
Sreerekha, Ms, 121, 140
Srikakulam, 30, 36, 117, 234
  uprisings, 54
Strategic United Front, 8, 78, 95, 100
Strategy of revolutionary struggles, 254
Strategy of total elimination of Maoists, 6
Student upsurge and massacre at Tiananmen Square, China, 239
Students Islamic Movement of India (SIMI), 95
Sujeet Kumar, 115
Sukhadeo Thorat, Professor, 43

Support extended by Maoist groups to Khalistan movement in Punjab or the secessionist forces like Jammu Kashmir Liberation Front (JKLF) in Kashmir or the insurgent outfits such as the United Liberation Front of Assam (ULFA), 149
Surya Sen, 70
Suryanelli case related to the abduction and sexual exploitation of a minor girl, 190

Tactical line, 26, 27, 71, 195
Team Solar, 189
Tebhaga movement, 25, 54
Telangana Rashtra Samithi (TRS), 65
Telangana uprisings, 25, 54
Telugu Desam Party (TDP), 63, 64, 65
Tendu leaf collection, 234
The Kerala Scheduled Tribes (Restriction of Transfer of Land and Restoration of Alienated Land) Act, 1975, 139-40
The National Rehabilitation and Resettlement Policy, 2007, 12
The Scheduled Tribes and other Traditional Forest Dwellers Act, 2006, 53, 226
The Wildlife Protection Act, 1972, 57
Theoretical foundation of Telangana movement, 25
Thettamala Krishnankutty, 79, 246, 253
Thiruvanchoor Radhakrishnan, former Home and Vigilance Minister, 190
Thomas Chandy, 200, 209, 212
tainted minister, 212
Threat of Islamic radicalization, 207
Thunderbolts, 91, 97, 225
Tiff between the CPM and CPI, 209
T Nagi Reddy, 31
Tom Jose, Additional Chief Secretary, 201, 202
TP Senkumar, DGP, 203
Training on Maoist insurgency strategy, 130
Tribal empowerment, 68
Tribal movement in Kerala, 122
Tribal rights, 122
Tri-junction, 90, 91, 92, 97, 106, 127, 217
bordering Kerala, Tamil Nadu and Karnataka, 220, 223
of Kerala, Karnataka and Tamil Nadu, 8, 165, 178
of Kerala, Tamil Nadu and Karnataka, 9, 97, 132, 216

Uday Kumar, 117
Ultimate victory of revolutionary forces, 26
Ultra Left radicals, 89
Under-developed agriculture, 46
UNDP India Report, 49
United Democratic Front (UDF), 100, 154, 186, 187, 188, 191, 195, 196, 197, 199, 202, 210, 211, 212
government, 189, 192, 202
regime(s), 100, 191, 196, 205
rule, 99
United Front(s), 28, 78
United Progressive Alliance (UPA) government, 186
'United Strategic Front', 68
Unity Centre of Communist Revolutionaries (UCCR), 31

Uprising of peasants and rural poor against Nizam of Hyderabad, 25
Using Adivasis as human shields, 132

Vanavakasa Samrakshana Samithi (Forest Dwellers Protection Committee), 131-32
Vanavasi Kalyan Parishad, 150
Vellathoovaal Stephen, 79
Vempatapu Satyanarayana, 36
Victims of oppression and exploitation, 34
'Vigilance Raj', 202
Violence in Kashmir, 5
Violent movement(s), 60, 104, 272
Viplava Sthreevadi Prasthanam (Revolutionary Women's Movement), 94
Viplava Vidyarthi Prasthanam (Revolutionary Students' Movement), 94
'Virginity', 248
VM Sudheeran, Kerala Pradesh Congress Committee (KPCC) President, 187, 188
VR Krishna Iyer, Late Justice – Legendary Personality of Judiciary, 121, 178, 181, 268-71
VR Raghavan, Retired Lt-Gen, 115
VS Achuthanandan, former Chief Minister, 196, 197, 252
Wayanad, 79, 80, 85, 91, 92, 106, 107, 108, 109, 121, 124, 127, 129, 131, 132, 134, 138, 139, 140, 141, 144, 150, 151, 154, 156, 157, 159, 160, 163, 164, 182, 184, 208, 209, 210, 221, 233, 238, 246, 250, 259, 261, 262, 264, 265, 267
  Adivasi belt of, 79
  Adivasi dominated areas of, 109
  Adivasi heartland of, 156
  Adivasi resettlement colonies in, 140
  eviction of farmers in, 266
  forest land in, 79
  pro-Maoist elements in, 130
Wayanad Adivasi Sangham (WAS), 150, 151
Wayanad Social Service Society (WSSS), 151
Western Ghats, 90, 91, 92, 97, 106, 127, 165, 251
  mountain rain forests, 106
Western Ghats Special Zonal Committee (WGSZC), 9, 91, 92, 132, 178, 216
'Witch-hunting' of people, 224
Witch-hunts of people, 11
World Bank, 90

Yogi Adityanath, Uttar Pradesh Chief Minister, 207
YS Rajasekhara Reddy, 63